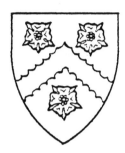

THE HARVARD ADVOCATE ANTHOLOGY

The HARVARD *ADVOCATE* Anthology

Edited by DONALD HALL

"If one seeks a monument to the little old paper, let him look about in the list of young writers, and see how many of them became famous."
—W. G. Peckham, '67, in *The Harvard Advocate; Fifty Year Book*, 1916

TWAYNE PUBLISHERS, INC. • NEW YORK

"An Ode for Richard Eberhart" and "Elegy on Yeats," by Harry Brown. From *The Violent,* reprinted by permission of New Directions.

"The Question," by Robert Hillyer. From *The Five Books of Youth* by Robert Hillyer. Copyright, 1920, by Brentano's, Inc. Copyright, 1948, by Robert Hillyer. The sonnet, "Even as love grows more," by Robert Hillyer. From *Sonnets and Other Lyrics,* by Robert Hillyer, reprinted by permission of Harvard University Press, publishers.

"The Zoo," by Howard Moss. From *The Wound and the Weather,* copyright, 1946, by Howard Moss. Reprinted by permission of Harcourt, Brace, and Company, Inc.

"Ballade of a Ship," "Villanelle of Change," and "Supremacy," by E. A. Robinson. From *The Children of the Night,* reprinted by permission of Charles Scribner's Sons.

"Memorare" and "Where Is the Clock to Tell my Time of Tears," by Dunstan Thompson. Reprinted from *Poems* by permission of Simon and Schuster, publishers. Copyright, 1943, by Dunstan Thompson.

"Corpus Est De Deo," by John Hall Wheelock. From *Poems, 1911–1936,* by John Hall Wheelock. Copyright, 1936, by Charles Scribner's Sons.

Manufactured in the United States of America by American Book–Knickerbocker Press, Inc.

PREFACE

THE HARVARD ADVOCATE HAS PUBLISHED SELECTIONS from its past volumes before, but the attitude of the anthologist has in each case differed from ours. In *Verses from the Harvard Advocate* (first, second, and third series, 1876, 1886, 1906), in *Stories from the Harvard Advocate* (1896), and in *The Harvard Advocate; Fifty Year Book* (1916), principal attention seems to have been paid to selecting the best material which had been published, irrespective of the later careers of the authors. Although the resulting choices were surprisingly good, they were perhaps only truly exciting in the cases where the selections of the "best" coincided with the work of men who had become well known in the field of literature or elsewhere. For this reason, our primary aim in selecting material for this anthology has been to form a collection of the juvenilia of outstanding men. Within this limit, we have generally tried to choose the best material available. It is to be hoped that the result will be, not only a curiosity, but of value to literary critics and historians.

In some cases, it should be stated, the editor has chosen not to print the best of a particular author's ADVOCATE work, printing instead work of his which has not been republished in book form.

Not all the prominent men who have written for the ADVOCATE are here represented. In some cases, their ADVOCATE writings were too inconsequential, or might prove embarrassing to them. Other authors have been impossible to contact; a few have declined to be included.

Many thanks are given all the authors who have given us permission to reprint their undergraduate writings. As Wallace Stevens wrote, in a letter to the editor, "Some of one's early things give one the creeps." Almost all of the men contacted felt similarly, but were willing, all the same, to display their juvenilia for the sake of Mother ADVOCATE.

We would also like to thank John Ciardi, not only for his encouragement and help as an editor of Twayne Publishers, but for the original suggestion for the book.

D. H.

TABLE OF CONTENTS

INTRODUCTION

The Harvard Advocate: 1866-1950

I

On the morning of May 11, 1866, students of Harvard college were delighted to see, tacked to trees, walls, and even to the side of the President's house, posters reading:

A NEW COLLEGE PAPER
for sale at Richardson's Bookstore
TOMORROW.

And on May 12, many of them did make the familiar trek to Richardson's; the first edition of the Harvard Advocate, 400 copies, was sold out.

But there was a definite air of secrecy about the first issue of Harvard's oldest publication. No editors' or authors' names were included. When Mr. Richardson was asked who had left the bundle of papers, he answered that he had promised not to tell. It was clear, then, that the editors feared a fate like that of the *Collegian.*

Only the previous Fall, in 1865, a lively weekly newspaper called the *Collegian* had been published by students who regretted that Harvard had no outlet for undergraduate opinion. But the editors, Gage and Peckham particularly, made the mistake of being too radical for the Harvard faculty of those days. Not only did the *Collegian* criticize the lack of student-faculty relations, and refer unmistakably to certain professors in terms that were said to lack a proper respect, but they dared to attack the tradition of compulsory chapel. An admirable Platonic dialogue, in which Socrates discoursed on the good of the many as opposed to the good of the few, ended:

> "*Glaucon.* I do indeed, by Jupiter! and, tomorrow morning, I will go to roll-call, and not to prayers. Come and breakfast with me, Socrates."

Punishment was slow to come but awful in the coming. The editors were forbidden ever to publish another issue on pain of expulsion. Although student reaction was vociferous, it was ineffectual. There were many who felt it intolerable that the undergraduates should have no voice. One of these, F. P. Stearns, took up the battle in the Spring of 1866 and organized the ADVOCATE. It was decided that former *Collegian* editors would not be allowed on the magazine, for their own safety, until the first issue had passed the faculty.

In an attempt to secure administrative approval, the new magazine, despite its pugnacious name and Latin motto, "Sweet is Peril," was less radical than the old. The most dangerous article in the first issue suggested that the faculty had been unjust and hasty in not allowing the *Collegian* to mend its own ways.

It may well have been that the faculty itself was coming to regret its former action. A faculty meeting was held, when the ADVOCATE appeared, and the case was argued lengthily on both sides. When the meeting was adjourned, word spread around the Harvard Yard that the ADVOCATE was to be allowed to continue publication. Years later, it was revealed that the chief supporters of the ADVOCATE in the faculty meeting that Spring had been James Russell Lowell and Oliver Wendell Holmes.

II

I

"If one seeks a monument to the little old paper, let him look about in the list of young writers, and see how many of them became famous." So wrote W. G. Peckham, '67, in the *Harvard Advocate; Fifty Year Book* in 1916. (Peckham, one of the founders of the *Collegian*, later joined the ADVOCATE.) If the statement was true in 1916, before Eliot, Stevens, and Cummings published their best work, it has certainly been doubly proved in later years. For the ADVOCATE has assumed a role of unique importance in American letters.

When it began, the student's ADVOCATE was an argumentative publication, fulfilling the designs of its founders. Most of each bi-weekly issue was editorial in function, with the remainder filled out by a poem or two. At the moment, the ADVOCATE is a literary magazine appearing six times a year, containing short stories, poems, criticism, and an occasional article of topical interest. While the change between the ADVOCATE of 1866 and ADVOCATE of 1950 is as great as it appears, it would be incorrect to assume that there has been a steady progression from the one to the other, or that the present direction of the magazine is final.

The magazine's emphasis grew to be chiefly literary in the 90's, and continued to be so with fair consistency through the teens. During part of the twenties, again, the magazine was largely argumentative. Switches from extreme to extreme are commonplaces in the history of the ADVOCATE, and are explained by the turnover of personnel and the shifts in undergraduate fashion. The format and schedule of publication have varied as much as the editorial policy.

Perhaps the only quality which the ADVOCATE has consistently displayed is its character as the nursemaid of genius, as the table of contents of the present volume will certainly attest.

Another distinguished list of ADVOCATE writers includes men who were not Harvard undergraduates at the time their material was published: Oliver Wendell Holmes, Edward Everett Hale, Bliss Carman, S. Foster Damon, Henry Miller, Ezra Pound, William Carlos Williams, Robert Lowry, Richard Eberhart, Archibald MacLeish, Theodore Spencer, John Ciardi, and Richard Wilbur.

With such a list of contributors, it was inevitable that the idea of reprinting should occur many times. Every ten years for the first fifty years of its existence the ADVOCATE issued an anthology. In 1876, 1886, and 1906, selections of the ADVOCATE verse of each ten-year period were printed, the first of the three edited by Charles Eliot Norton. In 1896, *Stories from the Harvard Advocate* appeared. In 1916, *The Harvard Advocate; Fifty Year Book* (prefaced with an essay on Harvard and preparedness by ranking ADVOCATE almunus Theodore Roosevelt) was published, containing for the most part selections from the prose and verse published during the 1906–1916 period. The current anthology, appearing in the ADVOCATE's eighty-fourth year, is the first since 1916.

Despite its distinguished alumni and its previous anthologies, the ADVOCATE is best known to the non-Harvard public for its parodies and special issues. *The Lampoon*, *The New Republic*, *The Dial*, *The Atlantic Monthly*, and *The Saturday Review of Literature* have all been accorded the dignity of parody. Probably the most successful was the *Dial* parody of 1925. The last stanza of "Portrait of an Ex-Lady," by T. S. Tellalot, went as follows:

[redacted]

"Ah! So Soon? Come in next Sunday."
China winks upon the shelves.
Somewhere in the Bay of Funday,
twenty gardeners drown themselves.

Special issues of the ADVOCATE have been printed in honor of T. S. Eliot (in 1938) and Wallace Stevens (in 1940). Both contained, besides critical articles and shorter tributes, selections of the undergraduate verse of the author in whose honor they were printed.

2

In 1948, Robert Rockman wrote his Senior thesis at Harvard on the subject: *The Poetic Renaissance and Harvard: Studies in the Harvard Advocate, 1915–1930.* Paying particular attention to articles on *vers libre* and attitudes expressed in book reviews, Rockman was able to chart the inroads of modernism by a close reading of the ADVOCATE in the period of change. Cummings' *The New Art* (see page 139), published in 1915, was a good starting point. Malcolm Cowley and Christopher LaFarge, as well as other and lesser known ADVOCATE writers, provided further material of interest. Secondarily, Rockman paid attention to the poetic content of the magazine itself, and described a gradual change.

There is room for further critical study of the past volumes of the ADVOCATE. Not only is there interest in watching large movements reflected in its pages, but there is some value in hindsight appreciation of writing by authors later famous. Much of the hindsight, it must be admitted, satisfies little but curiosity, but some authors provide significant clues to the origins of their mature work.

Perhaps the best example is the poetic progression of T. S. Eliot as an ADVOCATE writer. Juxtaposition of two examples may prove the point. Eliot's first ADVOCATE poem was called "Song," and appeared in May of his freshman year:

When we came home across the hill
  No leaves were fallen from the trees;
  The gentle fingers of the breeze
Had torn no quivering cobweb down.

The hedgerow bloomed with flowers still
  No withered petals lay beneath;
  But the wild roses in your wreath
Were faded, and the leaves were brown.

Now let us look at the final stanza of the last poem Eliot published in the ADVOCATE, "Spleen" (January, 1910).

And Life, a little bald and gray,
Languid, fastidious, and bland,
Waits, hat and gloves in hand,
Punctilious of tie and suit
(Somewhat impatient of delay)
  On the doorstep of the Absolute.

Prufrock is already with us, in 1910!

The process was gradual. Eliot's second ADVOCATE "Song," "If Space and Time as sages say," is probably his poorest, and since Mr. Eliot stipulated that the editor delete at least one poem from this collection, it has been omitted. "Before Morning," Eliot's next, is another lyric, successful but not exciting. In Eliot's fourth poem, "Circe's Palace," we hear the first indications of his later tone. In the first stanza, after describing the scene in traditional poetic language, the last line, "We shall not come here again," appears with the suddenness and flatness which Eliot later used with great effect. The last lines:

The peacocks walk, stately and slow,
And they look at us with the eyes
Of men whom we knew long ago.

are again Eliotesque in their simplicity and shock.

Eliot's next two poems, "Song" and "On a Portrait," are not so revealing. The former is either a throwback to an earlier style or was composed at an earlier date than appears. "On a Portrait," a sonnet, contains ironic surprises reminiscent of the mature Eliot, but is not a very successful poem.

"Nocturne," Eliot's seventh in the ADVOCATE, is his first "modern" poem. The young man's irony is full grown. The first quatrain of the sonnet, which is the best, is:

Romeo, *grand sérieux*, to importune
Guitar and hat in hand, beside the gate
With Juliet, in the usual debate
Of love, beneath a bored but courteous moon. . . .

It should be noted that here and in the rest of the poem, Eliot's fine sense of rhythm, which he had demonstrated in his first "Song" and elsewhere, has broken down, perhaps in the excitement of a new way of writing. "Humouresque," the next poem Eliot printed in the ADVOCATE, is technically more proficient. Perhaps most significant is its subtitle, "After J. Laforgue." We have already quoted from "Spleen."

Other writers do not display such neatness in their stylistic progression. But there are facts to be noted, and more comprehensive studies than this will be needed to exhaust them. A few facts of interest can be noted, however. There is Conrad Aiken's snow imagery in his early poems, compared to the phrasing of his celebrated short story, "Silent Snow, Secret Snow." From "To a Head in Marble" (1911):

> . . . at my pane
> The voiceless snow makes ceaseless whisperings,
> Yearning to tell of strange and demon things. . . .

And one should also compare these lines from "Le Penseur" (1910), which, though not about snow, use phrases similar to Aiken's later prose:

> Play me a song such as the headland hears
> Softly about its feet, in break of seas
> Enchanting it to dreams; dim surge and fall;
> Till, like the headland, I may lose the world,
> Hearing the song grow fainter at my feet.

"Silent Snow, Secret Snow" is concerned with a young boy who imagines that snow is constantly falling. Lying in bed each morning before school, he hears the steps of the postman faint and obscure on the snow. But when he gets out of bed, he sees that no snow has fallen. Each day he first hears the footsteps of the postman (who seems to represent sanity and contact with the actual world) at a point on the street nearer his own house. Constantly dreaming about the snow, hearing it talk to him and seeing it falling everywhere, he becomes absent-minded at school and at home. His parents become upset, and attempt, with the family doctor, to question him, but he runs away to his bedroom where he can be alone with his world of silent snow, secret snow. At the end of the story, the reader realizes that the boy will not hear the postman at all, that morning.

Here is some of the snow imagery from the story:

> . . . snow falling about him, a silent screen of snow between himself and the world. . . . Snow growing heavier each day, muffling the world, hiding the

> ugly, and deadening increasingly—above all—the steps of the postman. . . . The snow was much deeper now, it was falling more swiftly and heavily, the sound of its seething was more distinct, more persistent. . . . A ghost of snow falling in the bright sunlight, softly and steadily floating and turning and pausing. . . . This . . . combination of ethereal loveliness with a something . . . faintly and deliciously terrifying . . . as if the little hissing voice [of the snow] came from a slow white spiral of falling flakes. . . . The little white spiral was still there, still softly whirling, like the ghost of a white kitten chasing the ghost of a white tail, and making as it did so the faintest of whispers. . . . The darkness was coming in long white waves . . . the . . . floor was like a little raft tossed in waves of snow almost overwhelmed, washed under whitely, up again. . . . The seamless hiss advanced once more, the long white wavering lines rose and fell like enormous whispering sea-waves, the whisper becoming louder. . . .

And the last sentence of the story:

> The hiss was now becoming a roar—the whole world was a vast moving screen of snow—but even now it said peace, it said remoteness, it said cold, it said sleep.

The parallels between Aiken's ADVOCATE imagery and "Silent Snow, Secret Snow" are too numerous to cover thoroughly. The snow, in the short story, is compared to the sea, and at the end sounds much like the sea in the lines from "Le Penseur": "I may lose the world, Hearing the song grow fainter at my feet." The idea of snow as a shield from the actual world is especially present in both the prose and the verse. In the quotes from the early poems, snow and sea are visualized as communicating, in the one case whispering, in the other singing. Then there is also the "Yearning to tell of strange and demon things," of the quotation from "To a Head in Marble." The snow in "Silent Snow, Secret Snow," often represented supernaturally, wants to tell the boy a story. It seems that Aiken, in his short story, exploited emotions and ideas that had been close to him for many years.

E. E. Cummings presents another case of interest. His ADVOCATE article, "The New Art" (1915), is a sort of Baedeker of modernism in music, painting, sculpture, and literature, and contains appreciations of Amy Lowell and Gertrude Stein. Yet Cummings' ADVOCATE verse, written two years earlier, is traditional in form. By 1917, when some of Cummings' poems appeared in *Eight Harvard Poets*, the rudiments of his later style had already appeared.

It may be noticed that the three writers mentioned are all slight hints of his mature manner. His Spenserian stanza, "Summer Silence," ends with the phrase, "the untranslated stars," identifiable with later Cummings both by the use of the negative and by the romantic attitude expressed. The last line of "Of Nicolette" reminds one of Cummings' later amatory verse: ". . . the yellow wonder of her hair."

It may be noticed that the three writers mentioned are all poets. This would seem to be significant; reading through the back files of the ADVOCATE one finds evidence for the supposition that the talent for verse matures earlier than the talent for prose. Several ADVOCATE poets (notably E. A. Robinson, Arthur Davison Ficke, John Hall Wheelock, Robert Hillyer, James Agee, Robert Fitzgerald, Dunstan Thompson, and Harry Brown) were writing with a professional competency when they were on the ADVOCATE.

III

While the ADVOCATE was steadily building for itself a place in the literary history of America; while poets, novelists, and critics were graduating from the magazine and moving on to succeed or fail in the professional world, another side of the ADVOCATE was having its effect on every man who was a member. As far back as record exists, there is mention of initiations, of parties, of readings. Wherever the ADVOCATE had its Sanctum, with the names of past board members inscribed on plaques on the walls, whether it was on the top floor of the freshman Union, in the building on Dunster Street, or the building on Bow Street, the members would gather, generally with beer mugs in hand, for their various social affairs.

Initiations included little of the hazing generally associated with college organizations. A fair amount of liquor was generally consumed, and a play presented by the successful candidates. Though copies of none of the plays have survived, extra playbills from some of the productions are plentiful. One of the mildest titles was *How to be Happy Though Fully Clothed, or Hell Hath no Fury Like a Husband Horned.*

With the advent of the house system at Harvard, and the collapse of importance of the clubs and other organized social life, the ADVOCATE has lost much of its clubbiness. Initiations are no longer held; there are no more night-long beer parties where the members sit in the Sanctum and sing. But there are still the parties and readings at which undergraduates have an opportunity to mingle with Cambridge literati. In the past, the ADVOCATE has had "coffee nights" at which men like John Livingston Lowes and Charles Townsend Copeland would place themselves at the mercy of the undergraduate, and the conversations would sometimes last until early morning.

The first recorded celebrity party was in 1907, when Theodore Roosevelt, treasurer of the ADVOCATE in 1870, made his triumphant return to the Sanctum. Two years later, Mrs. Minnie Maddern Fiske, the actress, was entertained at a party in the Advocate House; also present were Irving Babbitt, Barrett Wendell, and George Baker. Since then, W. Somerset Maugham, T. S. Eliot, W. H. Auden, Dylan Thomas, Gertrude Stein, Amy Lowell, and many others have been guests of honor at ADVOCATE parties.

But parties and initiations have not provided all the excitement at the ADVOCATE offices over the years. In 1924, the ADVOCATE first achieved national publicity when it instigated a contest to find an epithet for upholders of the Eighteenth Amendment. With prohibition just beginning, a Harvard alumnus named Delcever King had offered a prize for a name to call "wets," and out of thousands of entries had picked "Scofflaw." Taking advantage of the newspaper notice King had aroused, the ADVOCATE, with its offer of twenty-five dollars for a counter-slogan, reaped a huge harvest of clippings, entries, and letters of denunciation. Although "Delcever" was the most popular suggestion, the editors decided that the winner was Miss Katherine Welling, a sixty-seven year old New York spinster whose entry was "Spigot-Bigot." On receipt of her prize money, Miss Welling wrote the ADVOCATE a grateful letter, adding that she was going to give the money to the Anti-Prohibition Society.

The phrase stirred up quite a tempest among the teetotalers. Delcever King wrote a nasty letter to the ADVOCATE about breaking the law. Amos R. Wells wrote a poem appearing in the *Christian Endeavor World* of which the opening couplet was:

So I'm a Spigot-Bigot because I uphold the law
And because I am trying to keep the young out of the
devil's maw!

It ended, sixteen lines later, with:

> And I'm a Spigot-Bigot and I glory in my name.

The next year, in 1925, a less self-induced dose of publicity occurred when the ADVOCATE's parody of the *Dial* was banned from sale in Boston and Cambridge. Cause of the banning was an extremely sketchy line drawing of a nude couple embracing, with the caption "Neo-Platonic Love." Postal authorities in Washington, appealed to by Boston police, affirmed the chastity of the ADVOCATE and refused to ban it from the mails. Local police still would not allow it to be sold on newsstands, but the issue was soon depleted, in one way or another.

Another banning took place just ten years later, in 1935. This time, short stories were the cause: "A Natural History," by James Laughlin, now editor-publisher of New Directions, and "Glittering Pie," by Henry Miller, the author of *Tropic of Cancer*, then an expatriate living in Paris. Both stories appeared in the registration issue, published in September. For a month, the issue sold undisturbed on the newsstands. Then, simultaneously, attacks occurred from two quarters. A former ADVOCATE editor wrote an anonymous letter to the *Crimson*, protesting the "barefaced indecency" of such "un-Harvardian trash." And outraged parents of Cambridge high school students who had bought the magazine complained to the police, who acted promptly. Assistant District Attorney Frank Volpe forced the five editors of the ADVOCATE to resign, threatening them with jail if they did not. Police rounded up all newsstand copies, and even made a visit to the ADVOCATE building to find any that remained.

The scandal was given prominence by the newspapers of the nation, particularly those of Boston. The *Globe* ran the resignation story as a page one headline. Volpe delivered a philippic which newspapers were fond of reprinting: "It is about time that college authorities maintained a rigid supervision over the childish literary efforts of these embryonic authors who seem to think it a mark of distinction and cleverness to dish up dirt for the edification of their immature readers." (Henry Miller was at this time nearing fifty in Paris.) ". . . Grotesque brain children of these college boys."

The story of the banning was mainly used by the local newspapers to play upon anti-Harvard feeling among the mass of Boston citizens. The ADVOCATE once again figured in a town-gown feud in 1938, when Cambridge City Councilman Mike Sullivan and others were engaged in trying to make Harvard a municipality separate from Cambridge. It was a time of facetious parades and demonstrations. Soldiers of the Free State of Lampoon, demanding a passage to the Charles, goose-stepped along Massachusetts Avenue. Mike Sullivan attempted to speak near the Lampoon building on Mount Auburn Street and was (allegedly) kicked by a student. Sullivan, enraged, hurried to a police station and swore out a warrant, but then had to withdraw it when he realized he had no idea who his assailant was.

Then came a brief reign of terror in Harvard Square. Local police, possibly alerted by the violated Sullivan, kept constant vigilance. A front page headline in the *Herald* put it:

TEAR GAS PATROL GUARDS HARVARD

At this point, the ADVOCATE issued a plebescite from its building on Bow Street. Members of the staff passed out small ballots which contained such questions as:

1. Do you prefer separation from Cambridge?
2. Do you approve of kicking councilors? (Answer yes.)

and ended with:

7. *Tantaene animis celestibus irae?*

which all the Boston papers translated differently.

But the town-gown difficulties, like all college sensations, had to end. In this case, it must be admitted, the ending was hastened by pressure from the administrative offices in University Hall. The ADVOCATE, never totalling the results of its plebescite, continued to exist as if nothing had happened, and has of late only put the clipping agencies to work by the election of two honorary presidents, Ann Sheridan and Elizabeth Taylor.

IV

The eighty-four years of the HARVARD ADVOCATE have produced much of which to be proud, but there are a few chapters the ADVOCATE would just as soon forget. If the magazine can claim for its sons such men as Eliot and Stevens, it can also blush to admit that it rejected Robert Lowell, when, as a Harvard freshman, he was a candidate for the literary board. Lowell reports that after he had registered as a candidate, the board members told him to come around and tack a carpet. After he had tacked the carpet, they told him not to come around any more.

But such occurrences were the exception. Mother ADVOCATE, who received the maternal title when she gave birth to the *Lampoon*, was generally kind to her young brood. Even rivals to the old paper, of which many have blossomed and withered during its long life, generally have been absorbed by the ADVOCATE at their eventual financial debacle. The most long-lived of these rival magazines was the *Harvard Monthly*, (1875–1917), which was avant-garde when the ADVOCATE was conventional, and printed two undergraduate authors that the ADVOCATE regrets having missed, George Santayana and John Dos Passos.

Whether on account of rivals, financial conditions, or the differences of individual boards, the ADVOCATE has had its financial ups and downs, too. At one time, ninety percent of the undergraduate body subscribed, and the magazine donated three hundred dollars a year to the Harvard Library. At other times, when debts have reached astonishing heights, help has been requested and received from ADVOCATE trustees and other alumni.

The ADVOCATE's success is, of course, attributable to the University of which it is a part. At least one Harvard student in three, if pressed, will admit that he is a poet. And Van Wyck Brooks has said of Harvard, "Nowhere are literary students so exclusively literary."

Now this specialism can have either good or bad effects. The ADVOCATE, since it is the nearest thing to an undergraduate literary center that Harvard has, is the best place to observe this literary exclusiveness at work. The student of literature is, on the ADVOCATE, in contact of some sort with the best undergraduate and graduate talents in his field in the area, which includes many of the foremost men of the nation. He is also in the most vulnerable literary position in what is probably the most literate undergraduate body in the United States.

These contacts, and this pressure, lead to a desire for perfection which can by a divorce from life produce the butterfly or the pedant, two extremes of literary worthlessness. But, on the other hand, the exclusive attention to perfection in one art or in one study can produce—and has produced—scholars and writers whose standards of achievement are unequaled.

And there is another force working on the ADVOCATE undergraduate, pushing him toward stronger effort, which cannot be ignored: the force of a tradition. Besides the valuable personal contact which the undergraduate receives through the ADVOCATE, there is a subtler kind of contact with past editors, great writers, whose names line the walls of the Sanctum. It is a tradition of success.

DONALD HALL
Cambridge, Mass.

AUGUST 1, 1950

The Origin of the *Advocate*

"Memorabilia," written by W. S. Gage and printed in the March, 1866, issue of the Collegian, *was a large factor in the decision of the Harvard faculty to force that magazine to cease publication. F. P. Stearns then organized the* Harvard Advocate *and printed the editorial "Our Paper," in the first number. "The Collegian," also from the first issue of the* Advocate, *was written by Stearns in collaboration with John E. Leonard.*

MEMORABILIA

(*Translation*)

SOCRATES: Good-morning, Glaucon.
GLAUCON: Good-morning, O Socrates!
SOCRATES: Tell me now, Glaucon, are you just from the temple?
GLAUCON (who has seen Socrates before): I should say so.
SOCRATES: Whether is the business there worship, or to see if any one of the young men be absent?
GLAUCON: Give it up.
SOCRATES: Is it not right that all men should be eager to learn?
GLAUCON: Most certainly, O Socrates!
SOCRATES: Are you not, then, a man?
GLAUCON (who has seen the Sphinx): You bet.
SOCRATES: It is plain, then, that you wish to listen to me.

GLAUCON (somewhat mixed): It must be so.

SOCRATES: Tell me, then, if you were to go into the Agora, and there see many citizens noting and discussing the affairs of the city, and only two or three who were selling figs, would you not say that the object of the meeting was politics, and not fig-peddling?

GLAUCON: Most assuredly. If I should deny it, I should be very foolish.

SOCRATES: And if there should be a crowd around me, some time in the Peireus, listening to my wise words, if perchance they might learn something, and two only should be matching obuli, of what would you say the crowd was composed? Ahem!

GLAUCON: Of your disciples, certainly, O most wise Socrates!

SOCRATES: Tell me, then, Glaucon, in the temple this morning how many were engaged in worship?

GLAUCON: One, indeed.

SOCRATES: Whether was one conducting the worship and many listening, or do you say that no one was listening?

GLAUCON: Not one, in truth, save by accident.

SOCRATES: And were there any who were busy marking the young men if they were absent?

GLAUCON: You will find no one to deny it.

SOCRATES: How many, then, were there?

GLAUCON: Four, O reverend sage!

SOCRATES: Then it seems that four were busy about the affairs of men, and one only about those things which concern the gods.

GLAUCON: Thus it certainly was.

SOCRATES: Do you not, then, say that in the temple, as in the Agora and in the Peireus, that the matter about which most were busy was the business of the meeting, and not that about which the few?

GLAUCON: I do indeed, by Jupiter! and, tomorrow morning,

I will go to roll-call, and not to prayers. Come and breakfast with me, Socrates.

MARCH, 1866

OUR PAPER

THE "COLLEGIAN" WAS STARTED TWO MONTHS AGO as a Cambridge newspaper, intended to represent the views and opinions of Harvard students. Its prosperity was great; it had a long list of honorable subscribers, among both graduates and undergraduates, and was favorably spoken of by the leading periodicals of Boston. Soon after the issue of its third number, the editors of the "Collegian" were summoned, and informed that their publication must be discontinued. No direct reason was assigned for this unexpected step; and all attempts at conciliation and compromise on the part of the editors, who offered to bind themselves to any restrictions whatever, were unavailing. Deterred from further pursuance of their undertaking by threat of a most severe college censure in case they continued it, the editors stopped their paper, and squared accounts with their subscribers. Impressed with a feeling that some such newspaper as was the "Collegian" is sorely needed here to express the wishes and opinions of the students, we propose to issue this, our present publication, as long as it is supported.

We do not make our attempt in any spirit of blind malignity to those who govern and instruct us, nor do we consider it mere school-boy sentiment which animates this appeal to our right of free journalism. As boys, we were prejudiced against our masters; and there may be some of that instinct lingering about us still: but we believe ourselves, on this occasion, to be actuated by other and more liberal motives. It seems to us as if "leave to plead our own cause" had been asked for, and refused. It is from no idle whim, nor in any spirit of unmeaning opposition, that we try to assert that we consider ourselves slighted by this relentless course of our rulers in overlooking our dearest wishes. The good order and correct discipline of the College is far more likely to be demoralized by one instance where all explanation of the disputed point has been refused, than it could be by many midnight revels in front of University. It is true that two or three articles in the "Collegian" contained indistinct allusions to those to whom we are rightfully expected to pay the highest deference, but such were hardly discernible to any save ourselves, and were not intended to be understood beyond the limits of a department or of a certain class. We admit that it may have been a mistake to have published such articles in the "Collegian," but we are positive that such a practice would have been entirely stopped as soon as it became known that they were a source of annoyance to their subjects. Harmless by-play the editors thought it, which no one need be offended at.

Here are four hundred young men, the greater number of whom have now passed that age at which the law prescribes that they shall become their own masters. All these have individual opinions, feelings, ideas, more or less, of their own. It would be absurd to attempt to gratify all their whims and tastes; yet, when a majority concur in claiming a right to this privilege or that privilege, we know there is some reason for it, which ought to be investigated. And we think, that, if we are able to be responsible at all, we ought to be allowed a voice, or at least some expression of appeal, on the subject of those rules and customs here which determine so nearly our habits of thought and action throughout life. We confess that undergraduates are inexperienced, and, as compared with older heads, are ignorant enough of the realities of the world. "Yet he that wears the shoe alone knows where the shoe pinches." The scholarly senior, who knows well where the discipline of each day serves him as an assistance and a guide, also knows best of all where the chafing of his harness impedes free motion. "Times change, and men change with them." Is it expected that we should find suited to our best purposes those regulations which were framed for the government of our grandfathers? If a change is to be allowed at any time, it is possible that one time may demand it as well as another.

We disclaim having received any assistance or co-operation in our project from the former editors of the "Collegian." Not even are they responsible for the original idea of our attempt. They were not alone in their belief that a newspaper of some sort was needed among the undergraduates, both for the purpose of expressing their sentiments to each other, and also their impressions of college matters to the world. We are not a small and insignificant minority, nor are the principals on which we act cherished within the breasts of a few proselytes. They have been for a long time echoed and re-echoed in college talk and society debates. We assure the public that our columns are open to all who desire to make fair, unbiased statement of their judgment on these subjects or on any others. Nothing abusive, nothing personally libelous, nothing which in the judgment of the editors would be likely to excite disobedience or disorder, will be received.

With this exposition of "our purposes," we intrust to the mercy of our readers the first number of the ADVOCATE.

MAY, 1866

THE COLLEGIAN

THE "COLLEGIAN" HAS BEEN SUPPRESSED. JUST AS IT was starting out upon a career full of hope and promise, its young life was crushed—crushed, so far as we have been able to learn, for the following cogent "reasons." 1st, Formal permission to publish it was not obtained from the faculty. 2d, It contained complimentary allusions to members of the faculty. 3d, It contained jocular ditto. 4th, It was conducted with no ability. 5th, It was not a fair exponent of the students' views. 6th, They (the suppressors) "did not think the said students had time for any such things."

We do not propose to endeavor to controvert the above "reasons." We submit that they are all lumps of wisdom, and so must stand, unscathed and unanswered forevermore. What we do propose is, to publish a paper in spite of the fate of our lamented predecessor, and regardless of the seven lumps of wisdom. We do not remember of ever having pledged ourselves not to publish a paper. So far from that being the case, we were well aware that divers papers had been published by students, from time to time; and, furthermore, that they were, for the most part, allowed to die a natural death. A few of them, indeed, committed suicide; but the "Collegian" was the first one which was ever murdered. We believe that this unfortunate sheet was not even allowed the poor privilege which the French despot grants his subjects; namely, a "warning," but was disposed of after the summary fashion of martial law. If we are infants, perhaps the act was justifiable; but if we are men, or even boys, it was not. We deny that the powers that be have any right to muzzle us in such a manner; or, even granting that they have the right, how much better it would have looked to have refrained from exercising it in such a case as this. They might have known that it would only serve to provoke ill-feeling between themselves and the students, and to bring the college into disrepute. We do not know of a single student, in any of the departments, who does not deplore the supressing of the "Collegian" as an act of arbitrary will. And the same opinion prevails everywhere. Several prominent gentlemen of Boston have declared that they never before imagined that the students were treated in such an illiberal manner. It is well known that the students are, for the most part, disposed to obey the laws of the college to the very

Theodore Roosevelt

Franklin Delano Roosevelt

Charles T. Copeland

George Lyman Kittredge

Advocate Board of 1880. Theodore Roosevelt is at top right.

Advocate Board of 1910. T. S. Eliot is third from left, front row. Conrad Aiken is fourth from left, second row.

Conrad Aiken

E. E. Cummings

T. S. Eliot

Maxwell Perkins

Robert Benchley

John Reed

Walter
Edmonds

James Gould
Cozzens

Edward A.
Weeks

Harry Brown

Malcolm
Cowley

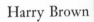

Robert
Hillyer

THE ADVOCATE GIVES A TEA

A *Lampoon* cartoon some time after Theodore Roosevelt was President and before 1917 when *Monthly* (lower right corner) expired. *Crimson* is represented at lower left, *Lampoon* by the jester at upper right. Pegasus is the name given to the literary editor.

Peter Viereck

Norman Mailer

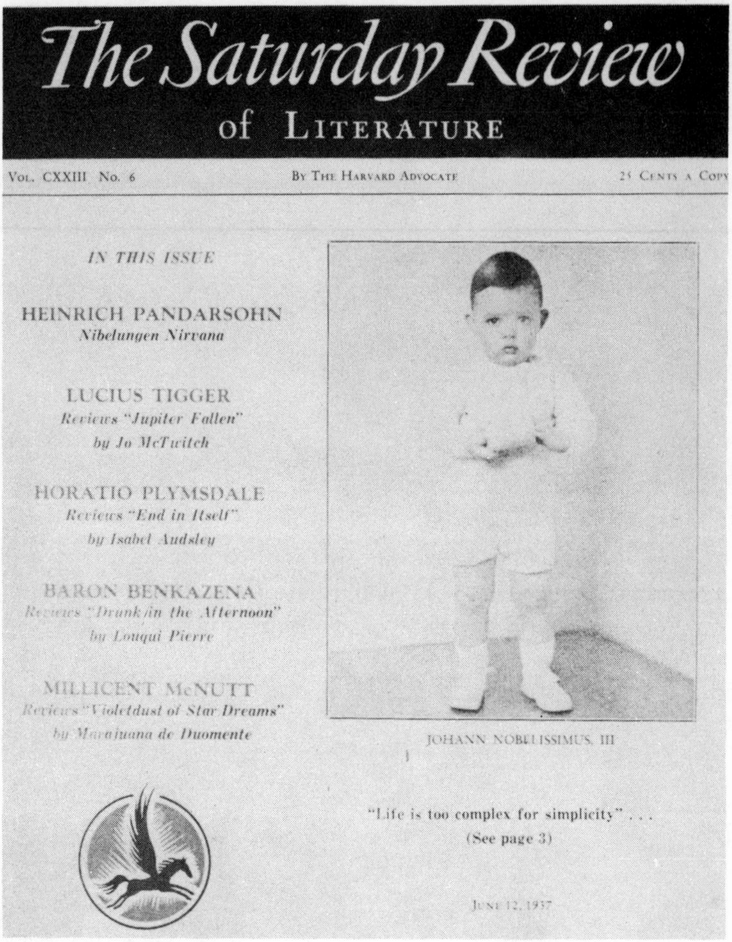

The Saturday Review
of Literature

Vol. CXXIII No. 6 | By The Harvard Advocate | 25 Cents a Copy

IN THIS ISSUE

HEINRICH PANDARSOHN
Nibelungen Nirvana

LUCIUS TIGGER
Reviews "Jupiter Fallen"
by Jo McTwitch

HORATIO PLYMSDALE
Reviews "End in Itself"
by Isabel Audsley

BARON BENKAZENA
Reviews "Drunk in the Afternoon"
by Louqui Pierre

MILLICENT McNUTT
Reviews "Violetdust of Star Dreams"
by Marajuana de Duomente

JOHANN NOBILISSIMUS, III

"Life is too complex for simplicity" . . .
(See page 3)

June 12, 1937

Cover of the *Saturday Review* parody issue of 1937.

On facing page: An Advocate playbill.

A
PLEASANT
CONCEYTED CO-
medie of How to Be Happy Though Fully Cloathed

OR

HELL hath no Fury Like an Husband Horned

by J. LeB. Boyle II

As it is Acted by the Gentlemen Servants of the Advocate

Sir Giles Scroughall	C. L. Barber
Socket	G. Piel
Mistress Philena Socket	R. Chafee
Captain Codpiece	H. B. White
Hotgut Twiddlestones	C. A. Haskins
Dr. T. S. Spencer	LeB. Boyle II

HARVARD ADVOCATE HOUSE

Febr. viii MCM.XXXIIII A.D.

Above: An ADVOCATE Sanctum of the twenties. *Below:* The current ADVOCATE Sanctum showing the President's chair. The plaques on the walls list the members of each past board. *Inset:* The founders' plaque over the fireplace.

letter, so long as they remain in force; but how absurd it is to say that they must not murmur, or have an opportunity to declare wherein these laws may be unjust and inexpedient!

MAY, 1866

THE HARVARD ADVOCATE ANTHOLOGY

Theodore Roosevelt, '80

1858–1919

Theodore Roosevelt was Treasurer of the ADVOCATE *in his Senior year at Harvard. Two years after his graduation, Roosevelt, a historian before he became a politician, published his first book. Years later (see Introduction) he returned as guest of honor to an* ADVOCATE *party, and published an article on preparedness in the* ADVOCATE's Fifty Year Book.

FOOTBALL AT OTHER COLLEGES

THE FOOTBALL SEASON HAS NOW FAIRLY OPENED, AND it is well to take a glance at what our rivals are doing. Yale has lost Thompson, who has twice turned the scale against us; but otherwise her team will probably be much the same as last year's, and there is plenty of good material from which to fill the vacancies. Captain Camp has already begun to put his men into regular training, running them in the gymnasium. Thirty men have been pledged to play against the team every afternoon, and games will probably be played with both Amherst and Trinity; so that there will be no danger of her men suffering from lack of practice. At present it hardly seems as if the team would be as good as last year's, but their playing is improving every day, and nothing but very hard work will enable our men to win the victory.

Princeton will undoubtedly have a good team, although the lower classes do not seem to possess very good material from which to choose; but it must be remembered that in Princeton, where there is no crew, all the best men go out on the football field, and work with a faithfulness not very common at Harvard.

At Cornell there has been some talk of organizing a team, but it is doubtful if it can be done this year. What Columbia will do, it is difficult to say. On the whole, the prospect should be by no means discouraging to us. We certainly have good teams to fight against; but there is plenty of excellent material in College, and our captain deserves most hearty praise, whatever be the result, for the pains he has taken, not only in keeping the men at work on the field, but in running them on the track every afternoon. What is most necessary is, that every man should realize the necessity of faithful and honest work, *every afternoon.* Last year we had good individual players, but they did not work together nearly as well as the Princeton team, and were not in as good condition as the Yale men. The football season is short; and while it does last, the men ought to work faithfully, if they expect to win back for Harvard the position she held three years ago.

OCTOBER, 1879

George Lyman Kittredge, '82

1860–1941

George Lyman Kittredge, famous philologist and Shakespearean scholar, was President of the ADVOCATE *in 1882. After his graduation, Kittredge first taught at Exeter, but returned to Harvard in 1888 as an instructor in English. Two years later he was made a professor, and for generations of Harvard students was beloved as "Kitty."*

DER PILGRIM VOR ST. JUST

(24. Februar, 1557.)
from AUGUST V. PLATEN

'Tis night; the storm comes on me more and more;
For God's love, fathers, open now your door.

Here let me rest, until the bell must needs
Call every monk to church to bid his bedes.

Make ready for me what your means can bear,–
A coffin and the habit which ye wear

Grant me a cell for my novitiate.
Half of this world once leaned upon my state!

The head that now submitteth to be shorn,
Full many a crown hath on its forehead worn.

The shoulder by this coarse-wove cowl embraced,
The ermine of an emporer has graced.

Now am I, living, likened to the dead;
And as I fall th' old empire bows its head.

APRIL, 1881

A TERRIBLE NIGHT

I HAD KNOWN HIM ONLY A FEW WEEKS, AND THOUGHT him a very jolly fellow. He reciprocated my feelings, and we passed many pleasant hours in one another's rooms, playing whist or discussing grave points in literature, art, science, philosophy, and tennis. One night (I think it is extremely doubtful–quite as doubtful, perhaps, as the championship problem–if I ever forget that night)–one night in March we were sitting before a blazing fire in his room, smoking and discussing the sonnet. The wind howled outside like mad and the chapel choir, but within all was calm save my new friend, who seemed strangely agitated. I wondered at this, for I could see nothing in the subject of our discussion to rouse agitation. Suddenly he sprang from his chair and with a sudden motion locked and barred the door. I had never noticed before that there was a bar, and was much surprised when I saw that it was arranged with a spring-lock attachment. "Elton," I cried, "what under heaven are you doing?" "Nothing, nothing, my dear fellow," and he laughed nervously, "I only thought I heard Shakespeare's walk outside, coming to dun me for my subscription to his sonnets, which I have never yet paid. Wait a minute and I'll show you the book." I was not much reassured by this reply, and watched Elton rather narrowly as he searched the bookcase behind me, but I finally turned round again, as it took him a good while, and sat as before, facing the fire.

Perhaps I had been sitting thus thirty seconds, when I felt myself violently seized from behind, while a mocking laugh sounded in my ears. I was taken altogether at a disadvantage, and didn't quite know what was up, but soon came to the conclusion that Elton was trying to tie me to the chair. I don't mind telling you that I'm a pretty strong and agile fellow, my muscles having been well developed by constant base-ball practice. I'm on the Freshman Nine, you know. So I kicked and struggled desperately, but to no purpose. Elton's constant exercise at tennis had given him strength against which mine, though my sinew had been toughened in the way just mentioned, stood no chance. I soon found myself bound hand and foot to the heavy chair and locked in a room alone with a madman. For Elton was mad. There was no doubt of it. I think the presiding genius at the office was never madder, not even when a venturesome senior asked her recently for his mark in Forensics. "Faredale," said he, "I have you now. You are in my power. You have often conversed with me on the sonnet, little suspecting I am a poet. But a poet I am. I have sent my poems in to various college papers. They have never been accepted. I hired my goody to listen to my odes at ten dollars a line; she heard three lines and fled. I bribed my janitor. He heard six lines and went out, borrowing my umbrella. I persuaded Connors, and he seemed to stand it pretty well, but it was too much for his bull-dog. It killed him. I had to pay Connors heaven knows how much damages. But now I have you. Ha! ha! Just listen to my beautiful poems." And he produced a well-bound and well-thumbed MS. and began:—

"OWED TO THE OFFICE

"O dread abode of doubt and dreary woe!
O dreary, doubting woe, and dread abode!
Why dost thou tear, torment, and torture so
The trembling toiler of this thrice-told ode?
Thou labyrinth of cave, thou cavy woe,
Why dost thou torture and torment me so?"

While reading this frightful production, poor Elton gesticulated and gyrated as I had thought nothing on earth could make a man gesticulate and gyrate, always excepting Dr. James's spiral swing. As for me, I was *in articulo mortis*. But I held my breath. "Is it not glorious?" shrieked the madman. "Yes, indeed," assented I. "Then just listen to this," and on he went:—

"LINES TO THE TUBULAR VU

"God bless thee, good old Tubular! God save and send thee rest.
The errors of my judgment long since I have confessed.
I used to think it dreadful (when I was young and green)
To figure out your mysteries and make my blank out clean—
But standing on one foot
At the bullention in U.
Has made me sigh for good old times
When each student, rich or poor, bond or free, without regard to age or sex, could, by simply calling for it, obtain at no expense, a copy of that invaluable manual for students known as the Tubular Vu."

"How do you like that?" said Elton. I was fast growing weaker, but I managed to gasp out, "Lovely. The wild and luxuriant redundancy of the last line, the sort of harmony blossoming itself to death, reminds me of—" "No matter what it reminds you of," burst out the madman, "listen to this. It is a

"THRENODY

"Scarce can I think that he is dead.
Who's dead? A Senior, he
Slipped up on his degree;
The mourners veil his head,
He's dead. No doubt he's dead.
Alas, why did he die?
Who can tell?
Dead he is, then let him lie,
Toll the bell."

"The bell," laughed Elton, "is to be tolled five minutes. You have no more prayer-cuts. You will go to prayers or be put on special." "I shall die," I groaned. "No doubt," said he; "here is another. Something of a magical nature:—

XXX

"Three friends came forth out of the West,
Out of the East came they,
There came three friends out of the South,
And thus began their say—"

"Help! help!" I shrieked, able to bear no more. At my words the door was burst open, and two men rushed in. They seized Elton and secured him after a desperate struggle. It was the janitor and a friend, who, supposing Elton out, were going to drop in for a quiet smoke. They saved me, any way. Elton was sent to —— Asylum, where he got over his poetry, and has since become a useful member of the community.

JUNE, 1881

Charles Townsend Copeland, '82

1860–

Charles Townsend Copeland and George Lyman Kittredge attended Harvard and were members of the ADVOCATE *during the same years. Copeland spent one year at Law School and did graduate work at Bowdoin. From 1893–1910 he was lecturer on English literature at Harvard, and in 1910 was made a professor. Most famous for his readings of favorite passages in prose and verse, Copeland has also achieved recognition as author and editor.*

THE STUDY OF ENGLISH LITERATURE

TO A GREEK OR TO A ROMAN THE PLACE WHICH ENGlish literature occupies in our education would seem absurdly small. Horace and Virgil were taught in the schools of Rome.

> "Quot stabant pueri, cum totus decolor esset
> Flaccus, et haereret nigro fuligo Maroni."

The Greeks learned Homer before they learned anything else, and we—learn almost everything else before we learn the masterpieces in our own language. There never was so fine a literature as ours, and never was a literature so neglected by those who possessed it. There are many college-bred men who have mastered Latin poetry and Greek plays, for whom Shakespeare continues to be Greek, and Milton but a stumbling-block.

The trouble begins in the lower schools, and is scarcely bettered in the higher ones. Latin and Greek, Arithmetic and Grammar, are studied with an assiduity which excludes all English, except what is gained through the exercise of writing "compositions"—an exercise, it is needless to say, which gives no acquaintance with literature. As long as such a state of things continues, so long will the greater number of young people have no acquaintance with their best writers, and candidates for admission to Harvard College (see an article by Professor Hill in *Good Company*) when asked to write on the "Style of Henry Esmond," will treat of the hero's clothes.

With such a preparation we are not surprised to find the matter in as bad a condition as it is in the colleges. Harvard College—and it is supposed to give more attention to the subject than any other college in the United States—has seven courses in English. Of these, three have to do with English Literature, but only one (English 7) deals with the subject from a *purely* literary point of view. In English 1 and 2 five authors are studied,—Chaucer, Bacon, Milton, Dryden, and Shakespeare. In English 7, which is a one-hour course, established within the last two years, the attempt is made to cover the literature of this century and the last; but, naturally, little is accomplished after 1800, and the literature of even one century must be hastily considered in so little time as is given to it. More courses and more instructors are evidently needed. Of interest there seems to be no lack. English 7, in spite of the fact that it is a one-hour course, and as much work is required in it as in most three-hour courses, is very popular. If there were two three-hour courses, one for the eighteenth and one for the nineteenth century, the class-rooms would no doubt be crowded. If Harvard College would raise its standard of admission in English, and then increase its own instruction, an improvement would be seen throughout this country. Cannot something be done? The production of *Oedipus* is expected to do much for the study of Greek. If a play of Shakespeare should, as has been proposed, be brought out in the old fashion next year, much might be done in the matter of "agitating" the subject.

MAY, 1881

ON DEAN SWIFT'S "A MODEST PROPOSAL"

FOR PREVENTING THE CHILDREN OF POOR PEOPLE IN IRELAND FROM BEING A BURDEN TO THEIR PARENTS OR COUNTRY, AND FOR MAKING THEM BENEFICIAL TO THE PUBLIC. 1729.

Startling as was this scheme–a plan for killing and eating the superfluous children of Ireland–and profound as was the impression it made on the public, it was not the first proposition of this sort to be found in literature. There was a popular belief during the civil wars in England that the Cavaliers were in the habit of eating children. Of Sir Thomas Lunsford, in particular, it was said that his favorite food was the flesh of children, and he was painted ogre-fashion, in the act of cutting a child into steaks and broiling them. He fell at the siege of Bristol in 1643, and the populace were told in rhyme,–

"The post who came from Coventry,
Riding in a red rocket,
Did tidings tell how Lunsford fell,
A child's hand in his pocket."

But this extraordinary fiction is chiefly elaborated in a comedy called the "Old Troop," of which the following forms part of a scene. The characters are some soldiers who are talking together, and a woman who announces herself thus:—

Woman.—By your leave, your good worship, I have made bold to bring you in some provisions.

Ford.—Provisions! where, where is this provision?

Woman.—Here, if it please you, I have brought you a couple of fine, fleshy children.

Cornet.—Was ever such a horrid woman! What shall we do?

Lieutenant.—Woman, art thou not troubled to part with thy children?

Woman.—Alas! sir, they are none of mine, they are only nurse children.

Lieutenant.—Whose children are they?

Woman.—A laundress that owes me for a year's nursing; I hope they'll prove excellent meat; they are twins, too.

Raggou (a French cook).—Aha, but! but begar, we never eat no twin shild; de law forbid dat.—*Old Troop*, Act III.

Whether Swift owed his idea to this delicate bit, is of no more importance than just how much or how little Shakespeare owed to this or that Italian tale. The "Proposal" stands alone. The modesty of it is scarcely less than the modesty of a certain other proposal made in good faith by the same writer, to the effect that the English language should be fixed in permanent form, no alterations thereafter to be made without more difficulty than lies in amending our Constitution. The "Proposal" is even more serious, in its grim irony, than "Gulliver's Travels." A certain business-like affability pervades it, the air of the well-meaning tradesman, who is determined to please at every hazard. The writer would seem to assure the reader by his very manner, that he is no visionary philosopher, but a man of affairs, and that his proposal, being made by such a man, is undoubtedly practical. Says he, "I shall now, therefore, humbly propose my own thoughts, which I hope will not be liable to the least objection." With an engaging modesty, speaking rather on another's authority than on his own, he goes on: "I have been assured by a very knowing American of my acquaintance in London, that a young, healthy child, well nursed, is, at a year old, a most delicious, nourishing and wholesome food, whether stewed, roasted, baked, or boiled; and I make no doubt (this, you will observe, is a logical addition of Swift's own) that it will equally serve in a fricassee or a ragout."

The effectiveness of the essay is further increased by the scrupulous and painstaking attention to detail. The benevolent Dean tells, with particularity, how many dishes a child will make at "an entertainment for friends," and how many when the family dines alone. He displays no narrow prejudice in regard to the fore and the hind quarter. Either will make "a reasonable dish." One advantage of adopting children as an article of diet (and, he might have added, an equal advantage in adopting them as one's own—every man being thereby his own butcher),—one advantage is, that "infants' flesh will be in season throughout the year." He says that shambles may be appointed in the most convenient parts of Dublin, but recommends, as a means of increasing the delicacy of the flesh, "buying the children alive, then dressing hot from the knife." If you are *fond of children*, the advantage of adopting a good many is again to be seen here. The author takes up considerable space with his "six advantages," exquisitely and even mathematically nice, but too long to be quoted. In conclusion, he earnestly recommends his proposal to Ireland as something "whereby we can incur no danger in disobliging *England*. For this kind of commodity will not bear exportation, the flesh being of too tender a consistence to admit of long continuance in salt." The candor of his last statement is simple and touching: "I profess, in the sincerity of my heart," says the honest soul, "that I have not the least personal interest in promoting this necessary work. I have no children by which I can propose to get a single penny; the youngest being nine years old, and my wife past child bearing."

The French, although reputed to be clever, are said to regard the "Vicar of Wakefield" as a description of actual country life in England; and we must all have heard of the respectable gentleman who thought De Quincey's essay on Murder as a Fine Art a malicious and dangerous publication. The "Modest Proposal," like these two productions, has not escaped misunderstanding, for, with such admirable skill is its ironical gravity maintained throughout, that "a foreign author is said to have quoted it as an instance of the extremity under which Ireland labored, that a man of letters, and a clergyman, had seriously recommended to the rich to feed upon the children of the poor."

DECEMBER, 1881

Thomas W. Lamont, '92

1870–1948

Thomas W. Lamont, the financier and philanthropist, wrote My Boyhood in a Parsonage *in 1946. Lamont was also the author of other books and pamphlets.*

AN INCIDENT OF THE CRIMEAN WAR

A FRIEND ONCE RELATED TO ME AN INCIDENT OF THE Crimean war which may bear repetition. It ran something like this.

It was during the siege of Sebastapol. A young Englishman was stationed in the city as war correspondent for the "London Standard." The city was under the surveillance of severe military rule, and it was a most dangerous piece of business to try to evade, in the slightest degree, the restrictions imposed by the military authorities. It was especially forbidden any one to send from the city dispatches, even of the most innocent kind, before an inspection was made of them by the officers detailed for the day. Thus it was, that all the correspondents for foreign papers were obliged to put their dispatches in the hands of the officers before sending them. The inspection was frequently delayed several hours, and sometimes it was a day after the articles had been written, before they reached their destination in London.

It was the account of a sudden and victorious sortie made

by the besiegers that the young English reporter determined to send to his paper in London, without waiting for the usual inspection. It was a dangerous experiment on his part, but if he should succeed, he knew that the "Standard's" account would be fully a day ahead of those of the other papers, and that his own advancement on the staff of correspondents would be ensured.

He was caught in the very act of sending the dispatches, and thrown into a dungeon of the prison which was situated immediately under the house of the military governor of the city. He was told that the penalty for his offense was death, and that he would be shot at dawn of the next morning. As he lay there in the darkness of early evening, he heard the sound of music coming from rooms of the governor's house far above him. He sent for his jailer and asked what the music was for. The jailer told him that it was being played at the birthday ball of the governor's young daughter. The prisoner, whom we shall call Bronson, sent for the governor and asked him if he might be allowed to spend his last night on earth at the ball. It was a strange request, but the governor granted it when Bronson gave his word of honor that he would not try to escape.

Bronson dressed himself in the uniform of the lieutenant of the guards, and was then led by the governor up to the ballroom. The governor told his daughter that there was a young Englishman who was to start at dawn on a most difficult and dangerous mission from which he might not return alive, and he asked her to be as kind as possible to him during the course of the ball.

Bronson was introduced to the girl, and danced with her many times during the evening. The ball had just broken up, almost all the guests had gone, and the grey of dawn was just beginning to show itself, as Bronson stood talking with the young girl. At that moment the governor came into the room, and walking up to the pair, said to Bronson, "Come, it is time you started." The young Englishman said goodbye to the girl, and at parting she gave him her handkerchief as a remembrance of the ball. He took it, and going down into the courtyard a few rods away, found the file of soldiers with muskets ready loaded. He took his position, and when all was ready, he gave the signal himself by dropping the handkerchief. The soldiers fired.

As the young girl, still standing in the ballroom, heard the report of the muskets, she said, "They are giving a salute to the brave soldier, as he starts on his journey."

MARCH, 1889

Edwin Arlington Robinson, 1891-93

1869-1935

Edwin Arlington Robinson, whose verse won him the patronage of President Theodore Roosevelt and three Pulitzer Prizes, attended Harvard for only two years. Robinson's poetic maturity came early; two of his ADVOCATE *poems, "Supremacy" and "Villanelle of Change," appear in slightly altered form in his* Collected Poems. *"Richard Cory," one of Robinson's best known poems, was written while he was at Harvard but was printed, unfortunately, in the* Harvard Monthly.

BALLADE OF THE WHITE SHIP

Down they went to the still, green water—
  The dim White Ship like a white bird lay;
Laughing at life and the world they sought her,
  And out they sailed on the silvering bay:
  The quick ship flew on her roystering way,
And the keen moon fired the light foam flying
  Up from the flood where the faint stars play,
And the bones of the brave in the wave are lying.

'Twas a king's gay son with a king's gay daughter,
  And full three hundred beside, they say,

Hurrying on to the lone, cold slaughter
  So soon to seize them and hide them for aye;
  But they danced and they drank and their souls grew gay,
Nor ever they knew of a ghoul's eye spying,
  Their splendor a flickering phantom to stray
Where the bones of the brave in the wave are lying.

Through the mist of a drunken dream they brought her
  (This wild white bird) for the sea-fiend's prey:
The ravenous reef in his hard clutch caught her
  And whirled her down where the dead men stay—
  A torturing silence of wan dismay;
The shrieks and curses of mad souls dying.
  Then down they sank to slumber and sway
Where the bones of the brave in the wave are lying.

L'envoi

Prince, do you sleep 'mid the perishing clay
  To the mournful dirge of the sea-birds' crying?
Or does blood still quicken and steel still slay—
  Where the bones of the brave in the wave are lying?

OCTOBER, 1891

VILLANELLE OF CHANGE

Since Persia fell at Marathon
  The yellow years have gathered fast—
Long centuries have come and gone.

And yet (they say) the place will don
  A phantom fury of the past,
Since Persia fell at Marathon;

And as of old, when Helicon
Trembled and swayed with rapture vast,–
Long centuries have come and gone–

This ancient plain, when night comes on,
Shakes in a phantom battle blast,
Since Persia fell at Marathon . . . .

With mouldering mists of Acheron
Long have her skies been overcast,
Long centuries have come and gone;

The suns of other days have shone–
The first has fallen to the last:
Since Persia fell at Marathon,
Long centuries have come and gone.

NOVEMBER, 1891

IN HARVARD 5

In Harvard 5 the deathless lore
That haunts old Avon's classic shore
Wakens the long triumphant strain
Of Pride and Passion, Mirth and Pain,
That fed the Poet's mind of yore.

Time's magic glass is turned once more
And back the sands of ages pour,
While shades of mouldered monarchs reign
In Harvard 5.

Thin spirits flutter through the door,
Quaint phantoms flit across the floor:
  Now Fancy marks the crimson stain
  Of Murder . . . and there falls again
The fateful gloom of Elsinore
            In Harvard 5.

DECEMBER, 1891

SUPREMACY

There is a drear and lonely tract of Hell
  From all the common gloom removed afar:
  A flat, sad land where only shadows are,
Whose lorn estate no word of mine can tell.
I walked among the shades and knew them well:
  Men I had scorned upon Life's little star
  For churls and sluggards; and I knew the scar
Upon their brows of woe ineffable.

But as I moved triumphant on my way,
  Into the dark they vanished, one by one.
Then came an awful light, a blinding ray—
  As if a new creation were begun;
And with a swift, importunate dismay,
  I heard the dead men singing in the sun.

JUNE, 1892

William Vaughn Moody, '93

1869–1910

William Vaughn Moody remained at Harvard the year after his graduation and received his M.A. degree. A teacher at Harvard and the University of Chicago, Moody achieved renown in his short life as an editor, poet, and dramatist.

SONG

I saw a knight fare gaily in the sun,
   Gold was his flowing hair;
And 'fore his steed did grace and glory run
   To speak him fair.
"I would I were Sir Knight," quoth I,
            With tear-dimmed eye.

I saw my Lord ride forth from out his gate,
   Gemmed all with jewels rare;
And forty thanes did follow him in state
   'Mid bugle glare.
"I would I were Sir Lord," quoth I,
            With moody sigh.

I met my Lady in the garden shade,
   Lent-lilies plucked she there;

And by her side a little love-eyed maid,
  Who smiled at me, I swear.
"I would I were none other 'neath the sky!"
      Quoth I.

NOVEMBER, 1889

Percy MacKaye, '97

1875–

Percy MacKaye, teacher, poet, and dramatist, recently received the Fellowship Award of the Academy of American Poets to complete work on his tetralogy for the theater, The Mystery of Hamlet, King of Denmark.

SONNET

Short-sighted Nature, thou unthrifty wife,
Why dost thou ply thy patient hands in patching–
With well-hid seams and nicely careful matching–
These garments that we mortals wear through life?
Yet when thou'st fashioned by long industry
A garb so wrought that it would grace the graces,
For charm and fair adaptability,–
Discarded, thou dost hide in mouldy places,
Flung in a box where must and mildew be,
And the lean worm that fattens on decay,
Wasting the toil of lifetimes in a day.
Doth this not shame thy praised economy?
Fie on thy thrift, unless–as some men ween–
Thou spinnest finer stuff, which is not seen.

MAY, 1895

Wallace Stevens, '01

1879–

Wallace Stevens, who was President of the ADVOCATE *while at Harvard, recently was awarded the Bollingen Prize for Poetry. The author of seven books of verse, Stevens in business circles is known as the vice-president of the Hartford Accident and Indemnity Company.*

In 1940, the ADVOCATE *published a special issue in honor of Stevens.*

SONNET

There shines the morning star! Through the forlorn
And silent spaces of cold heaven's height
Pours the bright radiance of his kingly light,
Swinging in revery before the morn.
The flush and fall of many tides have worn
Upon the coasts beneath him, in their flight
From sea to sea; yet ever on the night
His clear and splendid visage is upborne.

Like this he pondered on the world's first day,
Sweet Eden's flowers heavy with the dew;
And so he led bold Jason on his way
Sparkling forever in the galley's foam;

And still he shone most perfect in the blue,
All bright and lovely on the hosts of Rome.

APRIL, 1899

QUATRAIN

Go not, young cloud, too boldly through the sky,
To meet the morning light;
Go not too boldly through that dome on high—
For eastward lies the night.

NOVEMBER, 1899

SONG

Ah yes! beyond these barren walls
Two hearts shall in a garden meet,
And while the latest robin calls,
Her lips to his shall be made sweet.

And out above these gloomy tow'rs
The full moon tenderly shall rise
To cast its light upon the flow'rs,
And find him looking in her eyes.

MARCH, 1900

OUTSIDE THE HOSPITAL

See the blind and the lame at play,
There on the summer lawn—

She with her graceless eyes of clay,
  Quick as a frightened fawn,
Running and tripping into his way
  Whose legs are gone.

How shall she 'scape him, where shall she fly,
  She who never sees?
Now he is near her, now she is by—
  Into his arms she flees.
Hear her gay laughter, hear her light cry
  Among the trees.

"Princess, my captive." "Master, my king,"
  "Here is a garland bright."
"Red roses, I wonder, red with the Spring,
  Red with a reddish light?"
"Red roses, my princess, I ran to bring,
  And be your knight."

MARCH, 1900

STREET SONGS

I THE PIGEONS

Over the houses and into the sky
  And into the dazzling light,
Long hosts of fluttering pigeons fly
  Out of the blackened night,
Over the houses and into the sky
  On glistening wings of white.

Over the city and into the blue
  From ledge and tower and dome,

They rise and turn and turn anew,
  And like fresh clouds they roam,
Over the city and into the blue
  And into their airy home.

II THE BEGGAR

Yet in this morn there is a darkest night,
Where no feet dance or sweet birds ever rise
Where fancy is a thing that soothes—and lies,
And leads on with mirages of light.
I speak of her who sits within plain sight
Upon the steps of yon cathedral. Skies
Are naught to her; and life a lord that buys
And sells life, whether sad, or dark, or bright.

The carvings and beauty of the throne
Where she is sitting, she doth meanly use
To win you and appeal. All rag and bone
She asks with her dry, withered hand a dreg
Of the world's riches. If she doth abuse
The place, pass on. It is a place to beg.

III STATUARY

The windy morn has set their feet to dancing—
  Young Dian and Apollo on the curb,
The pavement with their slender forms is glancing
  No clatter doth their gaiety disturb.

No eyes are ever blind enough to shun them,
  Men wonder what their jubilance can be,
No passer-by but turns to look upon them—
  Then goes his way with all his fancy free.

IV THE MINSTREL

The streets lead out into a mist
  Of daisies and of daffodils—
A world of green and amethyst,
  Of seas and of uplifted hills.

There bird-songs are not lost in eaves,
  Nor beaten down by cart and car,
But drifting sweetly through the leaves,
  They die upon the fields afar.

Nor is the wind a broken thing
  That faints within hot prison cells,
But rises on a silver wing
  From out among the heather bells.

APRIL, 1900

NIGHT SONG

I stand upon the hills to-night
  And see the cold March moon
Rise upward with his silver light
  And make a gentle noon.

The fields are blowing with the breeze,
  The stars are in the sky,
There is a humming through the trees,
  And one cloud passes by.

I wonder if that is the sea,
  Rid of the sun's annoy,
That sings a song all bold and free,
  Of glory and of joy.

MAY, 1900

SONNET

Lo, even as I passed beside the booth
Of roses, and beheld them brightly twine
To damask heights, taking them as a sign
Of my own self still unconcerned with truth;
Even as I held up in hands uncouth
And drained with joy the golden-bodied wine,
Deeming it half-unworthy, half divine,
From out the sweet-rimmed goblet of my youth;

Even in that pure hour I heard the tone
Of grievous music stir in memory,
Telling me of the time already flown
From my first youth. It sounded like the rise
Of distant echo from dead melody,
Soft as a song heard far in Paradise.

MAY, 1900

BALLADE OF THE PINK PARASOL

I pray thee where is the old-time wig,
  And where is the lofty hat?
Where is the maid on the road in her gig,
  And where is the fire-side cat?
  Never was sight more fair than that,
Outshining, outreaching them all,
  There in the night where lovers sat—
But where is the pink parasol?

Where in the pack is the dark spadille
  With scent of lavender sweet,

That never was held in the mad quadrille.
  And where are the slippered feet?
Ah! we'd have given a pound to meet
  The card that wrought our fall,
The card none other of all could beat–
  But where is the pink parasol?

Where is the roll of the old calash,
  And the jog of the light sedan?
Whence Chloe's diamond brooch would flash
  And conquer poor peeping man.
Answer me, where is the painted fan
  And the candles bright on the wall;
Where is the coat of yellow and tan–
  But where is the pink parasol?

Prince, these baubles are far away,
  In the ruin of palace and hall,
Made dark by the shadow of yesterday–
  But where is the pink parasol?

MAY, 1900

QUATRAIN

He sought the music of the distant spheres
  By night, upon an empty plain, apart;
Nor knew they hid their singing all the years
  Within the keeping of his human heart.

JUNE, 1900

SONG

She loves me or loves me not,
  What care I?—
The depth of the fields is just as sweet,
  And sweet the sky.

She loves me or she loves me not,
  Is that to die?—
The green of the woods is just as fair,
  And fair the sky.

1901

Witter Bynner, '02

1881–

Witter Bynner, who has been both editor and teacher, is best known for his poems and translations. His latest book of verse is Take Away the Darkness, *published in 1947.*

A LEAF

The summer long I hung on a tree
    That kept me green and gave me life to dance:
The summer long I could not help to see
    I made no least advance.
Then a wind came creeping, came stealing—
And, suddenly reeling,
I loosened my hold and flew high, high, high,
In the wideness of sky,
In the freedom of wilderness, free,
                Looking down on the sea,
                    Down on the tree,
                        Free!
What tho' I fell in a fainting trance,
                        Free!
Tho' I lie, alas, at the foot of the tree,
Tho' I die in the grass, I was free,
                    I was free,
                        Free!

JUNE, 1902

LADY ROWENA

When Lady Rowena
Came over the sea
(Woe to the islanders! woe!)
Her flowery color
Grew fresh and free
Lusty as the roses grow.

The wind and the water
Were wet in her hair;
(Woe to the islanders! woe!)
Her glances were quick
As a swallow in air,
Blither than breezes blow.

Flashes of womanhood!
Flashes of wine!
(Woe to the islanders! woe!)
Like the liquor she poured him
Her eyes were a-shine,
And the blood of her cheek was a-glow.

She was worthily sister
Of Hengist in wile;
(Woe to the islanders! woe!)
King Vortigern prostrate
Lay slain by her smile—
O for the spear of a foe!

Heathen the mistress
That lay in his bed;
(Woe to the islanders! woe!)

Christian the heroes
That stiffly lay dead
        Where battle brought them low.

When Lady Rowena
Came over the sea,
        (Woe to the islanders! woe!)
There was all of the beauty
With all of the plea
        That lovers and poets know.

MAY, 1902

Franklin Delano Roosevelt, '04

1882–1945

Franklin Delano Roosevelt, at Harvard, gave some indication of what was to come. Besides being elected permanent chairman of his class, Roosevelt was editor of the Harvard Crimson, *the college undergraduate daily. Not a member of the* ADVOCATE *staff, Roosevelt contributed to its pages only "A Newly Discovered Fragment from a Voyage to Lilliput."*

A NEWLY DISCOVERED FRAGMENT FROM A VOYAGE TO LILLIPUT

BUT STRANGER EVEN THAN THESE NURSERIES FOR BOYS and girls past the nourishing age are the places where what the Lilliputians call "higher learning" is taught. Shortly after the fire in the Empress' wing of the palace, the Emperor, in order that I might not think him displeased with me, conferred upon me the degree of Doctor of Extinguishment, and commanded me to inspect one of these learned institutions which I have just mentioned. I found it situated in a pleasant marsh not far from the city of Axis—a town locally supposed to be the source and centre of all learning. The institution itself was called in the dialect a University, because, as I was told, it is the whole thing.

The earliest settlers of Lilliput founded this University soon after their arrival, chiefly for the purpose of a house of correction for the natives whom they found there. A few years later a worthy settler, dying, bequeathed a valuable set of printed notes to the institution which thereafter bore his noble name. Since then many life-like statues of him have arisen, all copied after an excellent sketch on the fly-leaf of a New England Primer, done of himself, by himself and for himself at the age of three and a half. His name also is frequently heard today, punctuated with sharp pleasure cries and given in chorus at a mystic sign from a six-inch giant who madly waves a cornucopia called in the language of the country megaphone. Owing, however, to a corruption of the name of the founder, the third letter, an r, is generally omitted by the inhabitants of Axis.

From a reformatory for the aborigines, the University has become the resort of thousands of Lilliputians, some even coming from the land of Blefuscu. Many of the inmates indeed come, not to study, but for the experience—"the finishing touch" which in many instances seemed to be indeed "the finishing touch." Some likewise go there for the sake only of exercise, but this practice has been lately discouraged because of a series of rules which it is said come down from Heaven, but which the Lilliputians to this day have been unable to interpret to their own satisfaction or that of anyone else. The University of the Big-Endians at Blefuscu is especially scornful of these rules, for they themselves have a rival set said to have been sent up to them by the Duskier God. The ill-feeling is further increased by the question of which can the better take exercise. The name of the Big-Endians itself is due to the swelling pride which these take in their victories in pushing a lima-bean through the ranks of the Lilliputians. On the other hand these latter, at the University I visited, because of a superior skill in killing fleas in mid-hop with a bow and arrow, claim to be the whole shooting-match.

In contests of needle threading, addition and subtraction, and reading aloud, the Little-Endians have also proved their mental superiority by victories for many moons. The needle-threading competition is especially thrilling, and the rapidity with which they passed the invisible thread through the invisible needle appeared to me quite out of sight. The enthusiasm at these contests is remarkable, very different I am told from what it was several moons ago. The din of the male students could be heard for many feet, while the co-educational members from the Sadstiff Annex signified their approval by "yum-yums" long and ponderous. I was told that the men who barked the loudest, and the lady students who yummed with greatest energy were as a rule the most liked in the University but that often in later life they did not come to high positions, probably because this form of strenuousness is not the best training to pass the great State rope dancing examinations.

The former custom of chorus singing at these matches is being superseded by hymns of praise sung alternately by a solo male and such a high female.

At the end of the contest the two umpires render diabolically opposite decisions, and the final result is announced many moons later by a partial Board of Arbitration.

Finally as a climax the two Universities rise as one man and sing their anthems. That of the Big-Endians started with the

"See such a mighty tail behind
And such a face before."

In the meantime my friends, starting at the same time in a deliciously different key sent heavenward their song—a beautiful diatribe composed of a sunset sonnet, a joke, and a communication, all taken from their leading University publications.

Such is the institution of highest learning among the noblest race in Lilliput—an institution which I would my own dear country would imitate.

On my return from Axis to the Capital I received another mark of the Emperor's favor.

[Here the manuscript stops.]

FEBRUARY, 1903

Arthur Davison Ficke '04

1883–1945

Arthur Davison Ficke was President of the ADVOCATE *while at Harvard. Best known as a poet, Ficke was also an authority on Japanese prints. Ficke's last book of verse,* The Tumultuous Shore, *appeared in 1942.*

NOCTURNE

Is it the wind that calls,
  Vague and far and low,
Or is it your yearning voice
  Out of the long ago?

Is it the night that lies
  So black on yonder hill,
Or but my yearning heart
  That sleeps in darkness still?

OCTOBER, 1903

THE WILD DUCK

A Japanese Frieze

The heron rises and circles,
The wild duck steadily flies
Past the shadowy lakes and marshes
Toward the yellow western skies.

The ripples murmur and travel
Onward in golden lines.
A wild duck flaps from the marshes
And rises over the pines.

Shadows sink on the woodland,
Mistily deepening more;
A wild duck flies toward sunset.
A wild duck lifts from the shore.

I am alone in this land of marshes;
I wander its silent streams,
Where I hear but the wild duck calling
And see but the yellow gleams.

Dark comes on the quiet waters,
The pine trees sink in haze.
Only the west is lighted
With ruin of many days.

Only the rushes murmur
On the water's mirror breast
As a wild duck hovers and turns him
Toward the open silent west.

JANUARY, 1904

Maxwell Perkins, '07

1884–1947

Maxwell Perkins in his many years at Scribner's edited the writings of Thomas Wolfe, Ernest Hemingway, and many other American authors. A volume of his letters, Editor to Author, *has recently been published, edited by John Hall Wheelock.*

ON GETTING UP IN THE MORNING

EVER SINCE MY EARLY SCHOOL DAYS, WHEN, AS A result of tardiness, I memorized a considerable portion of the United States Constitution, I have made a careful study of the different methods of getting up in the morning. These methods, though they have accumulated through the ages, have none of them, as yet, completely solved the problem, nor can I say that I have done so myself; however, since it has been my life study, so to speak, and since I have made certain advances, which, so far as I can ascertain, are original, I feel that it is my duty to lay them before the public. I therefore venture to offer these suggestions with the sincere hope that they may be of some use to my fellow-students, and particularly to Freshmen, or at least that they may direct some great mind into the proper channel for removing so great a source of unhappiness.

Before I go any further, I wish it to be distinctly understood that I am not preaching early rising. Whether it is a good thing or not is not for me to state. I have heard it said that it is a positive evil, for when a man does rise early he becomes so conceited, so puffed up with pride, that for the day at least he can do nothing but contemplate his own virtue. The inspiration of this essay, if such I may call it, is the unaccountable lack of consideration on the part of the college authorities. They enforce attendance, and then assign all those courses in which a gentleman can hope to attain the grade of C at such ridiculous hours as nine or ten. How illogical! How tyrannical! How—but I forget my subject.

The first scheme which I have found of great help is a very ingenious one, and I must, I regret to say, renounce all claims to its origin. Nor can I mention the name of its inventor, for, though he deserves great credit, he is too modest to allow publicity. His method was this: he always slept with the bedroom shades down, and before retiring, carefully placed a pair of old shoes upon a table by his bed. When he awoke in the morning he would reach out, take a shoe from the table and hurl it at the window. The sudden jerk which the blow of the shoe would give the shade caused the latter to fly up with a bang. The same performance was used with the same effect upon the other window. The sudden rush of light makes sleep impossible to unaccustomed eyes, and the exercise involved does much to facilitate the effort of getting out of bed.

Certain questions immediately arise in one's mind when first contemplating this plan.

"Wouldn't it break the window?" one might ask, or "Wouldn't it be as hard to move about and get the shoes as to get out of bed?"

As to the last question, my friend tells me (and I have since proved the truth of his word by experience) that you become so interested in your development as a shot, that you actually look forward to the hour when another opportunity will arrive to try your skill. My friend also says that such proficiency is acquired with constant practice that with but two motions of the arm, one in raising the boot, the other in swinging it toward the window, success almost invariably results. In his enthusiasm, he even asserts that one becomes so exasperated by a failure that pillows follow shoes, and that when all ammunition within reach has been exhausted, he himself has risen on more than one occasion, and procuring articles from a distance, persisted in his bombardment until success crowned his efforts. But my friend is more ambitious than the average.

Now in regard to the breaking of windows—of course that sometimes happens in the case of beginners, but this risk merely adds zest to the enterprize, and also makes the desired results more certain. For if the morning is cold, the ensuing fall in temperature makes a longer sojourn in bed out of the question.

The beauty of this method lies in the fact that you experience none of the disgust with self which you ordinarily feel, and sometimes to an intense degree, when you rise merely because you resolved to do so the night before. On more than one occasion I have been informed by my friends that I am not reasonable. It has even happened, especially in connection with money matters, that my own family has made this assertion. But never have I been more fully convinced of my own unreasonableness than when on a cold dreary morning I have dragged myself out of bed for no other reason than because I had a "nine o'clock" and had taken it into my head the night before that there lay my duty. One cannot escape this loss of respect for one's own intelligence by the ordinary tricks of counting ten or jumping, or by telling a friend to drag you out of bed. There is this advantage in the counting method, however. Make the number 25 or 50, and start to count when you awake; then if you do fall asleep before the fatal point is reached, it certainly is not your fault, and knowing that you would have jumped if nature had not intervened, you avoid the reproaches of Conscience. Conscience, the hardest of mistresses! to whom those of us who escape the bondage of tobacco (or some such paltry vice) are slaves! For we are all slaves to one thing or another, and it is a question in my mind if she is not the least desirable mistress of all.

In reading over what I have written up to this point with especial reference to the shoe experiment, an episode arises in my mind which is related to my subject and illustrates the change of view-point which one takes in the morning as contrasted to that which one holds at night.

I have a friend whom I much admire for a certain rare quality he possesses; that of arguing every question fairly and squarely with his conscience before he decides to do the thing he wants to do. Sometimes he feels that he is wrong and yields to Conscience, especially when necessity takes Conscience's part, and he is forced to acknowledge that their combined arguments are forcible. Generally speaking, however, he gains his point, for such is his power of reasoning that Conscience, while perhaps not quite persuaded—for she is a stubborn wench—at least lowers her voice to a whisper, audible only from time to time; and even in the event of her victory, he always forces her into some concessions. Some men obey this mistress absolutely, are her abject slaves. Others break away from her, ignoring her reproaches for the time, only to receive their lashes later. My friend, as you see, belongs to neither of these classes.

One evening I entered his room, and remarking that I had not been in town for some time, proposed the theater. It seems that he had been in on the previous night and in consequence had cut his nine o'clock. He could not go, he said, for the reason he had some work which must be done by ten the next morning. Did I write "he said"? It was not he who spoke it, it was Conscience. Immediately his native spirit of independence asserted itself. He argued eloquently. Well! he could get up early the next morning. He could always work better in the early morning anyhow, he said,–I think Conscience here embarrassed him with the question "What makes you think so?" He had just borrowed a book which would make his work twice as easy, he continued. Still Conscience was obdurate. Suddenly he sprang from his chair and from a drawer, produced a beautiful clock. It would ring until you got up and stopped it, he explained. Before so tangible an argument, Conscience could hold out no longer. We went in to town.

Jim, my friend, was not feeling very well when we returned, but he was still enthusiastic over his early morning plan. His roommate was away and we were to sleep in the same room. Just before retiring I said, "Jim, I'll bet you five dollars you don't get up at six tomorrow."

"I'll bet you I do," said he, and winding his clock, he placed it on the sill of the open window.

The next thing I knew there was a terrible hubbub. I thought very hard and remembered where I was, and recalled the alarm clock and the wager. I opened my eyes to see what effect the uproar would have on Jim. With a sort of cross between a grunt and a groan he rolled over and eyed the thing on the window-sill in much the manner in which I should imagine one would watch an infernal machine in operation, knowing that escape was impossible. Next he turned his eyes upon me, but I was feigning sleep. The clock had been going for a good ten minutes I should say, and was just getting into full swing. I opened my eyes again cautiously, and then I saw a sight I would not have missed for worlds. Jim was reaching out of bed and feeling about the floor. Now he raised his arm, holding a slipper in his hand, and still lying on his back, sent it flying towards the window. The weapon missed the clock by a foot or two. Jim lay still for a moment, an expression of great disappointment upon his face.

The alarm-clock seemed to be laughing at him, catching its breath every second, and going on in short spurts. Again Jim felt about the floor and procured a second slipper. This time he raised himself on his elbow, took steady aim, and sent it spinning straight as a die. The clock caught the blow right in the center. There was a crash and down it went, but game to the last, ringing away until it reached the pavement three stories below. I am convinced that nothing short of three stories and an asphalt pavement would have stopped that instrument of torture.

With the final crash and death rattle of the poor clock, which had met its fate only in doing its duty, Jim fell back on his pillow, a contented man. Then he must have remembered me: perhaps he heard me laugh. At all events he looked in my direction suspiciously. I was still as a mouse, watching through my half closed eyes. However, he raised himself, observed me doubtfully, and then got slowly out of bed and went into the next room. When Jim returned in a quarter of an hour looking fresh and pink after his bath, he asked me, eyeing me narrowly, "How about that bet?"

I looked him full in the face and, "It will just about buy you another clock and I'd gladly pay ten to see it over again," I said, and then we laughed and laughed until I was so thoroughly awake that I got up myself.

Now before I bring this essay to a close, I wish to say a few words which may benefit Freshmen. In my opinion the officers of the University are open to censure for taking no steps towards informing fellows who have just entered college of facts which everyone must know sooner or later. Some of these things are so closely connected with my subject that I take the liberty of recording them here.

In the first place, the shortest route across the Yard by actual measurement, from all points east of Holyoke Street lies to the east of Gore Hall and past Sever. In case there is snow upon the ground, it is shorter to go through the hall of Memorial, but under all ordinary circumstances, the path around the west end of that building is preferable for reaching the New Lecture Hall. Secondly, taking the time of each maid in the Oak Grove and Quincy, and getting an average on the service of boiled eggs, coffee and toast for both restaurants, I find that the former is faster by four minutes and thirty-three seconds. However, the tall blonde in the Quincy, who takes charge of the West counter, at the end nearest the street, holds the individual record; beating the best waitress in the Oak Grove by ten and two-fifths seconds on the average per week. Another point in favor of the Quincy is that the coffee there cools faster than that of the Oak Grove, whether through some intrinsic qualities of its own, or some superiority in the cookery, I am ashamed to say I have failed to ascertain.

There are many other points which should be made familiar to all undergraduates, but I have neither time nor space to give them here. In conclusion I merely add, in hopes that my suggestion may have some effect, that the University might furnish an information bureau where men could ascertain such valuable facts as I have just mentioned. In case they persist in their gross neglect, I suggest that some outsider apprise himself of such facts, and establish a bureau, and he might, at the same time find it advantageous to draw up ideal schedules to order, in accordance with the requirements of his patrons. I feel certain that such a venture would prove prosperous even though the charge were trifling. In the absence of any such institution, having, as I have already said, made a thorough study of these questions, I will put myself at the disposal of any who will send their questions to me through the mail, enclosing their addresses and stamps.

DECEMBER, 1905

Hermann Hagedorn, '07

1882–

Hermann Hagedorn, besides teaching and editing, has written poetry, drama, fiction and non-fiction. An authority on Theodore Roosevelt, he has also written biographies of E. A. Robinson and Albert Schweitzer.

WHEN THE SHADOW FALLS

When the star breaks in the melting sky,
  And the last dawn glows on a shattered world,
  To some new garden, peace-unfurled,
Our never-ending souls shall fly.

Because we loved, and loving knew
  A greater strength, a greater hope,
  Than lies within man's mortal scope
And fear-bound, death-encircled view,

We two shall find immortal days–
  Not in the gray ethereal heights,
  But in a world where old delights
Shall wait on unforgotten ways.

Let scholars speak of death that blends
  Men into one enmantling soul–
  For you and me the final goal
Must re-create the life it ends.

In some far island we shall learn
  The mysteries and runes of earth—
  Until beyond another birth,
Homeward, as one soul we return.

SEPTEMBER, 1905

FROM THE CLASS POEM FOR 1907

There's trampling of hoofs in the busy street,
  There's clanking of sabers on floor and stair,
There's sound of restless, hurrying feet,
Of voices that whisper, of lips that entreat—
  Will they live, will they die, will they strive, will
    they dare?—
The houses are garlanded, flags flutter gay,
For a troop of the Guard rides forth today.

Oh, the troopers will ride and their hearts will leap,
  When it's shoulder to shoulder and friend to
    friend—
But it's some to the pinnacle, some to the deep,
And some in the glow of their strength to sleep,
  And for all it's a fight to the tale's far end.
And it's each to his goal, nor turn nor sway,
When the troop of the Guard rides forth today.

The dawn is upon us, the pale light speeds
  To the zenith with glamor and golden dart.
On, up! Boot and saddle! Give spurs to your steeds!
There's a city beleaguered that cries for men's deeds,

With the pain of the world in its cavernous heart.
Ours be the triumph! Humanity calls!
Life's not a dream in the clover!
On to the walls, on to the walls,
On to the walls, and over!

JUNE, 1907

Van Wyck Brooks, '08

1886–

Van Wyck Brooks is the author of The Flowering of New England, New England: Indian Summer, *and other volumes of literary criticism. A selection of his writings in one volume,* A Chilmark Miscellany, *appeared in 1948.*

THE BOY AND THE OTHERS

THE BOY:

The lichen climbs upon the wall
To hear the hidden robins call:
Every cloud across the sky
Freely comes and passes by.

THE OTHERS:

Come in, come in, the stool is set;
Life give up and living get.

THE BOY:

Robins on the apple-limb
Are silent through these windows dim.

THE OTHERS:

Go forth as once you wished to do.
Nothing more is left for you.

THE BOY:

Give back my stool—I ask no more,
The desk, the pen I loathed before:
The lichen climbs not on the wall
To hear the hidden robins call.

OCTOBER, 1905

TO A MAN OF POMPEII

(*Petrified in lava, in the museum at Naples*)

Thy features, fashioned thus like mine, eclipse
These long two thousand years—the quiet grace,
The posture calm, the face
Fixed not to battle fate. Within thy lips
There lies this gospel: "I have lingered long
With cymbals and sweet song,
And I have wandered forth as yesternight.
These days have been to me
Between two screens as flecks of candle-light:
And I discern the near and ultimate shade.
Enough, I have delayed
Longer than such or such. The draught be deep!
Enough, let me compose my hands, and sleep."

What man has bidden Him give,
God sent him from on high:
Manna to those who once desired to live,
Ashes to those who trembled not to die.

NOVEMBER, 1905

LAST CHAPTER OF "SMITH'S DECLINE AND FALL OF THE WORLD"

It is evident to the reader of my previous chapter that any life on the earth was now only a question of days. Not only had its circular form become egg-shaped, but this violent contortion had erected vast toppling mountains, seven times higher than the Himalayas, and, from their proximity to the sun, white-hot and molten on the summits. Prodigious streams of blazing lava were rushing hither and thither, at a speed of some twenty miles a minute, and hissing like a million cobras. The Pacific Ocean could be spanned and scanned with the naked eye, being scarcely broader than a mill-pond, and all about it for thousands of miles its bed was a vile seething mass of slime. Bodies of vast sea-monsters lay festering among the stagnant weeds, many of them still breathing, ponderously flapping their ulcerous gills, gasping and squirming.

No better test for my aero-car could be conceived. Thanks to the efficient service of the Interplanet Wireless Company, I was able to keep in constant touch with Mars; my own appliances resisted the force of gravitation, and enabled me to remain poised at a distance of half a mile over any spot which demanded my investigation, while my air-tank supplied me with our delicious home-atmosphere, and my radium window-plates kept out the rank vapors and the insufferable heat. Thus I remained for three weeks pursuing my observation in perfect safety.

On the tenth day I passed over the wide valley which I had formerly known as the English Channel, and pushed southward along the coast of Spain. It occurred to me that, with the ocean completely dried up, I might easily find the lost continent of Atlantis. I had always suspected the Azores of being its surviving peaks, and accordingly steered in that direction. Towards evening, the land beginning to rise, I found it necessary to steer violently upward in order to avoid precipitating myself into the mud-hills which stood before me. The sun, which had gained so enormously in size that seven fissures were visible upon it, sank in the west. The ground beneath me now rose violently, so that it was necessary for me to pursue my course upward at an angle of seventeen degrees, and as the moon rose, I discovered myself at the foot of a steep ascent which sloped off indefinitely into the sky. At this point I threw out all my extra side-flaps and parachutes and decided to poise for the night. My sleep was disturbed at intervals by a jarring of the basket in which I lay, caused by the perpetual whir of the huge monsters below whose coiling and leaping produced a constant vibration in the air without.

At daybreak I continued my upward progress and towards noon, after rising perpendicularly for two or three miles, the mountain suddenly broke off into a wide plateau, which I recognized instantly from its shape as the island of Terceira. I ascended twenty or thirty miles to gain a bird's-eye view of the Azores, and to ascertain their relation to the rest of the continent. The islands were connected at a distance of not half a mile below the former water-line, and above this they defined themselves as upon a clay map. I approached the village of Angra, to find that the vast cathedral had melted like a candy house, its marvellous mosaics and colored marbles running in streams through the neighboring streets. In two hours I had crossed the entire archipelago. To the west for a thousand miles lay the continent of Atlantis, a flat stretch covered to the horizon in every direction with a layer many rods deep of decayed yellow sea-plants, swarming with life, now wilted and sickly from exposure to the sun. I dropped to within a hundred yards of the surface in order to watch two monstrous clams; when suddenly an unusual jolting of my car caused me to look around. Almost upright to the sky, towering like a water-spout, a vast snake was bearing towards me, his tail swishing along in the slime and weeds, his upper parts propelled by flaps or fins which supported him in the air. His long, sleek, hose-like body glistened, and in his mane or hair streamers of sea-weed were fluttering. I had but a second. Turning on the recoil-valve, my car darted upwards like an arrow, as I felt his hair brush against my hanging basket below. As I continued my flight I saw the huge tower topple, and his whole length fell with a violent splash, cutting the weeds like a sword, and gradually sinking through with a suction on both sides which stirred the mire for many acres.

Towards evening I discerned a distant mountain to the north-west and turning my course in that direction came just at dark upon what appeared to be a vast pyramid. The rise of the moon confirmed this conjecture. It was after the model of the pyramids of Egypt, though many times larger—quite regular in shape, and covered with barnacles of the size of a church spire. I was thus enabled not only to confirm my notions of the lost continent, but to reach rather definite conclusions as to the nature of its civilization.

During the following days, there was a perceptible change in the condition of the earth. The molten state was apparently drying and it was evident that in a few days the entire planet would be one great burnt-out cinder. On the sixteenth day I was in the neighbourhood of the South Pole. The snow having entirely melted, another great continent was exposed, which ran for two thousand miles across the pole and up on the other side from Franklin's Land. Almost exactly over the pole were a number of caves or long tunnels which ran into the ground. As I watched one with not unnatural curiosity, I saw a man, a human being, crawl out slowly, followed by a woman. They were scorched quite black and seemed to have lost all power of locomotion. I approached them with the idea of rescue, but seeing them diseased beyond any hope of recovery, and, moreover, in a contagious state, I thought it best in the interests of science to keep myself safe. In this distraction, I had not noticed that a sort of gray pallor was coming over the entire surface of the earth. The man saw it too, for he cried out "Just as I said!" and the woman fell down and worshipped him—and I am convinced that these were the last words spoken on earth. The skeleton of an echo rattled through the cinder hills, just as vast fissures opened everywhere; and suddenly in absolute silence the whole earth gave way. It shot from me with inconceivable speed, revealing more and more of itself, until in an instant I saw the globe spinning off like a cannon ball down the infinite void.

JANUARY, 1908

John Hall Wheelock, '08

1886–

John Hall Wheelock has been an editor at Scribner's since 1926. Verses by Two Undergraduates, *containing the poems of Van Wyck Brooks and John Hall Wheelock, appeared in 1905. Wheelock has published many volumes of verse, including his* Poems, 1911–1936.

CORPUS EST DE DEO

Lo—say the wise, say the very wise—
"Only the soul is of God" say they,
"She shall not perish or pass away—
But the flesh dies, but the fair flesh dies."
Corpus est de Deo.

This is the time, this is the sweet time,
How that Lord Christ was risen from Death,
All we shall sing, all we that have breath
In a glad rhyme, in a low glad rhyme.
Corpus est de Deo.

One Joseph said, and good Joseph said,
"That I might bear the body away

And the white body in sepulchre lay,
    And the heavy head, the heavy head!"
        Corpus est de Deo.

    With myrrh and spice, with fresh myrrh and spice,
And linen white the white body they bound,
This saw from a more removèd ground
    Mary's eyes and the Magdalen's eyes.
        Corpus est de Deo.

    With spices sweet, with fresh spices sweet,
In tomb they laid the body away,
"O piteous Lord, Master!"–cry they,
    And "the wounded feet, O the wounded feet!"
        Corpus est de Deo.

    With their own hands, with their own sad hands
They closed the tomb with a massy stone,
There none remained but the watch alone,
    –On his wrist, bands, on his feet grave-bands–
        Corpus est de Deo.

    Still was around, deep still was around;
There was none wept with a covered face,
There was none mourning about the place
    With a low sound, with a sad, low sound.
        Corpus est de Deo.

    Master arise, good master arise!
Nay, for a little a sleep is sweet.
Desire there was not in his feet,
    And in his eyes, no light for his eyes.
        Corpus est de Deo.

With sound of might, with sound of great might,
The white grave-clothes were rent in sunder,
With a terribleness and wonder
And a great light and fire of light.
Corpus est de Deo.

Be you all glad, be you now all glad,
Be glad in your soul for your great gladness,
His spirit sprang from the night and sadness
And was not sad—lo—and was not sad.
Corpus est de Deo.

Put by vain shame, put by your vain shame,
Loosen your hair, and your lips with song,
Out of the darkness that is most strong
His body came, his fair body came.
Corpus est de Deo.

Lo—say the wise, say the very wise,
"Soul is of God, the body a vain thing."
Dance with your feet, let your mouth sing,
Lift up your eyes, lift up your sad eyes—
Corpus est de Deo.

In every place, say they in each place,
"Soul is of God, the body of shame"—
Out of the dust his sweet body came
And blood to his face, to his sweet face.
Corpus est de Deo.

O wondrous thing! O most blessèd thing!
Body and soul of one great birth—
All ye that are of dust and earth
Lift up and sing, lift ye up and sing,
Corpus est de Deo.

APRIL, 1906

FOR A BOOK OF POEMS

I have made a garden out of dreams and song
  Where we may walk together, side by side,
  And whisper to each other till time has died
All the old words that we have loved so long;
For the strange world that bore us works us wrong,
  Keeping us from each other, unsatisfied;
  With classes and with custom and with pride
The world divides us and the world is strong.

But I have found this garden, where it lies
Out of the world and all her thousand eyes
  —The birds sing and the fountains make a sound.
O come with me from a lost Paradise,
Whose guardian angel wearies our cries
  And walk in this new world that I have found!

OCTOBER, 1907

THE GHOST TO HIS BELOVED

Can you not hear me now when I call you softly!
  Open your window, dear—I love you, I love you—
  Night is deep, the heaven is starry above you,
Can you not hear me now when I call you softly!

Open your window, dear, I am weary of waiting,
  Do you remember the words of the love we plighted;
  I must fly when the fire of dawn is lighted,
Open your window, dear, I am weary of waiting.

Ah did you think that I could ever forget you!
  Hurry, hurry, (the robin had given the warning)
  Before the wind has kindled the fire of morning!
Ah did you think that I could ever forget you!

Quiet you lie there sleeping under the starlight.
  O the body is passionate, strong and splendid,
  What do you care for me whose passion is ended!
Quiet you lie there sleeping under the starlight.

What do I see—hide me, cover me, hide me!
  Pity me, love, (poor ghost from a land forsaken)
  Gather me close! O do not let me be taken!
What do I see—hide me, cover me, hide me!

O it is cold, it is cold, will you not hear me—
  These are the very meadows we loved and walked in,
  These are the very bowers we sat and talked in.
O it is cold, it is cold, will you not hear me!

O black-hearted! O deceitful! O darling—!
  O you have forgotten me altogether!
  O you have forgotten me altogether!—

* * * * * * * *

NOVEMBER, 1907

H. V. Kaltenborn, '09

1878–

H. V. Kaltenborn, best known as a news analyst for CBS and NBC, has been Harvard-Berlin exchange professor in Berlin, and worked for many years as a journalist.

THE COLLEGE AND THE PRESS

NOT LONG AGO, THE PRESENT RULER OF ITALY, WHEN he was told about a particularly brilliant piece of newspaper work, cried out: "If I could not be a king I would be a journalist!" But I wonder whether such enthusiasm for the journalist's career could be carried away by any young man who spends four years in one of our large eastern colleges? Throughout his college course educated men have impressed upon him the venality and utter worthlessness of the American press. The undergraduate in Harvard College learns from his professors that newspapers are hopelessly inaccurate in their reports, and that their English is beneath contempt. If the "New York Evening Post" or the "Boston Transcript" is praised, it is only that the sins of the "New York American" or the "Boston Herald" may stand forth in bolder contrast.

This criticism of newspapers combines very naturally with adverse comment on the work of newspaper making. In college circles journalism is thought of as a possible stepping stone to literature or political life, a means to an end, and not as a career that presents good opportunities in and for itself. The very fact that reporters and editors often become great statesmen seems to cast some discredit on those who fail to rise. The professors of literature point out that the best fiction of the nineteenth century was written by such newspaper men as Thackeray, Dickens, Barrie and Kipling who forsook their calling to undertake literary work. One of our teachers of English Composition here at Harvard concludes his class-room work each year with a little advice to his young friends with regard to journalism. The gist of it is that newspaper work, like some medicines, is beneficial only when the dose is small.

How different from all this are the stimuli which drive men into other occupations. Technical courses of preparation are provided for them even in the college, and there are graduate schools for the preachers, miners, foresters, engineers, and within the past year Harvard has even established one for the bankers and brokers. Leading representatives of the medical profession, of the diplomatic service, of various kinds of business are summoned to the college to picture the advantages of their work. Only a few weeks ago our President Emeritus delivered from this platform an address which inspired every teacher that heard it with a greater love for his work, and turned more than one college man to look upon teaching as a possible career.

Thus the undergraduate is urged into such overcrowded professions as law and medicine because they are approved by his teachers and associates, because special efforts are made to interest him in them, and because there are professional schools to lead him from the blooming paths of college theory into the dusty highway of accepted business practice. He is turned away from journalism—which, with the growing number of magazines and daily papers is a field of expanding opportunities, because he does not wish to do a kind of work so generally condemned, because no one makes any special effort to rouse his interest in journalism, and because he must enter the newspaper office fresh from college, where he has acquired a haphazard mixture of culture and information, but no technical preparation for his work.

As the result of this difference, journalism has lost and is still losing the services of many able college graduates, whose tastes and talents incline them to write for the press, but who have been made to believe that success in newspaper work involves the sacrifice of self-respect. Even among those college men who enter journalism, many do so half-heartedly, without resolving to see it through, ready to shrink back at the first sight of an unattractive piece of work. In view of this hesitating spirit it is small wonder that these men fail in a calling where hearty devotion, and whole-souled enthusiasm are the first essentials.

The newspapers, on their part, have become suspicious of the college man. Even today, the great majority of editors are not college men. They are graduates of the remorseless school of experience, and have little respect for the Bachelor's degree. The office boys whom they have trained, never assume knowledge where they have none; the college man likes to think that he knows what he should know, but since his training has been general and not technical he often makes foolish mistakes. To be sure, the exceptional man who has a passion for journalism overcomes all handicaps. Skilfully and unobtrusively he learns to apply his college training where it counts, and soon the world sees a Dana, a Lamont, or a Hapgood—to mention only three Harvard men—who has made his way to the top. And in the offices where these men have worked, the staff is more patient with the young college graduate. There they have found out that when college men have once learned the rudiments of the business their work excels that of the former office boys. But in general, the editor still distrusts the college man just as the college man distrusts him.

It is bad for journalism and bad for the public that this mutual distrust exists. Of course, there are newspapers with which no self-respecting college man should associate; papers which require their employees to tell lies and steal photographs, just as some business houses require their salesmen to misrepresent goods and rob customers. But such practices are everywhere exceptional and misunderstanding rather than malfeasance is the root of this distrust. Much of this misunderstanding has come about because the public—especially that part of it which pays three cents for its newspaper—fails to consider that publishing is a business. Somehow, just as soon as a business man becomes a publisher, he is expected to abandon his former business habit of selling the public what it wants, and to turn out an article which a few persons of superior taste think the public ought to want.

This demand is a high compliment to the past conduct and achievements of our press. A business enterprise that has taught the best elements in our public to expect it to represent only the most enlightened public opinion, to depend only upon the cold light of reason, and to body forth the highest ideals of a nation must look back upon a glorious history. But in looking back into newspaper history, in remembering Garrison and his "Liberator," Greeley and his "Tribune," Godkin and his "Post," we must also remember that the conditions under which these men worked no longer obtain. The "Liberator" was the voice of Garrison, the "New York Tribune" was the printed expression of Horace Greeley. These papers were small. The owner was the editor. He was responsible only to himself. He wrote much of what his paper contained, and passed upon the rest. Sometimes he even took a hand in the work of the press-room. How is it today?

The "Tribune" and the "Post" have become million dollar

enterprises. They are owned by companies of capitalists, they are directed by a score of editors, and instead of the living voice of a single man, they have become ponderous collections of news, comment, and advertisement made to sell at a price. We may regret this change, but there is, after all, little use in quarreling with what is only one phase of business progress. Twenty editors work to greater advantage when they coöperate, and hence the business men, who are organizing the world as economic laws demand, have brought them together. We can no more go back to one-man newspapers than we can return to one-man burden bearing or one-man store-keeping.

Editors like Garrison and Greeley might well say, as Luther said to Reuchlin: "Nihil timeo, quia nihil habeo."—The modern newspaper, if it is to go on, must consider the capitalists, who founded the enterprise, the unions that control its mechanical departments, the advertisers who supply the major part of its income, and the readers, who contribute little money, but who read advertisements. All these interests have a right to be considered, and the newspaper, if it is to continue, must pay some attention to their varying demands. It need not truckle, it need not barter its independence, but so long as the newspaper is a private and unendowed enterprise it must show a decent respect for the opinions of those portions of mankind that own it, or make it, or buy it.

The college man should not turn his back upon all newspapers because he thinks some are sensational or grossly commercial. Let him work on one that is fairly good, and do his best to make it better. The life of Mirabeau shows us a man who entered journalism when this was at its worst. No newspapers in the world's history appealed so generally to man's lowest instincts as those of the French Revolution. And when Mirabeau, the promising young statesman, the gifted orator, member of a leading house of France, decided to become a journalist, his friends and family were horrified. He replied that journalism, practised by worthy men, had done great things for England and should be made to do great things for France. "There is not among the English a man of merit," he said, "who has not worked for a long time at these periodic writings. These flying pages that our instruction disdains, have everywhere produced the great changes in things, the great revolutions in ideas, the great effects upon men. I cannot then find myself humiliated in doing what the best blood of England has always done, what it is doing today."

In our large eastern colleges we need greater toleration for the press, more generous recognition of the difficulties by which it is beset. If these colleges will adopt a more reasonable attitude, if they will encourage young men to look towards journalism by recognizing that profession in their courses of study, the army of newspaper workers will enroll more well-equipped recruits, more men whom we can trust with the responsible task of guiding the King of America—Public Opinion! As much as ever in the past, the American press needs men who can teach a great truth by telling a simple story, men who are able, fearless, and warm-hearted, who, while working "in the world and for the world, can keep themselves unspotted from the world." We depend upon our colleges to supply these men.

JUNE, 1909

T. S. Eliot, '10

1888–

T. S. Eliot, Secretary of the ADVOCATE *in 1910, is probably the* ADVOCATE'S *most distinguished literary alumnus. Eliot took his M.A. at Harvard in 1911, and did further graduate work at Harvard, the University of Paris, and Oxford. Currently an official in Faber and Faber, Ltd., British publishers, Eliot received the Nobel Prize for literature in 1948.*

In 1938, the ADVOCATE *published a special issue in honor of Eliot, containing his own undergraduate poems, several critical articles, and tributes from many authors and teachers. (See Appendix.) "Gentlemen and Seamen" is reprinted here for the first time. Eliot's poem, "Humouresque," is here presented for the first time accurately, without the two major misprints of 1910.*

SONG

When we came home across the hill
    No leaves were fallen from the trees;
    The gentle fingers of the breeze
Had torn no quivering cobweb down.

The hedgerow bloomed with flowers still
  No withered petals lay beneath;
  But the wild roses in your wreath
Were faded, and the leaves were brown.

MAY, 1907

BEFORE MORNING

While all the East was weaving red with gray,
The flowers at the window turned toward dawn,
Petal on petal, waiting for the day,
Fresh flowers, withered flowers, flowers of dawn.

This morning's flowers and flowers of yesterday
Their fragrance drifts across the room at dawn,
Fragrance of bloom and fragrance of decay,
Fresh flowers, withered flowers, flowers of dawn.

NOVEMBER, 1908

CIRCE'S PALACE

Around her fountain which flows
With the voice of men in pain,
Are flowers that no man knows.
Their petals are fanged and red
With hideous streak and stain;
They sprang from the limbs of the dead.—
We shall not come here again.

Panthers rise from their lairs
In the forest which thickens below,
Along the garden stairs
The sluggish python lies;
The peacocks walk, stately and slow,
And they look at us with the eyes
Of men whom we knew long ago.

NOVEMBER, 1908

SONG

The moonflower opens to the moth,
  The mist crawls in from sea;
A great white bird, a snowy owl,
  Slips from the alder tree.

Whiter the flowers, Love, you hold,
  Than the white mist on the sea;
Have you no brighter tropic flowers
  With scarlet life, for me?

JANUARY, 1909

ON A PORTRAIT

Among a crowd of tenuous dreams, unknown
To us of restless brain and weary feet,
Forever hurrying, up and down the street,
She stands at evening in the room alone.

Not like a tranquil goddess carved of stone
But evanescent, as if one should meet

A pensive lamia in some wood-retreat,
An immaterial fancy of one's own.

No meditations glad or ominous
Disturb her lips, or move the slender hands;
Her dark eyes keep their secrets hid from us,
Beyond the circle of our thought she stands.

The parrot on his bar, a silent spy,
Regards her with a patient curious eye.

JANUARY, 1909

NOCTURNE

Romeo, *grand sérieux*, to importune
Guitar and hat in hand, beside the gate
With Juliet, in the usual debate
Of love, beneath a bored but courteous moon;
The conversation failing, strikes some tune
Banal, and out of pity for their fate
Behind the wall I have some servant wait,
Stab, and the lady sinks into a swoon.

Blood looks effective on the moonlit ground–
The hero smiles; in my best mode oblique
Rolls toward the moon a frenzied eye profound,
(No need of "Love forever?"–"Love next week?")
While female readers all in tears are drowned:–
"The perfect climax all true lovers seek!"

NOVEMBER, 1909

HUMOURESQUE

(*After J. Laforgue*)

One of my marionettes is dead,
Though not yet tired of the game,–
But weak in body as in head,
(A jumping-jack has such a frame).

But this deceasèd marionette
I rather liked: a common face,
(The kind of face that we forget)
Pinched in a comic, dull grimace;

Half bullying, half imploring air,
Mouth twisted to the latest tune;
His who-the-devil-are-you stare;
Translated, maybe, to the moon.

With Limbo's other useless things
Haranguing spectres, set him there;
"The snappiest fashion since last spring's,
"The newest style on Earth, I swear.

"Why don't you people get some class?
(Feebly contemptuous of nose),
"Your damned thin moonlight, worse than gas–
"Now in New York"–and so it goes.

Logic a marionette's, all wrong
Of premises; yet in some star
A hero!–Where would he belong?
But, even at that, what mask *bizarre!*

JANUARY, 1910

SPLEEN

Sunday: this satisfied procession
Of definite Sunday faces;
Bonnets, silk hats, and conscious graces
In repetition that displaces
Your mental self-possession
By this unwarranted digression.

Evening, lights, and tea!
Children and cats in the alley;
Dejection unable to rally
Against this dull conspiracy

And Life, a little bald and gray,
Languid, fastidious, and bland,
Waits, hat and gloves in hand,
Punctilious of tie and suit
(Somewhat impatient of delay)
   On the doorstep of the Absolute.

JANUARY, 1910

GENTLEMEN AND SEAMEN

THOSE OF US WHO CAN CLAIM ANY NEW ENGLAND ancestors may congratulate ourselves that we are their descendants, and at the same time rejoice that we are not their contemporaries. Their sombre faces, with an inflexible contraction of the lips, as they have been stiffened and conventionalized in oils by forgotten artists, suggest natures difficult and unyielding, as the consequence of religious principle and of interminable struggle against the narrow resources of New

England. The men of whom I am thinking are the patriarchs of the smaller towns, rather than the merchants of Boston, whom affluence often left more genial than the never prosperous countryfolk. But the representative New Englander is not exclusively a city man by descent, and has quite as much reason for taking pride in his rustic ancestors.

One notable characteristic of those hardy folk is the success with which they supported, in the conflict with misfortune, a gentlemanly dignity. Tradesmen and farmers, most of them, by descent, they were farmers in America; yet here they founded and maintained successfully a plebeian aristocracy, without the training of generations, and under adverse fates. Any task which necessity compelled them to undertake, in their hands became honorable; no privation and hardship lowered their pride or social position. So they were found as merchants and tradesmen, as farmers and printers, according to circumstance, without losing a jot of their dignity. There were many sacrifices. Straitened means confined noble ambitions, and their passion for education was not always gratified. In one of those white clapboard houses which look so tranquil in their decay lived a boy of good family, a hundred years ago, whom lack of means thwarted from his ambition the college education. So, at the age of fifteen, he killed himself.

But most of our New Englanders were stronger, and turned to what vocation they could find; the farm, the printing-press —a hundred years ago there were many local presses—or to the sea. The merchant marine was not the least important career in which New Englanders found distinction. They were the men who carried American commerce to the Levant, to India, to China; who from the Revolution till after 1812 made America an ocean power in war and peace. They built the fine old ships which we know only from contemporaneous engravings. How stirring are those antique woodcuts. The "Ajax," two hundred ton brig, entering Algiers under full sail with a thundering salvo from the city; the ensign very large, triumphantly shaking out its thirteen stars from the end of a yard-arm. Or the "Poor Richard," off the coast of Africa repelling pirates; the native feluccas very small in contrast; or the "Samuel Adams," passing a sea-serpent in the Bay of Biscay. Built and manned and commanded, every one of the boats, by Yankee seamen; and for them was built the handsome old custom house at Salem, now slumbering in proud uselessness.

Go to Salem and see a town that flourished a hundred years ago in the hightide of New England's naval energy. It seems now to be always in dignified mourning for its former grandeur, for the ships which do not leave and the ships which do not return. One feels that noisy mirth is a profanation there, the town is so populous with ghosts. Where is the China fleet now? the clumsy barks that sailed to every part of the world? Every day, a hundred years ago, the crowsnest watched for another homecomer bending past Baker's Island. Of the freights which the boats carried in are left only the shawls, the ginger-jars, the carved ivory which the captains brought back from the Orient, the gifts which their descendants are proud to display. From New Brunswick to Florida today lounge the coasters, manned with Irish and the "blue-nose"; the mackerel fleet slants out to the banks under Irish skippers, and the cargoes of the world are borne in steamers owned in Europe. The sea trade of the Yankees is gone.

The captains who handled the old fleet were just the sort of aristocratic plebeians of whom I spoke. Very young, at fourteen or fifteen years, they would enter the service, at the bottom of the nautical *cursus honorum.* They often rose quickly; there were many like the youth who sailed a bark from his father's Portsmouth ship-yard to Savannah for lading, thence to London, where he sold ship and cargo at a good profit; and this when he was aged nineteen. His log-book, kept in a neat small hand, shows that he was an able and a conscientious navigator. Such were the men who handled the shipping of New England.

Though we must regret the commerce which has fallen to Germany and to England, we must regret still more the virtues of the old skippers. Thrown from youth among the roughest adventures, with the crudest companions, they emerged at the end as good gentlemen, often, as the more fortunate college-bred. Of these yeomen ancestors we are apt to think as the infantry whom the drums beat to Charlestown, or as the gunners who raked the "Hornet," rather than as the founders of commerce or the pioneers of education. But that is half of their importance. We may well mourn for the enterprise which sent American shipping round the world, and started the printing-press in many small communities. Nowadays we are thankful that more congenial occupation is open to the industrious gentleman, however needy, than was possible to some of our New England forebears. If along with greater luxury, with more generosity and geniality than was theirs, we have preserved the spirit of our old plebeian aristocracy, we should give them the grace of recognition.

MAY, 1909

John Reed, '10

1887–1920

John Reed, author of Ten Days That Shook The World, *was an editor and war correspondent. He published one volume of verse,* Tamburlaine and Other Poems.

THE WEST

Gulls to their home on the aged rock
  Wheeling athwart the spray,
Thrill of the wind from the isles of Ind
  In the heart of the dying day.

Dreams in the depths of the solemn pines
  Ancient before our birth,
Hearing the speech of the plains that reach
  To the ends of the happy earth.

Out of the years that have passed away
  Out of the days to be,
Night brings the pang of the salt air's tang
  And the call of the West to me.

JUNE, 1908

THE SEA-GULL

Wet with the stinging spray he skims the deep,
A livid gleam of life, and scans afar
Where the great breakers pound across the bar,
Beneath the headlands where his nestlings sleep.
Above the light the keeper sees him sweep
From fog to fog, and vanish like a star
Down where the unknown ocean monsters are,
And hears his mournful crying on the steep.

And when on winter days he rises high
Against the squall, and swift on-coming night,
And bares his gleaming armor to the fight,
Then are the sailors startled by his cry;
Darting spear-like athwart the dark'ning main
To ride the helmet of the hurricane.

OCTOBER, 1908

Conrad Aiken, '11

1889–

Conrad Aiken, President of the ADVOCATE *while he was at Harvard, has published novels, short stories and criticism as well as his poetry. Recipient of the Pulitzer Prize for verse in 1929, Aiken's most recent volume of poetry is* Skylight One.

ME AND HER

WELL, DICK OUGHT TO HAVE KNOWN BETTER, ANYway; of course he ought. Dick is a jolly chap, and I am proud to be his room-mate; but once in a while he makes an ass of me by the most innocent means, and I take the consequences. Now this afternoon he might have known that I would put my foot in it if I had the least chance in the world. That's my way. So he gave me exactly the best chance in the world. That's his way.

He asked me this morning if I was taking anybody to the game. He knew I wasn't; that was merely his deft method of closing loop-holes before I could get my bearings.

"Well, then," said he, "I have an unexpected pleasure for you. You know Gilbert was going to take my cousin Dorothy to the game; but he's just telephoned me that he's sick and can't go. So the pleasure is to be yours!"

"Mine! Why, my dear boy, I'm going to sit in the cheering-section with Norton. Besides, which cousin is it? That little one I met up at North-East six or seven summers ago—pig-tails down her back, talks in a squeaky voice, and says 'ain't'?—what the English call a 'flapper'?"

"You remember her? Well, you just wait till you see what alchemy seven years can do. You've *got* to take her,—there's nobody else."

"Touching tribute! Well, if you're stranded as badly as that, I suppose I've got to help you out."

So I took Miss Channing to the game. Dick was right; seven years had brought miracles to pass. I could hardly believe that this was the same gawky girl whom I had once seen pulling her brother's hair. She was still slight, but where was her former awkwardness? She was as graceful as a kitten,—and that's extraordinarily flattering, I assure you. I won't try to describe her, you know,—but I might remark "in passing"—as father Cicero used to say,—that her eyes were aquamarine or glaucous, and redolent of summer by the sea; her voice was argentine, and her hair a kind of spun sunlight—in fact, though I shan't detain you by useless portraiture, she was perfectly bewitching. Even I, a hardened old bachelor (as you know) must confess it.

We had fairly good seats, and from the very beginning she followed the game with an intelligence exceeded only by her dogged interest.

"Heavens, look at that blue man run! He's got him! What a perfectly terrible fall! Do you think he's killed?"

" 'Fraid not," I murmured absently.

"Why, you weren't even looking!" she reproached me.

"Of course I was; haven't I *two* eyes?"

"Now don't be idiotic; watch the *game*."

At this juncture out of a blue and crimson whirlpool popped a man bereft of his jersey, and the players grouped themselves about the victim.

"Poor Tom's a-cold!" I stammered.

Miss Channing fought gamely against a blush, which rose like a cheer for Harvard over her cheeks and white temples, and I felt my own cheeks,—particularly my ears,—giving a cheer also. Other people in the neighborhood were doing likewise, and there was a general silence, except for the merry chuckle of a fat man below us, whose collar made a white line on his purple neck.

"Why don't they hang a Harvard flag on this side, like that Yale one over there?" Miss Channing ventured timidly.

"Would be a good idea," I answered, to help out; but then went on maliciously, "there goes the new sweater! Why, they do it rather cleverly!"

I looked at the group of red and blue mannikins, between whom one could catch a glimpse of the victim, waving his arms. Beside me, another Harvard cheer went up.

Presently, however, the game was resumed, amid feeble plaudits. The signals came sharply, bodies clashed against canvas-covered bodies with the crash of armor, and the fight went murderously forward.

I watched the rest of the game,—by proxy. The bulletins were very interesting, and vivid as the real thing. Besides,—well, never mind, you know.

After it was all over, cheering and snake-dance, and all,—we ploughed back, with me manfully in the lead: for Dick had told me, (as an additional little surprise) that we were going to have a tea in our rooms. Miss Channing and I finally sifted over Boylston Bridge, and, positively, before I knew it, we were safe in my own room. Dick's mother was there, but I knew scarcely anybody else. I tried to talk with some of them, —but what was the use? They seemed so deadly stupid.

Miss Channing, however, was pouring tea in one corner of the room. After I had given up three attempts at conversation with other people, I—well, I wandered over in her direction.

"Ah, you are pouring?" I asked with delicately arched eyebrows (as though I had not kept my eye on her for the last quarter of an hour!)

"Yes, Richard said I *must*. Won't you have some tea?"

I took a chair near the table.

"Wasn't it a glorious game, Mr. Cholmondeley? Of course, I'm no judge of foot-ball;" (correct!) "but I don't think I ever saw such a game in all my life."

"Oh, it was a jolly good game, in the main."

"In the main? Why are you always so cautious, all of you?"

"Cautious is never caught," said I, with my accustomed cleverness. (But I'm afraid I'm too subtle.)

"Oh, you ought to have some real enthusiasm. If I had been you, I should have gone just wild."

"I fancy I shouldn't look a *bit* well, if I went wild."

"Now you are silly about it."

"Well, how about the snake-dance? Was that enthusiastic enough?"

"That was *much* better. But you weren't in that; can't you show your feelings in some other way? Or perhaps you haven't any."

"Oh, I imagine I have a proper degree of unshorn emotion hidden away in me somewhere."

She arranged the cups in symmetrical rows.

"Then you don't dare to show it," she said with patent sarcasm.

"Or perhaps I don't care to show it," I corrected.

"Then it is selfishness, and that is a great deal worse. Do you know what I really think is the matter?" she added, dropping a lump of sugar with a splash into my cup.

"I should be delighted to learn."

"The trouble is that you aren't sincere. You aren't sincere with yourself or with other people. You are too much afraid of what other people say and think. If you feel glad about a foot-ball game, why don't you show it?"

"Well, I am going to express my feelings about the game, then, and never mind what you say. Heartless as it seems, I'm glad that my friend Gilbert had his little ill turn this morning."

"Now you're being silly again. And besides, you were influenced by my being here."

"How so?"

"Oh, you,—I'm not going to answer such a foolish question. But you don't seem to be able to say anything original and direct without thinking of what other people will say. Try now; I don't believe you can." Her tone was coaxing.

"May it be about anything I please?"

"Anything in reason; only you mustn't be silly."

As I said in the first place, you know, the whole fault is Dick's; he ought to have known better than to get me into such a scrape. Of course she expected an extravagant and flattering answer. This is what,—ah, brutal one,—I said.

"Miss Channing, why do you wear that hat? It's stylish, you know, but not at all becoming or artistic. Are you afraid of what people would say if you wore a hat out of style?"

Now I really didn't mean to be rude; but she sat up straight, and asked in a freezing voice, "Lemon or cream, Mr. Cholmondeley?"

What did I tell you?

NOVEMBER, 1909

"LE PENSEUR"

I made a statue; out of formless marble
I fashioned him to image in my brain
With smooth, white muscles, cunningly, and brow
Unluminous with mind. I made him sit,—

This thing uncouth,—and wrestle with his thoughts;
And then I dreamed I heard him stir, and cry,—
Baffled and hopeless in his quest for truth,—
"Why do you hew me out of the marble, Man?
Surely I did not cry to you in sleep—
For I have lain long aedolons in chains
And whimpered not, nor sorrowed in my soul;
And I have slept a deep and peaceful sleep.
And yet there comes an alien god to me,
Some meddling god, who seeth with his soul,
And speaks to me, and bids me stir; in dreams
I feel his presence near me, strange and strong,
And know him for a Messenger of Pain.
His fiery hands burn through the snows of sleep,
He tortures me to restlessness; his brain
Afar off knows me, pictures me, conceives
My power of limb and powerlessness of thought.
My eyelids, sealed for centuries in stone,
Feel now his icy chisel, and unclose
To rims of fire, inquisitorial Light.
The world breaks on me like a stormy sea
And crushes me,—before one breath is drawn,
Before my head is raised from fume of dreams,
Or heavy limbs unchained from lethargies.
Unhappy spirit who created me!
Play me a sweeter song than this you learned
To charm me out of marble, and to wake
My dreaming ears; the sunlit world is sweet,
And it is sweet to crush with careless hands,
To break, to snare, to kill, to overcome,—
But oh, my soul is filled with weariness.
Play me a sweeter song, oh mighty god!
Of Lotus flowers, forgetfulness, and peace—
Bring back my thousand thoughts, my vagrant dreams,

Where they have wandered in the search for truth,–
Yea, I am sick of questioning the stars.
So play to me that I may be enthralled,
And pause, and dream, and close my eyes, and sleep
Once more the sleep of marble; lose once more
The world and thee and all unhappiness.
Play me a song such as the headland hears
Softly about its feet, in break of seas
Enchanting it to dreams; dim surge and fall;
Till, like the headland, I may lose the world,
Hearing the song grow fainter at my feet."

FEBRUARY, 1910

LE REVEUR

Bring me the chisel! Hot is the impulse now,–
One fiery stroke will work a miracle,
Yea, like a magic, change this shaggy brute
Into a god! Ho, boy–thou heartfree elf!–
Bring me the chisel, where it lies and gleams
There by the grindstone; yea, and I will smite
Such master-stroke as never Phidias smote
Among his Parian marbles: feel such bliss
As God once gloried in, when out of dust
He fused a beautiful man and laughed to see!
O thou dull brutish shape of marble! Clod,
Spiritless clod of manhood, pitiful thing
Who knowest nothing of heaven or of song:
Base crawling thing, blinker upon the sun,
Whose happiest pleasure is to count the stars
As one counts bees, with pointing finger, so!
(Bring me the chisel, quick, thou lazy boy!

Thinkest thou noon is all eternity?)
Thou thoughtless killer of all soft things that live
In sunlight, thou whose hairy hands are red
With blood of birds and animals thou hast slain:
One sharp ecstatic torture of my steel
Driven by all my soul and thou art changed
To something beautiful; a light will shine
From those wide eyes where dullard cruelty
Basks like a serpent now; and in thy face
Will shine a new intelligence of heaven,
A love of stars, a glory in the sun.
Already with that master stroke I thrill;
Already do I feel my nostrils flare
In ecstasy of sensuous bliss,—I know
Already how my breath will sear my lips,
My tongue go dry, my hand go tremulous
With frenzied happiness! And thou shalt stand,
Upright and strong and beautiful and pure,
Looking beyond me to the sea and sky
Which through the doorway gleam, and lo the sun,
Falling upon thee slantwise out of heaven,
Will fire thy face to splendor. Warm and soft,
Who knows but it will open thee thy lips
And give thee power of hymn to praise the world
Wherein thou livest; loosen in thy breast
The prisoner song which lodges there in gloom,
That song which came from heaven to sleep in thee.
Thinkest thou life so fruitless, O thou clod?
Under my chisel dost thou writhe and burn
In anguish, like a sleeper stirred from dreams?
For thee is everything so profitless,
And life so filled with pain? And art so weary
Of feeling with dull fingers after truth?
Nay, look not at me with so hard an eye!

Dream not of snarling at me! I am strong
To make or mar thee with a touch, a breath,–
To lift thee out of sorrow with a song
Or charm thee slowly into endless sleep
With some smooth euthanasia.–Ho, thou boy!
This brute hath glowered at me long; bring here
My chisel, where it sparkles in the grass.
Unto the genial sun will I unfold
His spirit, till it gulps like thirsty flower
That cordial golden wine; till it becomes
Drunk and reeling with utter happiness;
O, I will make him luminous with soul,
This starless creature pale with dreams of stars. . . .
What if it pain him, or he long to sleep?
Hot is the impulse, now–bring me the chisel!

JUNE, 1910

TO A HEAD IN MARBLE

Tumultuous is the midnight, with no stars;
  The elm trees, burthened deeply with soft snow,
Mourn for the Spring, for Youth's gay-tongued guitars,
  And dream of loves that blossomed long ago.
Tumultuous is the midnight; at my pane
  The voiceless snow makes ceaseless whisperings,
  Yearning to tell of strange and demon things,
But yearning still in vain;
While I, envisioned, turn a starry page,
And read the glories of a buried age.

Thou virgin head, with forehead sculptured smooth,–
  In those breath-parted lips, those dream-dimmed eyes,

Soft with the fleeting sadnesses of youth,
  Tender with new-winged hopes and memories—
Some passionate lover, with impetuous hand,
  Phrased the ephemeral glory of his love,
  Nor little dreamed that it would last, above
The gods of that gray land;
Ah, little thought he, when he shaped this flower,
That it would bloom beyond his own brief Hour!

When those stone lips, forever now entranced,
  Burned with a sigh, or cooled with ocean air;
When those unlustred eyes illumed and danced,
  And soft in the wind and sunlight flew thy hair—
In that red dawn of earth thou sawest then
  The galleys from far battle surging home
  Green garlanded, and drenchèd cold with foam;
Thou sawest the sun-dark men
Hymn for the gods their praises to the skies,
The heifer slain, the bleeding sacrifice.

Maiden of marble,—charmed,—immutable!
  Whose temples cannot beat with cloudy pain!
Whose lips can never stir, nor ever tell
  Their happiness to mortal ear again!
I sicken of these human agonies,
  These hates and loves that breed within my breast,—
  These vampire passions that vouchsafe no rest,
These pale-eyed ecstasies;
I too would turn to stone, and leave behind
Earth's griefs that open wide our eyes, earth's joys that blind.

Thou serene loveliness of youth and bliss
  Immortalized forever in fair shape,

To feel forever Time's impassioned kiss,
  His panting breath,—yet ever to escape:
To see forever faces new, and eyes
  That hunger for thy love, as now do mine:
  To tremble like a goddess in her shrine
Dizzy with sacrifice:
Oh dreamless soul, sweet languor without end,
And gracious neck that still begins to bend,—

Would I, or thought of me, could last as long
  As high and changeless, as untouched of years,
As thou hast been! The music and the song
  Perish with lute and voice, like laughter, tears:
The flesh is changed to rose or violet,
  The kingdoms blow away, like wind and rain:
  Yet thou, oh odorless flower, dost still remain,
Nor will men soon forget;
Oh may I have from Death the last redress
To dream forever of thy loveliness.

Even in death I will remember thee;
  Though I dissolve in dust and wander far
Behested by the winds, yet I will be
  Still mindful of thy glory, like a star
Beaming upon my darkness; tender still,
  And still of youth the sweet embodiment;
  Gazing on life with musèd wonderment
And calm, unaltered will;
So, dreaming on thy steadfast beauty, I
May haply share thine immortality.

Blow on, thou wind, and fall forever, snow!
  Ye sombre elms, still nurse your dreams of spring;

Thou canst not touch this Soul of long ago
  Oh haggard mistral! with thy cruel wing.
Thou voiceless sleet that frettest at my pane,
  To human ear thy words can never come,–
  Thy demon warnings are forever dumb,
Thy yearnings are in vain;
This night will pass, its storm remembered not;
To-morrow dawns, this darkness is forgot.

FEBRUARY, 1911

Robert Benchley, '12

1889–1945

Robert Benchley, at Exeter, was asked to write an essay on how to do something practical. He came forth with, "How to Embalm a Corpse." It seems that there was always only one Benchley; the selections here already bear the familiar trademarks. "The Ivy Oration" is a humorous speech given each year on Class Day by a graduating Senior. The review of "The Lottery Man" is included as an illustration of early Benchley dramatic criticism.

"THE LOTTERY MAN" AT THE MAJESTIC THEATRE

THE CAUSE OF DRAMA IN AMERICA HAS BEEN NEITHER appreciably furthered nor seriously retarded in the bringing forth of "The Lottery Man," but some Friday night, after a section-meeting, when you are not especially keen about the cause of the Drama, and want to buy a few hearty laughs, you couldn't find a safer investment for your money.

"The Lottery Man" is a farce pure and simple (these words are used advisedly) of the type that affects the hysterical lady behind you to such a degree that she has to be led out by an usher during the second act. The plot is delightfully impossible, and very easily forgotten, but there is a refreshing breeziness about the whole piece that marks it as the product of the pen of a clever woman who writes for the fun there is in it, in pleasing contrast to some of the machine-made, union-labelled pieces that are being turned out by the ream as mere vehicles for stars.

Cyril Scott seems to have caught the genuine spirit of the author in his characterization of the young journalist, but the blue-ribbon for originality and fun-making may, without question, be pinned on "Lizzie," the splinter-like spinster, as portrayed by Miss Helen Lowell. "Lizzie" is more than a mere part in a play; she is an experience. And, between you and me, as one businessman to another, Miss Bartlett as the heroine is very good to look upon; but that is beside the point, and quite out of place here.

And even when you have forgotten the plot, and are no longer haunted by the vision of "Lizzie," you will be surprised to find that during the performance, when you weren't looking, there were administered to you one or two little doses of sermonizing on such topics as the infectious charm of a happy disposition, and the futility of dissimulation in matters of age and appearance, and if you can remember these, certainly it was an evening well-spent.

MARCH, 1911

IVY ORATION

IMAGINE MY SURPRISE—MY CONFUSION—AT JUST NOW being called upon to address you at this meeting. Nothing could have been farther from my thoughts as I sat listening to the other speakers here this afternoon, than that my modest voice should be desired to lend a touch of dignity to this occasion. Why, a quarter of an hour ago I was sitting in my room, looking for a position for next year, when the Bursar, that Prince of Good Fellows, that Shylock of Melancholy Dane, came bounding up the stairs, and laying a sympathetic hand on my shoulder, said "Bob, old man, aren't you coming down to say a few words to the Big Red team? The boys are all calling for you down there." Then it all came over me like a flask—this was Class Day! I did remember having seen a program of the week, in which somewhere between ball-games with Yale and Phi Beta Kappa Exhibits there was made casual mention of a Class Day Exercise, but I understood that it was to be held only in case the ball-game at New Haven was called off on account of rain, and besides, I really did not dare to leave the Yard, for fear lest I had not the right colored ticket and that, once out, I could never get back in again to get my clean clothes for the summer vacation. So here it was Class Day, and there I was in my room, hemming napkins. Quickly I drew on a pair of shoes and my cap and gown, and breaking into a run—and a perspiration, soon found myself, unless I am mistaken, here.

On this day, when all minds are turned to the National Prize Ring in Chicago, where Harvard and Yale are again demonstrating that the rules of the game need changing before next season, and at a time when the air is so charged with personal politics that it threatens to destroy the crops, what could be more out of place or thoroughly disagreeable, than for me to give my speech a political flavor? With true Harvard indifference then, I shall proceed to deliver a political speech, which our paternal and conservative Administrative Board refused me permission to deliver in the Thayer Common-Room, stigmatizing it as unnecessarily impolite and improper propaganda.

I shall divide my speech into three quarters, or halfs; 1st the Peroration, containing what I consider to be one of the most virulent attacks against the Malefactors of Great Health yet voiced in the present campaign. 2nd the Oration Proper, or

Improper, dealing in the large with the great issues of the day, such as the Class Day Issue of the Lampoon and the Recall of Faculty Decisions. In this I shall embody a sweeping denunciation of the goodies. Thirdly, and inevitably, will come the Anti-Climax or Oporation, in which, with a burst of mature rhetoric seldom found in one so young I shall revile in bitterest terms the Social Usurpation of our Colleges, dealing with the underground method in which the Social Set at Harvard derives its stimulus from Boston, the annual, exclusive, five-day cruise of the Yale crew along the Themes, to be celebrated again Friday, and the recent election and inauguration of Sam White as President and Fellows of Princeton, on the magnanimous endorsement of our intrepid cheer-leader, our heritage from the class of 1911. These are vital questions, Classmates, and must be met at Harvard Squarely.

You have my ultimatum. If you are resigned and ready, I shall proceed, without further parsley, to dissect my Peroration. If there are any timid or super-sensitively nervous ladies or members of the Harvard Equal Suffrage league present in the arena, they may retire now inconspicuously by the trapdoor opposite, where the elephants enter. I will answer any questions that may be put to me after the lecture.

1st Peroration: Roman numeral I–small letter (a).

Voters and Votaries–and Conservative Republicans.

We are gathered here today in this June sunshine (if it had been raining I should have been quick-witted enough to substitute for that, "We are gathered here in this June rain." By a lucky coincidence the "June" part would be equally fitting in both cases, you see.) We are gathered here in this June sunshine, under the leafy boughs of these grand old elms, to celebrate the fourth anniversary of the passing of our entrance English examinations. As our witty Latin orator so aptly puts it "Non sequebantur, sed in felicitate demonstrandum nunc nobis ad libitandum esse." What more can be said? Father

Garcelon, in his prime, from his taxi-chariot, could say no more. Were it not for the fact that all you nice people had melted all the way down here just to hear my words and to say that they weren't nearly so funny as you expected them to be, I should let it go at that, and call the whole thing right off now. But I will not. Rather will I turn from this, our Peroration, to the second section of the speech—the Oration Proper. If the Malefactors of Great Health do not like what I have just said about them, they may petition the Administrative Board at its next secret practice.

Oration Proper—Section A, under the General Heading of Cotton Goods and Steel Rails. Roman numeral V. (Personally, I think the speech drags a little at this point.)

As I look into your bright young faces here in the shade of these grand old rock maples, I am oppressed with the conviction that never before in her history has our country been face to face with such a grave financial crisis. It is with the customary Class Day mingled emotions of pleasure and regret that we bask here today, and with eyes dimmed by Boylston St. dust look back over the seventeen pre-digested courses that have consituted our educational banquet. Let us ponder ponderously on these things. What have we accomplished? What new visions have we seen? When and why does all this mean? O, Brothers, we are all unthinking in this extremity. We have waited and the innumerable caravan has gone without us. We have sung, and the echo has not come back. And now I ask you, what has the Republican party ever done for you—the working man? Temporary platforms, unfilled pledges and dinner-pails, and these mute, defenseless colonnades confront us, and with tier upon tier cry out "Give us the man."

You are brave men. You have given your lives without a murmur to the Class Album Committee, lives padded, it is true, by Vice-Presidencies of the Soap and Brush Club, but lives, nevertheless, young, virile lives. Even now, with that intrepid fearlessness born of youth you recline here in the new-mown grass before this altar raised to machine-made wit, defying at once hay-fever, and Owen Johnson's accusation that Harvard's social set is based on the dry grass of the fields, which, like Memorial toast, is cast into the oven and withereth away.

You have heard with calmness the dictatorial warnings of the Class Day Committee that pajamas are not to be worn under the caps and gowns until the caps and gowns have been removed, and that anyone attempting to leave the Yard by more than one gate at a time without a yard mileage ticket properly endorsed by the Secretary of the Navy, will have to stay in the yard all night, and cry himself to sleep under the red-oak saplings, or else leave the yard immediately. And yet we are Romans, and this is Rome, that from her throne of beauty ruled the world! O, ingrates! Sluggards! Undesirable citizens!

And now I think that you will agree that I have come logically to the crux of my argument on which I base my claim for the nomination. You have gone through much, besides your June allowances. You have survived the embroidered salmon of last night's spread, where your class-mates and their class-mates tread on your light fantastic toe. You have gone through that most democratic of institutions, the Senior Picnic, where one sees more of the other men in one's class than at any other gathering. And right in connection with the Senior Picnic, I wish to make the announcement that I have learned the name of the man who slapped me on my sun-burned back the morning after the Picnic, and I give him warning that I shall hound him today, from spread to spread, forcing him to eat one dollar's worth of food at each place, till at last I see him sink bubbling beneath the banana-strewn Red Sea at Beck.

And now, as Tupper's lightning artist says, as the one-thirty bell rings on a lunchless noon, "Now for the last and best!" My speech so far has dealt mainly with the economic aspects of the matter at hand. I shall now close by a few concrete references to the proposed Freshman Sanitarium, and the Conservation of our National Resources in general.

As a result of a clubbing offer with the HARVARD ADVOCATE I shall omit this section of my speech in delivering it here this afternoon, but a complete copy of it, with footnotes and errata, may be found in the current issue of the ADVOCATE on page 409. It is for sale almost everywhere, and offers two prizes—a second and a third prize, the amounts to be announced at its awarding for the best essay on "How the Ivy Oration (printed in this number) might be improved."

I do not claim that the principles enunciated in this speech will take effect immediately. You are young men yet. But think them over, Brothers. Take them home and confront yourselves with them when you are alone tonight shaking the confetti from your clothes, standing on a packing box full of old neck-ties which Max won't buy and which you hate to throw away. Then, in the silence, ask yourself if your life has been such that you could face with calmness a disclosure to the world of all that Terry knows about you.

When the time comes to fee the goody with an I.O.U. and when, with some one else's diploma in one hand, and a Bursar's card, to show that you are a real Harvard man, in the other, you sit on the old college fence, and gaze over your Lyendecker Arrow collar across the old college campus to where the sun is setting in a crimson glow behind the old college pharmacy, then allow a tear to trickle unnoticed down your cheek, and thinking of what I have said today about the Ideal College man and the community, give a regular Harvard cheer for yourself, gird up your loins and be brave.

Go forth now, and, like the gypsy-moth, spread to your heart's content. The only distressing feature of Class Day is now over. Go and live today out to its fullest measure, rejoice and be glad, for you are existing today in that Golden Age, to which, when again we assemble here as a class, we shall longingly refer as the good old Halcyon Days when we were in College.

JUNE, 1912

E. E. Cummings, '15

1894–

E. E. Cummings, poet and painter, took his M.A. in 1916 and left America to drive an ambulance in France. Besides his many books of verse and fiction, Cummings has had several one-man shows of his painting.

OF NICOLETTE

Dreaming in marble all the palace lay,
Like some colossal ghost-flower, born by night,
Blossoming in white towers to the moon;
Soft sighed the passionate darkness to the tune
Of tiny troubadours, and, phantom-white,
Dumb-blooming boughs let fall their glorious snows,
And the unearthly sweetness of a rose
Swam upward from the moonlit dews of May.

A Winged Passion woke, and one by one
There fell upon the night like angels' tears
The syllables of that ethereal prayer.
And as an opening lily, milky-fair,
When from her couch of poppy petals peers
The sleepy morning, gently draws apart
Its curtains to reveal the golden heart,
With beads of dew made jewels by the sun,

So one fair, shining tower, which, like a glass,
Turned light to flame, and blazed with silver fire,
Unclosing, gave the moon a nymph-like face,
A form whose snowy symmetry of grace
Haunted the limbs as music haunts the lyre,
A creature of white hands, who, letting fall
A thread of lustre from the opened wall,
Glided, a drop of radiance, to the grass.

Shunning the sudden moonbeams' treacherous snare,
She sought the harboring dark, and, catching up
Her delicate silk,–all white, with shining feet,
Went forth into the dew. Right wildly beat
Her heart at every kiss of daisy-cup,
And from her cheek the beauteous courage went
At every bough that reverently bent
To touch the yellow wonder of her hair.

MARCH, 1913

SUNSET

Great carnal mountains crouching in the cloud
That marrieth the young earth with a ring,
Yet still its thoughts builds heavenward, whence spring
Wee villages of vapor, sunset-proud.–
And to the meanest door hastes one pure-browed
White-fingered star, a little, childish thing,
The busy needle of her light to bring,
And stitch, and stitch, upon the dead day's shroud.
Poises the sun upon his west, a spark
Superlative,–and dives beneath the world;

From the day's fillets Night shakes out her locks;
List! One pure trembling drop of cadence purled—
"Summer!"—a meek thrush whispers to the dark.
Hark! the cold ripple sneering on the rocks!

MARCH, 1913

SUMMER SILENCE

(SPENSERIAN STANZA)

Eruptive lightnings flutter to and fro
Above the heights of immemorial hills;
Thirst-stricken air, dumb-throated, in its woe
Limply down-sagging, its limp body spills
Upon the earth. A panting silence fills
The empty vault of Night with shimmering bars
Of sullen silver, where the lake distils
Its misered bounty.—Hark! No whisper mars
The utter silence of the untranslated stars.

MARCH, 1913

BALLADE

The white night roared with a huge north-wind,
And he sat before his thundering flame,
  Quaffing holly-crowned wine.
"Say me, who is she, and whence came
The snow-white maid with the hair of Inde?
  For I will have her mine!"

"She was crouched in snow by the threshold, lord,
And we took her in (for the storm is loud),
 But who, we may not know.
For, poorly-clad, she is strangely proud,
And will not sit at the servants' board,
 But saith she comes of the snow."

"She shall sit by me," he sware amain;
"Go, ere another ash-stick chars,
 Ask of her whom she loves."
"We ask her, lord, and she saith, 'The stars.' "
And he sware, "I will kiss with kisses twain
 Those cheeks which are two white doves."

The wind had tucked in bed her earth,
And tiptoed over valley and hill,
 Humming a slumber-croon;
And all the shining night lay still,
And the rude trees dropped their hollow mirth;
 Silently came the moon.

He rose from the table, red with wine;
He put one hand against the wall,
 Swaying as he did stand;
Three steps took he in the breathless hall,
Said, "You shall love me, for you are mine."
 And touched her with his hand.

White stretched the north-land, white the south . . .
She was gone like a spark from the ash that chars;
 And "After her!" he sware . . .
They found the maid. And her eyes were stars,
A starry smile was upon her mouth,
 And the snow-flowers in her hair.

APRIL, 1913

THE NEW ART

(COMMENCEMENT PART)

THE NEW ART HAS MANY BRANCHES,—PAINTING, sculpture, architecture, the stage, literature, and music. In each of these there is a clearly discernible evolution from models; in none is there any trace of that abnormality, or incoherence, which the casual critic is fond of making the subject of tirades against the new order.

It is my purpose to sketch briefly the parallel developments of the New Art in painting, sculpture, music, and literature.

I.

Anyone who takes Art seriously, who understands the development of technique in the last half century, accepts Cézanne and Matisse as he accepts Manet and Monet. But this brings us to the turning point where contemporary criticism becomes, for the most part, rampant abuse, and where prejudice utters its storm of condemnation. I refer to that peculiar phase of modern art called indiscriminately, "Cubism," and "Futurism."

The name Cubism, properly applied, relates to the work of a small group of ultra-modern painters and sculptors who use design to express their personal reaction to the subject, i.e.—what this subject "means" to them,—and who further take this design from geometry. By using an edge in place of a curve a unique tactual value is obtained.

Futurism is a glorification of personality. Every so-called "Futurist" has his own hobby; and there are almost as many kinds of painting as artists. For instance, one painter takes as his subject sounds, another, colors. A third goes back to old techniques; a fourth sees life through a magnifying glass; a fifth imposes an environment upon his subject proper, obtaining very startling effects; a sixth concerns himself purely with motion,—in connection with which it is interesting to note the Japanese painters' wholly unrealistic rendering of the force of a river.

The painter Matisse has been called the greatest exponent of Cubist sculpture. At the 1912 exhibition the puzzled crowd in front of Brancusi's "Mlle. Pogany" was only rivalled by that which swarmed about the painting called "Nude Descending a Staircase." "Mlle. Pogany" consists of a more or less egg-shaped head with an unmistakable nose, and a sinuous suggestion of arms curving upward to the face. There is no differentiation in modelling affording even a hint of hands; in other words, the flow of line and volume is continuous. But what strikes the spectator at first glance, and focusses the attention throughout, is the enormous inscribed ovals, which everyone recognizes as the artist's conception of the subject's eyes. In the triumph of line for line's sake over realism we note in Brancusi's art the development of the basic principles of impression.

II.

Just as in the case of painting, it is a French school which brought new life to music; but at the same time, Germany has the honor of producing one of the greatest originators and masters of realism, Richard Strauss.

The modern French school of music finds its inspiration in the personal influence of César Franck. Debussy, Ravel and Satie all owe much to this great Belgian, who (like Maeterlinck and Verhaeren), was essentially a man of their own artistic nationality.

It is safe to say that there will always be somebody who still refuses to accept modernism in music, quoting in his defense the sovereign innovator, Beethoven! On a par with the sensation produced by the painting and sculpture of the Futurist variety was the excitement which the music of Strauss and Debussy first produced upon audiences. At present, Debussy threatens to become at any moment vulgarly common; while Strauss is fatuous in his clarity beside Schönberg; who, with Stravinsky, is the only god left by the public for the worship of the esthetes.

Erik Satie is, in many respects, the most interesting of all modern composers. Nearly a quarter of a century ago he was writing what is now considered modern music. The most striking aspect of Satie's art is the truly extraordinary sense of humor which prompts one of his subjects, the "sea cucumber," to console himself philosophically for his lack of tobacco.

The "Five Orchestral Pieces" of Arnold Schönberg continue to be the leading sensation of the present day musical world. Their composer occupies a position in many respects similar to that of the author of the "Nude Descending a Staircase." I do not in the least mean to ridicule Schönberg;—no lawlessness could ever have produced such compositions as his, which resemble bristling forests contorted by irresistible winds. His work is always the expression of something mysteriously terrible,—which is probably why Boston laughed.

I have purposely left until the last the greatest theorist of modern music,—Scriabin. Logically, he belongs beside Stravinsky, as leader of the Russian school. But it is by means of Scriabin that we may most readily pass from music to literature, through the medium of what has been called "sense-transference," as exemplified by the color music of the "Prometheus."

This "Poem of Fire" is the consummation of Scriabin's genius. To quote the Transcript: "At the first performance, by the Russian Symphony Society, on March 20, for the first time in history a composer used a chromatic color score in combination with orchestration. . . . At the beginning of the orchestration, a gauze rectangle in about the position of a picture suspended on the back wall became animated by flowing and blending colors. These colors were played by a 'color-organ' or 'chromola,' having a keyboard with fifteen keys, and following a written score."

III.

The suggestion of an analogy between color and music leads us naturally to the last branch of the New Art,–to wit, literature. Only the most extreme cases will be discussed, such as have important bearing upon the very latest conceptions of artistic expression.

I will quote three contemporary authors to illustrate different phases and different degrees of the literary parallel to sound painting–in a rather faint hope that the first two may prepare the way for an appreciation of the third. First Amy Lowell's "Grotesque" affords a clear illustration of development from the ordinary to the abnormal.

> "Why do the lilies goggle their tongues at me
> When I pluck them;
> And writhe and twist,
> And strangle themselves against my fingers,
> So that I can hardly weave the garland
> For your hair?
> Why do they shriek your name
> And spit at me
> When I would cluster them?
> Must I kill them
> To make them lie still,

And send you a wreathe of lolling corpses
To turn putrid and soft
On your forehead
While you dance?"

In this interesting poem we seem to discern something beyond the conventional. The lilies are made to express hatred by the employment of grotesque images. But there is nothing original in the pathetic fallacy. No one quarrels with Tennyson's lines

"There has fallen a splendid tear
From the passion-flower at the gate"–

Let us proceed further,–only noting in the last three lines that brutality which is typical of the New Art,–and consider the following poem by the same author:

"THE LETTER"

"Little cramped words scrawling all over the paper
Like draggled fly's legs,
What can you tell of the flaring moon
Through the oak leaves?
Or of an uncurtained window, and the bare floor
Spattered with moonlight?
Your silly quirks and twists have nothing in them
Of blossoming hawthorns,
And this paper is chill, crisp, smooth, virgin of loveliness
Beneath my hand.
I am tired, Beloved, of chafing my heart against
The want of you;
Of squeezing it into little ink drops,
And posting it.
And I scald alone, here under the fire
Of the great moon."

This poem is superb of its kind. I know of no image in all realistic writing which can approach the absolute vividness of the first two lines. The metaphor of the chafed heart is worthy of any poet; but its fanciful development would have been impossible in any literature except this ultra-modern.

I shall now quote from a sonnet by my second author, Donald Evans:

"Her voice was fleet-limbed and immaculate,
And like peach blossoms blown across the wind
Her white words made the hour seem cool and kind,
Hung with soft dawns that danced a shadow fête.
A silken silence crept up from the South,
The flutes were hushed that mimed the orange moon,
And down the willow stream my sighs were strewn,
While I knelt to the corners of her mouth."

In the figure "Her voice was fleet-limbed," and the phrase "white words," we have a sought-for literary parallel to the work of the "sound painters." It is interesting to compare Dante's expressions of a precisely similar nature, occurring in the first and fifth cantos, respectively, of the Inferno—"dove il Sol tace," and "in loco d'ogni luce muto."

From Donald Evans to Gertrude Stein is a natural step,—up or down, and one which I had hoped the first two might enable us to take in security. Gertrude Stein subordinates the meaning of words to the beauty of the words themselves. Her art is the logic of literary sound painting carried to its extreme. While we must admit that it is logic, must we admit that it is art?

Having prepared the way, so far as it is possible, for a just appreciation, I now do my best to quote from the book "Tender Buttons," as follows:

(1) A sound.
Elephant beaten with candy and little pops and chews all bolts and reckless, reckless rats, this is this.
(2) Salad Dressing and an Artichoke.
Please pale hot, please cover rose, please acre in the red stranger, please butter all the beef-steak with regular feel faces.
(3) Suppose an Eyes

. . . .

Go red, go red, laugh white.
Suppose a collapse is rubbed purr, is rubbed purget.
Little sales ladies little sales ladies
Little saddles of mutton.
Little sales of leather and such beautiful, beautiful, beautiful beautiful.

The book from which these selections are drawn is unquestionably a proof of great imagination on the part of the authoress, as anyone who tries to imitate her work will discover for himself. Here we see traces of realism, similar to those which made the "Nude Descending a Staircase" so baffling. As far as these "Tender Buttons" are concerned, the sum and substance of criticism is impossible. The unparalleled familiarity of the medium precludes its use for the purpose of esthetic effect. And here, in their logical conclusion, impressionistic tendencies are reduced to absurdity.

The question now arises, how much of all this is really Art?

The answer is: we do not know. The great men of the future will most certainly profit by the experimentation of the present period. An insight into the unbroken chain of artistic development during the last half century disproves the theory that modernism is without foundation; rather we are concerned with a natural unfolding of sound tendencies. That the conclusion is, in a particular case, absurdity, does not in any way impair the value of the experiment, so long as we are dealing with sincere effort. The New Art, maligned though it may be by fakirs and fanatics, will appear in its essential spirit to the unprejudiced critic as a courageous and genuine exploration of untrodden ways.

JUNE, 1915

Robert Hillyer, '17

1895–

Robert Hillyer holds the distinction of being the only undergraduate ever to have a book of poems published by the Harvard University Press. Sonnets and Other Lyrics *appeared in 1917. Formerly Boylston Professor at Harvard, Hillyer is now a visiting professor at Kenyon.*

TRIOLET

I praise the dainty triolet,
So courtly and so gay;
I know it's trivial, and yet
I praise the dainty triolet.
A wisp of song, a moment set
In loveliness away,–
I praise the dainty triolet,
So courtly and so gay.

FEBRUARY, 1917

SONNET

Even as love grows more I write the less;
Impelled to speak, unable still to voice

The lyric thoughts like angels that rejoice
Attendant on thy godlike loveliness.
Stay the bright swallow high in airy poise,
Carve out of stone an infinite caress,
Garner the fruits of tears and happiness,
Make bloom forever what an hour destroys,—

Then shamed by such unprecedented skill
I may find words to name thee, and to sing
Such praises of thy beauty as shall fill
The listening world with floods of carolling;
Till then thou art like starlight in the air,
Or clouds at dawn, unutterably fair.

MARCH, 1917

THE QUESTION

Now the sick earth revives, and in the sun
The wet soil gives a fragrance to the air;
The days of many colors are begun,
And early promises of meadows fair
With starry petals, and of trees now bare
Soon to be lyric with the trilling choir,
And lovely with new leaves, spread everywhere
A subtle flame that sets the heart on fire
With thoughts of other springs and dreams of new desire.

The mind will never dwell within the present,
It weeps for vanished years or hopes for new;
This morn of wakened warmth, so calm, so pleasant,
So gaily gemmed with diadems of dew,
When buds swell on the bough, and robins woo

Their loves with notes bell-like and crystal-clear,
The spirit stirs from sleep, yet wonders, too,
Whence comes the hint of sorrow or of fear
Making it move disquiet within its narrow sphere.

This flash of sun, this flight of wings in riot,
This festival of sound, of sight, of smell,
Wakes in the spirit a profound disquiet,
And greeting seems the foreword of farewell.
Budding like all the world, the soul would swell
Out of its withering mortality;
Flower immortal, burst from its heavy shell,
Fly far with love beyond the world and sea,
Out of the grasp of change, from time and twilight free.

Could the unknowing gods, waked in compassion,
Eternalize the splendour of this hour,
And from the world's frail garlands strongly fashion
An ageless Paradise, celestial bower,
Where our long-sundered souls could rise in power
To the complete fulfillment of their dream,
And never know again that years devour
Petals and light, bird-note and woodland theme,
And floods of young desire, bright as a silver stream,

Should we be happy, thou and I together,
Lying in love eternally in spring,
Watching the buds unfold that shall not wither,
Hearing the birds calling and answering,
When the leaves stir and all the meadows ring?
Smelling the rich earth steaming in the sun,
Feeling between caresses the light wing
Of the wind whose fragrant flight is never done,—
Should we be happy then? happy, adorèd One?

But no, here in this fragile flesh abides
The secret of an infinite delight,
Hidden in dying beauty there resides
Something undying, something that takes its flight
When the dust turns to dust, and day to night,
And spring to fall, whose joys in love redeem
Eternally, life's changes and death's blight,
Even as these pale, tender petals seem
A glimpse of infinite beauty, flashed in a passing dream.

APRIL, 1917

Malcolm Cowley, '19

1898–

Malcolm Cowley was associate editor of the New Republic *from 1929 to 1944. Author of non-fiction and verse, his latest volume of poetry,* The Dry Season, *appeared in 1941.*

TO A GIRL I DISLIKE

Ever since I was a very little boy,
I have known a path that wound away through the birches
and hemlocks;
And I remember
How I always feared to follow it,
And liked to dream instead what lay at its end—
An Indian burying-ground, perhaps;
Or a cave of robbers, stored with fabulous riches;
Or a rotting cabin that had nursed some great hero.
And one day I followed the path,
Walking slowly out of fearfulness;
Starting back when I roused a covey of quail
From the maple scrub around the spring;
Only to find at the end of it,
Among the hemlocks and mossed birches,

A pigsty—
Like a piece of yellow glass set in filigreed platinum,
Or like your heart
Beneath the mysterious immobility of your beauty.

NOVEMBER, 1916

AN OLD FELLOW TO HIS FRIENDS

When I am dead, and you have heard the news,
You'll spend an evening in a darkened room,
Perhaps, all thinking of me, and afraid
To break the silence with a word. And then
Somehow your minds will slip to other things;
Poems, press-notices, and love affairs,
And yet your faces still will wear, I know,
The self-same gloom, the same hypocrisy—
And can't you hear me laughing in the shadows?

Forget the silence and the darkened room,
Old friends, when I am dead. Perhaps instead
You all might meet as we all used to meet;
With cards and glasses and a haze of smoke—
And then the time to jest and jibe at me.
Then tear apart my poems as of old,
Show their essential weakness; take my prose,
That never could grow up, and jeer at it.
And when all that is criticized enough,
Turn to my person, laughing louder still;
Bring forth my foibles and my prejudices. . .

Then maybe one of you will want his glass,
And reaching find it emptied silently,

Mysteriously. Then you may know my ghost
Has emptied it, and ghosts, the old tales say,
Grow tipsy easily. And when you laugh
At some remembered foible, you may hear
A tipsier laughter echoed back. Then know
My ghost is laughing with you merrily
From out the shadows, at his own dead self.

FEBRUARY, 1917

TO A DILETTANTE KILLED AT VIMY

Years of small sorrows and of small endeavor;
Years of great plans, and mental cowardice;
And we that hoped they would not last forever:—
That's all. To cut the whole thing short, came this.

And yet the petty muddle you made of it;
The pose; the brave dreams foundered in a sea
Of idle talk, now seem to us resolved
Into clean metal by catastrophe.

FEBRUARY, 1918

Christopher LaFarge, '20

1897–

Christopher LaFarge was an architect until 1932, and has been writing ever since. He is author of The Sudden Guest *and many other books.*

TO MY GODDESS

My stream has had its course through open field,
Through banks where birches slenderly lean out,
Through woods and swamps where sodden thickets shield
The lady-slipper's tender growing sprout;
Over rock bottoms where split eddies shout,
Over the sand whence murmurous music comes,
Under cool ferns where lurks the radiant trout;
Tumbling from ledges where the water strums
On hollow-echoing rocks resounding like deep drums.

My stream has many songs that all men know:
Some that are tender when the raindrops fall,
Some that are sad, sung where the rushes grow
And make vibrating harp strings, slender-tall.
But if in symphony were gathered all
And tuned to make a perfect melody,

Then lovelier than the hermit-thrush's call,
  Than whippoorwill's insistent threnody,
Would rise a love-song, Goddess, fit to honour thee.

APRIL, 1918

SONNET

IN APOLOGY FOR A CURIOUS HANDWRITING

Lady, I know my curlicues perplex,
And that my writing is most hard to read,
But rapid letters to the gentler sex
Do not conduce to a fine, flowing screed.
What with a fluttering heart and beating head,
Imagination makes the pen to wobble,
And hasty expurgation of what's said
Lames the poor thoughts as slow they outward hobble.
Could I but write whatever to my mind
First comes and bravely damn the consequence;
Shackles which the conventions strictly bind
About my writs, throw off, with common sense,—
Such a wild letter would I write you then
As would atone for wobblings of the pen.

JANUARY, 1919

John Brooks Wheelwright, '20

1896–1940

John Brooks Wheelwright, author of four books of verse, was Pegasus (literary editor) of the ADVOCATE *in 1920. His* Selected Poems *was published by New Directions in 1941.*

MY FATHER'S BRIDGE ON THE CHARLES

This euphonious bridge
tells of ages when men will revere it
as builded by giants . . .

Such a pile in the past would have smiled, a kingly palace—
would have sneered at the mob,
but its grace and grandeur of granite and steel
proclaim to callous passers
that theirs is the robe, globe, diadem.

Erosion can only crown it with romance,
change will make it prophetic;
sombre and proud, a pagan,
affliction will sanctify.
Let time toss an elegant turret
into the basin!

the brothers will rise with more exquisite song.
Or let him shatter
an open-work archway,
the sisters will cling in silence made solemn by tears;–

Voice of my father speaking through metal and granite
to an esoteric as to an heedless child;
love speaking to love from one world to the other,
death speaking to life in the language of love.

NOVEMBER, 1919

David McCord, '21

1897–

David McCord, as an undergraduate, was more of a Lampooner than an ADVOCATE *man, but "The Ups and Downs of Skiing," luckily, was printed in the* ADVOCATE *after McCord had delivered it as his initiation part for the Signet Society, Harvard's literary club. McCord, best known for his humorous verse, has edited an anthology of light verse,* What Cheer, *and is editorial chairman of the* Harvard Alumni Bulletin.

THE UPS AND DOWNS OF SKIING

SOME PEOPLE HAVE A PECULIAR AND WHOLLY UNnatural liking for snow. What it's good for is beyond me—the very sight of it reminds me of the most miserable experience in my life. (This from a retiring old bachelor whom I have known as long as I can remember.)

Several years ago, when I could still wear a belt in place of suspenders, a friend of mine—at least he *was* a friend then—invited me up to the Adirondacks for the winter holidays. "We'll go sheeing," he said. "Sheeing?" said I. "What do you mean by that?" "Ah," he replied, "you are an American and the 'k' is hard." "What 'k'?" I asked. "Why, the 'k' in sheeing—you pronounce it 'skiing.' " Unfortunately I accepted this explanation and the invitation as well. I had no skis, but my enthusiastic friend told me where they could be had.

Next day I went in quest of them in a large sporting goods store. "Let me see some shees–skis," I asked nervously. The clerk looked at me with that penetrating, withering look that only clerks have, and decided on the spot—without any reservations—that I was *not* a fearless ski-jumper fresh from the land of the slippery Alps. A moment later he had spread before me a heterogeneous mass of narrow boards with bent ends, rawhide thongs, and what not. I have always felt just a little pride, when buying a new golf club, in pointing out its merits and defects to the salesman, and in swinging it in excellent form for the latter's especial benefit. Now, however, I was at a loss. I knew nothing about skis. I didn't want to. Something told me that the pointed end goes to the front. The most I knew with certainty was that they were worn on the feet. With this fund of information at my disposal, and with the help of numerous suggestions on the part of sympathetic customers (I know now *why* they were sympathetic), I decided upon a slender, speedy-looking pair that seemed to match both my stature and complexion, and left, trying all the while to make my unwieldy purchase seem as much like a walking stick as possible.

A week later I arrived in the mountains. I don't consider myself in the least a prophet, but somehow coming up on the train I felt that everything wasn't going to be just right. Nor was it. For the first day or so my host contented himself with taking me on walks, miles long—and even longer—so that I might get broken in on my new conveyors. I feel now that he meant broken up, but of course I can't be sure.

Then one bright, clear morning he said we were ready. God knows he may have been—but not I. Never have I felt so far from being ready for anything. Skiing, it seems, is an art not akin to the earth alone. Like the playful porpoise the true skier must now and then forsake his native heath and plunge off recklessly into space, to descend at last, as best he may, a new and vastly happier man for his trip aloft. I took a long and unenthusiastic look down the slide and the jump at the bottom.

My feet had been cold for some time, but a wave now spread over my whole frame with great rapidity till my teeth chattered so loudly I could hardly hear what my companion was saying. "Get a good shove-off with your pike," he told me, "keep your feet together, good balance, and don't worry. This is only the beginner's slide anyway."

Amid a torrent of similar advice, and in more or less of a daze, I slid out and would have given myself some kind of a send-off with the aid of the pike had not gravity beaten me to it. I was off! Like a true thoroughbred my right ski took a course straight down the slide, but the left one, dissatisfied with things in general, or else displeased with its running mate, shot off in another direction. Unfortunately my foot was not consulted in the matter and had to follow blindly. Thank the Lord my body remained neutral, and though it almost split on the issue, I was saved by being prostrated on the ground and finishing the unhappy journey on whatever portions of my anatomy nature found suitable.

Little more remains to be told. In a dizzy condition I was escorted once more to the starting point, and pushed off once again on my way. Things went better. Faster and faster I slid. Lord, how the wind whistled! Down! Down! Wow! Ye Gods, I was over the jump! I seemed to fly to pieces. My skis dangled down like the legs of a stork; the earth shot up to meet me like a rebounding punching bag. Something told me I wasn't landing just right. I wasn't. I didn't. In fact, I must have made quite a failure of it, for the next I knew was three hours later when I woke up in bed to find only one limb out of a possible four functioning properly. They said that between me, my skis, and my clothes I had presented a knot that took great skill to unravel. And, as I said before, snow was at the bottom of it all.

DECEMBER, 1920

W. Ellery Sedgwick, '22

1899–1942

W. Ellery Sedgwick, nephew of the Atlantic's *Ellery Sedgwick, was the author of* Herman Melville, the Tragedy of a Mind.

SLUMBER SONG

Roses born in early June
Shall not see the harvest moon;
Birds that in the morning sing,
Sleep at eve 'neath folded wing;
Soon the summer sun will set,
And the soul will soon forget
All its faith in that to be,
And the heart its constancy.

Sleep, my child, while wandering winds
Passing by, thy face caress,
Lost art thou to all these tears,
Lost to all the hungry years,
In thy charmed forgetfulness.

JUNE, 1919

E. A. Weeks, '22

1898–

E. A. Weeks, Secretary of the ADVOCATE *in 1922, has been editor of the* Atlantic Monthly *since 1938. An author as well, Weeks is a trustee of Wellesley and an overseer of Harvard.*

BATHOS

WE HAD FINISHED DINNER, AND THE CHILDREN had gone upstairs to their lessons. Rica was tracing out a pattern on the damask cloth with the tip of her coffee spoon. The soft light of the candles shadowed the faint imprints of time, she was very handsome, and I loved that characteristic poise of her head. She looked up and I smiled at her.

"Saw Jim Parkman today. He hasn't changed a hair."

"Did you, Ned? Dear old Jim! Has he made good yet?"

"Why, Rica, he's never made anything else!"

"Which means, of course, that he hasn't. How you men do stand up for each other! I wonder if you know that Lelia hasn't had a new evening gown for five years?"

She rose, deposited a fleeting kiss on the bald spot which I'm trying to train my hair to cover, and a few moments later I heard her at the piano . . . Rica does play well.

I settled a little lower in my chair and lighted my cigar.

Jim not made good—it's absurd—I first met Jim two or

three nights after the opening of college in my freshman year. Tom Carrol, my room-mate, had gone in town on a "party," and I had been unpacking until fairly late in the evening. The contents of my trunk and boxes were piled about in a heterogeneous collection on the chairs and the couch. I must have been engrossed in my labor, for I remember starting when the door suddenly opened. Before me stood Tom, swaying slightly, disheveled,—hopelessly drunk. He was supported by a slender, thin-faced chap, whose luminous black eyes attracted me, and whose paleness of skin was in marked contrast with Tom's flushed countenance.

"Better give me a hand with him, he's pretty far gone. I found him down in the entry."

But Tom with a "Thanks, ol' man, thanks vera much," had lunged forward and subsided full length on the couch. Between us we finally got him to bed and then, because Tom's erratic movements upon the couch had raised havoc with the fruits of my unpacking, the stranger gave me a hand in straightening things up. He introduced himself as Parkman, said he was rooming upstairs and "wouldn't I drop in and see him some time"—I liked his smile, and I knew that I was going to like what was behind it.

We roomed together the last three years of college—I always said I boarded with him, which came fairly close to the truth. He chose the rug, and the chintz curtains, bargained for our near-mahogany furniture, and adorned the walls with his etchings and wood cuts. . . . "Listen, Ned, you ass, that slop"—indicating a choice collection of posters and "prep-school" photographs,—"goes all very well in your bedroom but this is a gentleman's study."

Jim made many nodding acquaintances but few deep friends. I'm afraid he set too high a standard.

"He's a nice enough chap, Ned, but he's stupid. His

world is composed of three elements: football, his club, and women. . . ."

He didn't care much for club life but could usually be found curled up on the window-seat with a book, or scribbling verse—his hair more touseled than ever.

And how he used to walk! He knew every back alley and "cul-de-sac" for miles about Boston. It was a treat to accompany him,—though it made you realize that your wind was not what it should be. He'd lead you through a labyrinth of dingy grey streets to show you some old relic of Colonial architecture, the while discoursing on his Utopian ideals. His imagination was never still a minute—How he detested "modernism" or "money grubbing Americanitis," as he called it.

In his senior year he began to write sonnets, with a far-away look in his eyes—It was generally understood that he and Lelia Curtis were engaged.

The night of our graduation Jim had delivered the Class Poem and early in the evening I'd seen him and Lelia wandering about the yard. Gorgeous moonlight. I came in about midnight and had started to grope my way to the switch, when I saw Jim, stretched out on the window seat, his head buried in a mass of pillows. I thought he was asleep, and tiptoed across to my bedroom.

"Hello, Ned," came a muffled voice, "turn on the light, will you?" He sat up. "Been far down in the depths. God, what a mess this life is! Four wonderful years, yet how have they molded me? A half-baked poet. Damn it, Ned, I've got to make some money! Lelia and I are going to be married in two years—I'm not worth a punched nickle to a business man—God knows, I don't want to sell soap, or manufacture suspenders—I want to write."

Jim didn't prove much of a business man even in his early days. He caught hold soon enough, and his personality carried him up a few rungs, but he was never "in the game." He considered it all in the light of a necessary evil, and he suffered accordingly. His firm noted his conscientiousness, his mind for details, and his stability—and shelved him into an office position. But Jim's head and heart were too full of Lelia and his poetry to be aware of his niche.

They were married, just as they had planned, two years after his graduation—It was a beautiful wedding—the church, a mass of white roses and apple blossoms. I was best man, and Lelia's younger sister sat on my silk hat. Lelia was radiant, Jim pale as a ghost, his eyes like coals—And how disgustingly drunk Tom Carrol was! Tom's retired from the Street now, with two millions. . . .

They settled down in a tiny little apartment up in Cambridge. Jim's "Sonnets and Lyrics" appeared that year and were received rather favorably.

Rica is playing the "Caprice Viennoise" . . . "Junior" arrived—Yet, as I look back on it, it wasn't until after Betty was born, that Jim and Lelia commenced to draw away from us. They came in and dined with us, and we paid occasional visits to their tastefully decorated little house, but they accepted few of their Beacon Street invitations and, as a consequence, they received but a few. I'd see Jim at a Vestry Meeting, or downtown, or semi-occasionally at the Country Club, but I was in a rut of my own affairs and Rica usually attended to our parties. So two or three years slipped by before it came to me, with a twinge of pain at my own carelessness, that I hadn't really seen Jim, that I hadn't had a talk with him for ages. Rica was at a Suffrage Dinner, so I thought I'd run out alone and surprise them. They were glad to see me. "June" and "Betts" were "piggy-backed" up to bed, and we had a delightful dinner topped off with some apple pie of which Lelia was justly proud. After coffee, she went upstairs to hear the prayers, and Jim and I chatted long over our cigars. A University instructor and his young wife came in shortly, and

I pleaded a fictitious club engagement and left them to their "auction"—But I had noticed some little things—the lines of fatigue in Lelia's face, though not a trace of it appeared in her smile; a ragged fuzz on Jim's tie, that bespoke long usage; and the enamel woodwork that showed traces of youthful grimy fingers. I knew that Jim had nearly reached the apex of his salary. Now and again one of his poems would appear in "Contemporary Verse," or even Harper's, and he was trying to induce Brentano's to publish his second book. He'd given up his golf. "You see, Ned," he said smilingly, "with golf balls at their present price it's either a question of humoring that cursed slice of mine, or sending 'June' to college. I take the whole family walking instead."

We met Lelia and Jim one late Sunday afternoon this fall after a concert—I think it was Kreisler. They were chatting like happy children. I offered them a lift home in the car.

"No thanks," smiled Lelia, "it's such a glorious evening I think we'll walk along for a while."

Jim patted my shoulder as we separated. "Harper's sent me a birthday check," he whispered in my ear.

Later, Rica asked if I had noticed poor Lelia's hair—and I said that I thought they were one of the happiest married couples I'd ever seen. Yet as Rica says, Lelia hasn't had a new gown for five years, and the children go to the public school.

"Ned, do come away and let Brower clear the table! And dear, you haven't forgotten that we're playing cards with the Nelsons this evening?"

I dislike "auction."

JUNE, 1921

John Mason Brown, '23

1900–

John Mason Brown, besides being dramatic critic for the New York Post, Theater Arts, *and the* Saturday Review of Literature, *has taught at Breadloaf, Yale, and Harvard.*

GREASE-PAINT AND PURITANS

PHILIP BARRY'S "YOU AND I" HAS JUST OPENED IN New York. It is a Harvard Prize Play, and being such it quite properly elicited from a prominent dramatic critic there an announcement in his columns, with "whatever that may mean" as a legitimate query. He was puzzled. Why a prize-play and why from Harvard? Moreover he was busy. A dramatic critic leads a hard life. He must go to the theatre three or more times a week, and write intelligently about what he sees for the morrow's paper. And to do that he must keep abreast of the times. No wonder, then, that this particular critic was puzzled, and annoyed. What was this "upstart crow" from New England? He certainly was not alone in wondering what Harvard had to do with the theatre, and why a prize play. Hearsay and tradition have it that Calvinistic Cambridge with its frigid creed would never have had a weakness for the tinsel and corruption of the theatre. But history may at times be at odds with hearsay and whispered tradition. Harvard in a modest way has had long dealings with the theatre.

As early as 1665 there is a record of amateurs being summoned to court for presenting a play in the Colonies. Even then the conflict! Even then the amateur was doing the unusual thing! But that is not Harvard. Harvard's first claims to dramatic distinction can be traced to 1690 when the first play written by an American was staged in Cambridge by those lantern-jawed, and stern Puritan ancestors. It was Benjamin Colman's "Gustavus Vasa," and was performed just sixty-two years before the coming of Lewis Hallam's first professional English company of note to New York, Philadelphia, and Williamsburg.

Needless to say, between that pioneer performance and the productions of the 47 Workshop and the Dramatic Club of today, has come no unbroken record of theatrical performances. The tradition for open-mindedness and liberality has, however, in most cases, been observed. The reactions against the theatre were all-inclusive in those early days. They seem utterly preposterous to most of us today, but the colleges naturally felt them and were affected by them. Laws against theatrical performances became current in many of the colonies, including Massachusetts. To the defense of drama came John Gardner in a speech delivered before the Massachusetts House of Representatives in 1792. With that admirable rationality of the legendary Puritan, he remarked that "the illiberal, unmanly, and despotical act which now prohibits theatrical exhibitions among us, to me, Sir, appears to be the brutal, monstrous, spawn of a sour, envious, morose, malignant, and truly benighted superstition." Even so mild a rebuke did not change the administrative attitude of American colleges to the theatre. As late as 1824, President Dwight of Yale could say in an "Essay on the Theatre" that "to indulge a taste for play-going means nothing more or less than the loss of that most valuable treasure, the immortal soul."

It is not in the dead record of early plays, nor even in those justly dead compositions—amusing as literary curios and comments on the tastes of our much-praised forebears—that we are interested. It may be worth mentioning that Royall Tyler's "The Contrast" (1787), the second native play professionally produced in this country, came from a Harvard graduate and was advertised as "written by a citizen of the United States." That same astonishment, when an American writes a good play, is observable even today. And if the colleges, and among them Harvard, had not given some dramatic training, our bill-boards might still read in that manner. To understand fully what the colleges have done in America is to appreciate the difficulties that lay in the path of officially recognizing the theatre and the drama, particularly in practice, as parts of a college's equipment. Tradition and polite scruples have always damned the theatre to the layman. Newspaper scandals have had their hand. Actors and actresses have become famous overnight by commercialized eccentricities as mild as milk-bath habits or as wild as human thought can imagine. Certainly for the colleges to fly in the face of such misconceptions was no easy thing. And Harvard had its part in the revolt.

Professor Baker was one of the first to teach the history of dramatic literature in this country. He was also the first to give courses in play-construction. Inspired by the success that attended the Abbey Theatre adventure in Dublin, he set out to establish a play-writing course, and by 1907 was giving his now famous English 47, at Harvard and Radcliffe. It was not until 1912, that the 47 Workshop, which produces plays written in the courses at the two colleges, was founded, giving to dramatic workers a chance to experiment and test before an audience. Before that time the Dramatic Club had produced the original plays. But after that, with a student company and stage force, the student plays were produced under Professor Baker's direction. The process involved the happy custom of making the audience cooperate by writing criticisms of the plays and thus giving to the authors a chance to study their plays in relation to an audience. Mr. Baker has tried "in the light of historical practice merely to distinguish the permanent from the impermanent in technique." In the classroom, "by showing the inexperienced dramatist how experienced dramatists have solved problems similar to his own, to shorten his time of apprenticeship," he has given to the embryo dramatist the same "instruction in art granted the architect, the sculptor, the painter, and the musician." All this in its way has given answer to the critic's query of "why a prize play" and "why from Harvard?"

Such work, and the work of other teachers of the drama, won for the doers the title of "St. Pauls of the drama," from Henry Arthur Jones. Professor Brander Matthews at Columbia, Professor Phelps at Yale, Professor Kochs at the University of North Carolina, and Professor Dickenson at Wisconsin are a few of the more prominent men who are actively teaching drama in this country now. The list could be extended to include almost every state university or college. And the remarkable thing is that we have been much quicker to take the feared, despised, and condemned trappings of the theatre under academic wings than has England. The work here has been going on for twenty years and more. In fact dramatic instruction has become almost a platitude with us, and for that reason obscured the struggle and enlightenment that brought it into being. Within the last two years, the first chair of dramatic literature in an English university was given to Granville Barker at the University of Liverpool.

Out of the instruction given at Harvard, and out of Harvard have come some few men and women who have created a slight stir in theatrical circles, even in New York, and perhaps, elsewhere. Among the earlier or pre-Workshop dramatists was William Vaughn Moody, who is known by many for "The Great Divide" (1906) and the "Faith Healer," both significant plays, that had their essence in native problems, and that have had their effect on what has followed them. Percy MacKaye—whose "Sappho" was written and acted when he was in undergraduate Cambridge, and performed with the help of Wellesley—was another. To him the civic masque and community drama of this country owe something, the recognition due the leader. His "Caliban" (1916) and "The Scarecrow" (1908) are perhaps not forgotten. Still another of these earlier dramatic writers was Edward Knobloch, who gained attention by his picaresque "Kismet" (1911) and followed it with the technically interesting "Milestones" (1912) written in collaboration with Arnold Bennett. From Radcliffe at that time came Josephine Preston Peabody, whose "Marlowe" (1901) opened the Agassiz Theatre, Radcliffe, and whose "The Piper" won the first prize, among the fifteen hundred manuscripts submitted, as the best play with which to open the Memorial Theatre at Stratford.

In the actual literary output of the Workshop dramatists who have received dramatic instruction here, an admirable catholicity of subject and treatment shows that no definite school or stamp has been arbitrarily established. Free rein has been granted to the embryo dramatists. The list includes some names of interest. Edward Sheldon's is among the earliest. In 1908 he wrote "Salvation Nell" while still an undergraduate, and in 1909 had the pleasure of seeing "The Nigger" produced at the ill-fated New Theatre in New York. "Romance" (1914), played for eight years by Doris Keane, here and abroad, his adaptations of "The Jest" (1919) and "The Czarina" (1922) are still fresh in our memories. Perhaps Eugene O'Neill, master of phrase and character, leader in both realistic and expressionistic schools of play-writing, equally adept in the short and long play, and three times winner of the Pulitzer Prize for the best American play of the year, may be pointed to with pride. He harks back to no European tradition. He writes without artistic forebears. After a year at Princeton and several years at sea, he came to the Workshop (1914–1915). There is a noticeable change in his work after that year, a mellowing, an improvement. "Bound East of Cardiff" was written while he was here, and it is different from the O'Neill of "Fog" and "Thirst." "Beyond the Horizon" (1920), "The Straw" (1922) and "Anna Christie" (1921)—examples of his realistic writing,—and "The Emperor Jones" (1920) and "The Hairy Ape" (1922)—examples of his expressionistic tendencies—are too well-known to warrant comment.

The New York critic wanted to know "why a prize play?" He had forgotten in his rush and worry that John Craig and Oliver Morosco had both offered production and $500 to the best play written in the 47 courses during a year. Craig started the competitions, Morosco followed him, and now Richard Herndon is conducting them. They have been of unquestionable value in giving impetus to dramatic composition at Harvard, and some of them have not yet faded from memory. Frederick Ballard's "Believe Me, Xantippe," (1915), and Cleaves Kinkead's "Common Clay" (1916) were among the Craig plays. Rachel Butler's "Mama's Affair" (1920) was probably the best-known of the Morosco winners.

Among the long plays of Workshop origin or by graduates of English 47 are Edward Massey's "Plots and Playwrights" (1915), which won a considerable following when given by the Washington Square Players, Frederick L. Day's "Makers of Light," produced last spring at the Neighborhood Playhouse, Hubert Osborne's "Shore Leave" and "Rita Coventry," and Lewis Beach's "The Square Peg," all of the present season.

The one-act play has also been studied at Cambridge. "The

Clod" of Lewis Beach, "Will O' The Wisp" (1916) and "The Playroom" (1915) of Doris Halman, "Torches" of Kenneth Raisbeck, "The Hard Heart" of Mark Kister, are fine contributions not unknown to the Little Theatres and amateur stages. So, too, are "Three Pills in a Bottle" (1917) of Rachel Lyman Field, "The Florist Shop" (1915) of Winifred Hawkridge, and "Two Crooks and a Lady" (1917) of Eugene Pillot. Impetus to the short play has been given by production within the Workshop and the published volumes of Harvard Dramatic Club and 47 Workshop Plays.

Play-writing has not been the only way in which Puritan Harvard has touched the theatre. Along with it go the other arts of the theatre. And the critic mentioned above must have been tired indeed when he forgot that Robert Edmond Jones and Lee Simonson studied here. Jones, whose settings for "The Jest," "Hamlet," "Macbeth," and "The Hairy Ape" have merited no little attention, was once an instructor in Fine Arts here, before he studied under Reinhardt and designed his set for Granville Barker's production of "The Man Who Married a Dumb Wife." Simonson, first with the Washington Square Players and now with the Theatre Guild, has done notable work as scenic artist in "He Who Gets Slapped," "Back to Methuselah," "R.U.R.," and "Peer Gynt."

In a modest way, too, founders of Little Theatres and teachers of the drama have come from Harvard. These men have brought to communities far from the pulse of a New York theatrical season, the best that the theatre has to offer in the form of either local productions or lectures. Among them are Sam Hume and Irving Pichel at the University of California, Louise Burleigh in Richmond, Frederick Koch at the University of North Carolina, and Samuel Eliot at Smith.

Papers and publications have often turned to the Harvard-bred for dramatic critics. Needless to say, the critic first mentioned was not from Harvard, but there are other critics who are read. In New York one finds Walter Prichard Eaton, John Corbin of the "Times," Kenneth Macgowan, whose "Continental Stagecraft" and "The Theatre of Tomorrow," written with Jones, are fascinating annals of the newer methods in the theatre; Hiram K. Moderwell, whose "The Theatre of Today" was significant as first catching hold of the new movement, and phrasing the reaction against photographic realism to "inscenierung"; Robert C. Benchley, a master of the lighter critical vein, and Heywood Broun. It is interesting in passing to note that in 1911 Benchley was on the Executive Committee of the Dramatic Club, when Macgowan was President, and R. E. Jones was an honorary member. In Boston, H. T. Parker, noted musical and dramatic critic, of the "Transcript," came from Harvard.

Among the actors, Walter Hampden is most important. The tradition that demanded that actors and actresses first appear as Cio-Cio-San's present from Pinkerton or a truly little Eva is passing. Yearly more and more college graduates are turning to the theatre. Among New York producers, Winthrop Ames—who once directed a Pudding show—is prominent. Theresa Helburn and Maurice Wertheim, who have been courageous in their management of the Theatre Guild, have studied in Cambridge, as did Agnes Morgan of the Neighborhood Playhouse.

So much for those who have gone in the past. The record is not one of which one should be ashamed, branching out as it does into all the departments of the theatre, and including an electrical artist and specialist such as Munroe Pevear. And there are still signs of dramatic activity in Cambridge. Here is the 47 Workshop with its six annual productions. Here is the Dramatic Club producing notable foreign plays for the first time in this country, and the Cercle Français, performing distinguished French pieces. Here, also, is the Circulo Español. In the lighter field of musical comedy there is the Hasty Pudding and the Pi Eta. The last two have theatres, small and private, but for the housing of the production of the first three organizations, cramped Agassiz, beamed Brattle Hall, or echoing Jordan Hall serve as temporary shelters.

Perhaps, after all is said, the critic who was preplexed by the announcement of a Harvard Prize Play, who wondered why Harvard in connection with the theatre, and why a prize play, was tired and over-worked. Perhaps, in his daily rush he had not the chance to trace college alliances in men of the theatre. To give a list of Harvard and Radcliffe graduates, prominent in the theatre, is not to claim that Harvard or Radcliffe endowed them with their talents. It is to explain the length and importance of that list, in the light of the laboratory work done at colleges, where a chance for dramatic expression, experimentation, and practice has been given. It is to realize the importance of a college's admission of the theatre and the drama as legitimate parts of an education. And even a weary dramatic critic, who has to write wisely of what he sees in the course of a season's play-going, might find such a background helpful and significant.

MARCH, 1923

Oliver LaFarge, '24

1901–

Oliver LaFarge, archeologist as well as writer, was President of the ADVOCATE *in 1924. His* Laughing Boy *won the Pulitzer Prize in 1929. A member of the American Association on Indian Affairs, LaFarge was a lieutenant colonel in the Air Corps in World War II.*

CAPTAIN TOM AND MOTHER CAREY'S CHICKENS

IF NEITHER YOU NOR YET ANY OF YOUR ANCESTORS have ever dug for clams, if there is in you no blood of men who have piloted fishing-sloop or schooner or dancing brig on a murky night into some New England harbour, with the taste and smell of the bottom on your lead for a guide, nay more, if you have never sailed in Rhode Island harbours and your ear is not attuned to Rhode Island speech, this story is not for you. If you are not one of the elect, you will read it and smile, because you will not know how to believe it. Then hastily forget, or else eschew the sea, for sure as the passage of the black duck over Wesquague Pond in April, the stormy petrel will haunt you for your unbelief.

This tale should be told only in one place, and under special circumstances; so if I, cheating, tell it to you, you must promise faithfully to remember all the time that you are sitting in the forecastle of an old, full-breasted two-master, anchored just off Austin's Hollow in the Western passage of Narragansett Bay. You are in here finding a partial haven from a smoky sou'easter. This is the easiest place to drop anchor on your way down to the Eastward, and the only shelter this side Sakonnet Harbour that does not take you way off your course.

The wind howls in the rigging, and great, low-flying clouds scud overhead. The moon peeps through for wan moments, lighting up the sheltering ridge of bleak Conanicut Island, showing for a second your main-topmast wagging crazily at the clouds, and gleaming faintly on the froth of jumbled waters between you and the shore.

The ground for the story has been prepared by the mate—come foreward to avoid the wrath of the skipper, involved in intricate mathematical calculations concerning the wages of another hand, the cost of a fore top-mast and the profit of speed gained thereby. The mate, sitting in the forecastle doorway, has just ended.

"And so he jumped right off the cliff, and the last Block Island seen of him he was sailing off to sea in the burning ship, with one of the fiery horses on each side of him, and he was never seen by mortal men again."

The forecastle lamp swings in great circles from the ceiling, casting irregular, jumping splashes of light and shadow on the bunks and ceiling. Now it brings out clearly the dark, keen face of the Portugee cook, now hides him in the shadow till all you see are the glints of light on his earrings and the flash of his white teeth.

There is a general scraping of boots and shifting of warm, lazy bodies as the story ends. The hand, from East Greenwich, reputed talkative, true to his form, remarks,

"Wa-all, wa-all, wa-all."

The rest say nothing.

There is a moment's pause, and in the comfortable, warm,

damp atmosphere you can feel heavy thoughts and opinions being brought into order. Then the Oldest Sailorman coughs, and all are still. Slowly and solemnly the Oldest Sailorman extracts from the cavernous recesses of his pockets a black, shapeless hunk and a broken, ancient jackknife. With razor-keen stump of blade he hews himself a morsel of "dark B.L." and stows it neatly under his brown moustache.

The two hands, knowing that the great tale is coming, crumble sticky strips of "Driver's Cut Plug" into their battered pipes. The mate does even as the Oldest Sailorman, save that his plug is a light brown—"light B.L." The Portugee shoves forward the tin full of his gingerbread, so that its odor may take pleasant place with the other forecastle smells, rich tobacco, salt water, tar, and humanity. You hastily suppress your desire for a cigarette, and fill your pipe from your pouch, conscious of a polite interest in your actions, and polite contempt of the chopped hay you call tobacco.

Then, in the comfort and friendship of the cabin, the low voice of the Oldest Sailorman, with its genial accent of the born clam digger, takes up the tale, while the faintly heard storm outside seems to keep up a running commentary thereon. I cannot reproduce his speech nor give word for word his story, but as nearly as I can remember it, I pass it on to you.

The credit for the whole thing lies between the Alonzo Gorgee that then was, and the Mother Carey's chickens. Ever since anyone can remember there's been an Alonzo here, just like the fellow that come out past us in that cat-boat this evening, setting traps. They ain't never changed, they all walk bow-legged and shuffling, they all talk like they had potatoes in their mouths, and all have shapeless, fuzzy moustaches. And this one, like the rest, spent his time on shore drinking, and on the water doing things no other man could have done. He was town drunkard—used even to get drunk with the Indians

—and could catch fish when all others came home empty handed, and foretell the weather when all others were wrong.

In those days everybody had a hand in running the rum. They ran it in where the old breakwater is below South Ferry, and hid it up by the Johnson house back of the marsh. But that wasn't a proper harbour, the land being too low to break the wind from the westward, and it was right open to winds from the South and east. There wasn't any Bonnet Cliff there then, and where we be was a big, rocky, treacherous headland sticking out.

But the real trouble was Alonzo's mortal enemy, Captain Tom Pearse. He was the worst man ever was in Rhode Island. He had a smart little brig that was supposed to be a revenue cutter, and a crew of rapscallions that were supposed to be the King's men. And he used to catch us running in and take our rum, and narry a drop the King saw. Nothing riled old Gorgee so much as having his rum taken excepting when Captain Tom took his fish.

And that wasn't the worst of it, neither. You see Wesquague Beach as you come in this evening, how it lies all open to the ocean, and how in this southerly blow the great waves go a-roaring in, hell bent for leather. No holding ground, just a long, smooth bottom of sand for the waves to pile up on, and not being any Bonnet Cliff, just low land to Northwest of it, it was as bad in a northeaster, and a westerly storm coming down over the open marsh and dunes would carry the misguided vessel that anchored in that slipping sand right out again to break to bits on Joneses Ledge. Well, Captain Tom built him a house in back of Wesquague south of the marsh, and raised him a light on the dunes, and let the weather do the rest.

A fine barquentine called the Lizzie Smith out of Charleston went ashore there one night, and when we found her in the morning—Captain Tom was the only soul who lived in sight of the beach—she'd been stripped right down to the copper rivets.

No one darst cross him, because he was so strong. He used to could take a mainmast in his hand the way you'd take a marling spike and drop it into its hole and step it just as easy! No, no one darst cross him.

Then one foggy day when no one else would have put out, Alonzo was down in his sloop fishing off the Old Man. And the first thing he sees floating on the water is one of Mother Carey's chickens that's been shot. And he broke right down and cried. Then he whistled, and a couple more chickens came and perched on his gunwale.

"How come," says Alonzo, "How come George's been killed?"

"Captain Tom Pearse did it," says one of the birds. "And we're a-going to get him. There'll be no wind and no lifting of the fog 'til he's starved to death off Brenton Reef." There wasn't any lightship there in those days.

"That ain't right nor hardly fair," says Alonzo. "What about us, that you like?"

The birds scratched their heads and allowed that that was right.

"Now you listen to me," says Alonzo, "you get a-hold of Peter"—Peter's the big wave that lives just under Whale Rock —"and all the birds, and you figure out how to block up Wesquague beach so's to make us a harbour that his big boat can't follow us into and other boats can't get wrecked in, and he'll lose all his business and go away. Then ye can becalm him somewhere else."

Before the fog lifted there was a great confabulation of birds, with Peter as moderator and Alonzo listening and suggesting. There were chickens, clever and sharp, and great gulls, wiser and more dependable but not so quick, and terns, and coots making no sense at all, all talking at once. Finally they decided to put it up to Mother Carey herself, and the oldest of her chickens went flying northward to tell her all about it.

As for Alonzo, he put back into Willettville with a hold full of Bluefish when no one else was getting anything but tautog.

When Mother Carey heard about it she went on knitting for a while—she was busy turning out some extra fine Northern lights on account of a man she liked being up in Baffin Bay—and then she sent her fastest gull down to the Great Grandfather of all the waves who lies under the Sargasso sea, ready to go north or south as the case may be. He comes up in the very biggest storms, roaring and raging mountains-high all across the Atlantic, with littler waves big enough to sink an ordinary vessel swirling in the wake of his great, smooth green back. The fringes of his right flank beat all along the French coast and go swashing up the Channel, and the fringes of his left flank throw the ships around off Hatteras like a man tossing salted cod. All the way up to the great ice-fields he sweeps, then comes a-roaring and a-crashing down on them, and there's your next season's crop of icebergs all ready made. After which he'll slip under the floes and lie there, talking to Mother Carey as man to man, until it's time for him to go south again.

But this time, being it's all calm, he just slithered north as quiet as he knew, and a strange sight he must have been towering over quiet seas.

When he got to the ice he slid up on top, and set there scratching his white head with one big, green flipper, forty fathom wide, and says,

"Well, Mother, here I be."

And the tide sunk a foot all round the world.

Mother Carey explained everything to him, and they sat and planned and talked for it might be two days. Then he slipped back into the ocean, the tide everywhere rose a foot, and a lot of people all over the world got their feet wet.

That night off Rhode Island there was a tempest out of the southeast that would make this gale look a flat calm. The clouds came a-scudding by overhead so low you could almost hear them a-swishing, and the great breakers went a-roaring and a-shouting into Wesquague Beach and a-rushing up on the dunes, with their long, green fingers curling around the bones of the Lizzie Smith as if they wanted to feel their work and be sure it was thorough.

Then Alonzo puts out in his little boat, and there off Whale Rock he meets Peter and the Great Grandfather of all the waves, and the chickens and the gulls. When the big waves get inside the bay the water rises about a fathom, and Mrs. Yardley's cellar is flooded and her cat drowned. Barring that, there was no harm done save to Old Daddy Briggses dory. Old Daddy Briggs was too mean to get him a proper anchor-line, and he had her moored so short that at high tide there wasn't no scope at all. When the extra fathom hit her, her bow went right straight under, and all you could see was her stem sticking out, with the rudder kind of thumbing itself at Daddy jumping up and down on Willettville dock when he found her in the early morning.

Meantime Alonzo and the waves and the gulls were a-working like all get out. They took rocks from over by Beaver-Tail and down by Narragansett Pier up by Narragansett and piled them up in a great line from the tip of the Wesquague crescent to northward—where the Bonnet is now—clear across to Joneses Ledge. The Mummies are the remnants of them. Then they got more rocks and built them out from Watson's Pier to the southward, until they had as nice a breakwater and harbour for small craft as ever you can see to Sakonnet or down to Point Judith Point. Inside it was all sweet and calm, too shallow for a revenue cutter to follow, with the sand beach to land on and the marsh behind to drop things in if you were in a hurry.

By that time it was late in the morning, so Peter and the big wave quit, letting Narragansett Bay get back to normal again. The storm moderated so that fishermen could go out. Then the chickens told Alonzo that the rocks weren't sot yet, and so for one more night they must be watched. He's to come down the next night and anchor off of them and then all would be fine.

But Captain Tom was no fool, and as soon as ever he saw what had been done, he fell a-thinking. Not so much for any good reason as just because it seemed a good idea, off he went and put a hole as big as your fist in Alonzo's sloop. Put a sail-maker's palm on his hand, he did, and then punched a marling-spike in and out like he was putting stitches in a worn out studding-sail.

Alonzo didn't figure out how it happened; he just cussed a lot, got him another jug of rum, and went that night to keep his watch on land. And on land Alonzo was just a drink-sodden old coot, which Captain Tom well knew.

By the time it was dark the storm had risen again to the last night's violence. You could see the breakers rearing up on the breakwater, and hear them thundering curses at being kept out. By the middle of the dog watch Alonzo was fast asleep, dead drunk, and Captain Tom had carried him a mile inland, out of the way.

Then Captain Tom walked out to the rocks over Joneses Ledge, and began heaving them away. He worked 'til he was down to the reef itself, and there he planted his feet and got set for the real labour. No one saw him, but you know what it must have been like. This great man, tall as his own cross-jack yard and broad as the two flukes of the Bower anchor on a ship, with great legs wide apart straddling the rock, the water now hissing out in white foam round the ankles of his cowhide boots, now thundering past his shoulder in a black wall, and he reaching out to right, and left, picking up rocks as big as whaleboats and throwing them through the smother of spume onto either shore. The moon didn't get a chance to look out at all that night, all the sign there was of a moon's being there at all was the succession of pale-grey lines along the fringes of the clouds as they passed under.

When Alonzo had waked up in the morning and got back to Wesquague, there were the high Bonnet Cliffs to Northward, and the nasty rocks of Watson's pier—that the *Lulu Epps* was wrecked on last March—just as Captain Tom had built them. The waves were running clear into the beach again, slapping the dunes on the back sort of, as if to say,

"Wall, wall, here we be back again. And haow's Lizzie Smith this morning?"

Alonzo sat right down on the top of the Bonnet with his legs stuck out in front of him and his fist in his eye, and began to bawl and blubber like a kid. Bye and bye the petrel came round and they give it to him good and proper. When after awhile he felt better and had got around to cutting himself a plug of tobacco, the oldest gull said to him,

"Wall, Alonzo, looks like you'd got the lines pretty wall snarled up this time. Ain't no use crying 'bout it, the big wave's gone back, and Mother Carey won't take all that trouble over ye again. But we're with ye, Alonzo, and we'll see what we can do. Next time Captain Tom's down to Block Island or perty well out to sea you just stick a knife in your mast and whistle up a westerly wind, then maybe we can do something."

So four or five days passed with Alonzo keeping by himself and not even drinking more than enough to wash down his johnnie-cakes. Come one day, however, Captain Tom's gone out beyond Block Island trying to get some swordfish. When the birds tell this to Alonzo where he's anchored off Beaver-

Tail he takes his old knife and runs it into the mast. Then he whistles and whistles until he has as nasty a wind blowing out of the northwest as you could meet from here to the Bay of Fundy.

Captain Tom hadn't seen hide nor hair of swordfish nor any other fish since he killed the petrel, and every day he come home with empty hold he got madder and madder. So coming back from Block Island he was pretty well set for trouble.

Every wave that broke on the brig sent a splash of spray on his lips. The salt clung to him, and the wind blew wisps of froth into his mouth when he opened it to bellow a command. He got thirstier and thirstier, and so did all the crew. So he had up some of the rum he took off of Alonzo the last time. But the more they drank the more the spray flew at them, and the more they wanted to drink.

By the time they got into Narragansett Bay it was dark, black dark, so's you couldn't see your hand before your face. The boat was leaping and shaking with the big seas, every rope aboard her was singing and screaming with the wind that rolled her down, and skipper and crew were boiling, howling drunk.

Captain Tom sees his false light over Wesquague, and he grins wickedly. Then he looks over to the pile of rocks on Conanicut, and on them he sees two lights, a-waving and a-dancing like anchor-lights on ships in the lee of the wind but not in still water. He starts cursing something awful, and crying out that someone's trying to spoil his trade, and by God he'll teach them.

"By God," he sings out, "if I can tear down one pile of rocks I can sail over another. And I'll take my vessel through that there point if it's the last damned thing I do on earth!"

Then he swings her head round and comes a-boiling down at those lights. No one sees it save Alonzo, and he tells afterward how she tore along, the wind a-whooping and a-screeching in the rigging and the crew a-yelling and a-cursing below. A leak of moonlight through the clouds, or maybe it was some kind of hell-fire, picks out every rope and spar of her in dim, wavy light, standing out against the purple-black sky; the white water under her foot and her whirling wake is all a-gleam, and greenish white fire is pouring out of the binnacle lamp onto Captain Tom's face where he stands at the wheel. She strikes the shore and never trembles, but goes on pitching through the rocks, crashing and grinding, and the land sinking beneath the seas that shoulder along under her dolphin-striker. Suddenly, as she comes to the middle of the island, she's gone, and the wind drops, and the moon comes out lighting up Austin's Hollow, ready-made refuge in a southerly blow.

And that's why if ye'd looked out the star-board port-hole at I did a minute or two ago, ye'd have seen a shining brig with a northwesterly gale of her own behind, and black clouds wreathing her top gallant-masts, go gliding past us, and running in over the shoal water 'til she disappeared just at the land's edge.

OCTOBER, 1922

Corliss Lamont, '24

1902-

Corliss Lamont has taught at Columbia, The New School for Social Research, Cornell, and Harvard. The author of many works of non-fiction, Lamont's latest book is Humanism as a Philosophy *(1949).*

IDEAS FOR IRRECONCILABLES

The formation this spring of a college division of the League of Nations Non-Partisan Association has been one of the most hopeful occurrences of the year in college circles. The Division was spontaneously started by college undergraduates who themselves originated the idea and later brought it before the Association's executives for ratification. The very fact that this Division has been organized should be encouraging to all thinking persons, because it shows that college students are beginning to stir from their apathy towards American politics, and towards foreign affairs, which are now inseparably linked up with our country's life. Even the most vehement irreconcilable must admit that an organization which tends to break down student indifference towards politics has some value. And, though the arousing of undergraduate opinion along general political lines is not the College Division's chief purpose, it is a most important consideration.

For pro-Leaguers the formation of the Division is reassuring, because it proves that there is a strong sentiment towards the United States entering the League among the most intelligent and enlightened group of young people in the country.

The aims of the College Division can best be explained by first outlining the principles and purposes of the Non-Partisan Association itself. In simple terms, the Association is a group of men and women of different party affiliations who are seeking to cultivate "such a public opinion as will induce the present administration, or if not this, the next one, to enter the League of Nations" either with or without reservations. The Association has already organized committees in every state, plans to do the same in every congressional district in the Union, and purposes to secure the insertion in both the Republican and Democratic party platforms in 1924, of a plank favoring entrance of the United States into the League. It is also an object of the Association to secure approval by the members of the Senate of President Harding's World Court recommendation.

Most emphatically the Association does not accept the statement that the Republican majority in 1920 meant repudiation of the League by the voters of the country. As Samuel Colcord, a Republican, points out in "The Great Deception," the League was, by a natural confusion of ideas associated in the minds of a great mass of voters with other parts of the Treaty of Versailles, which were particularly offensive to the foreign element. This confusion sent many votes to the Republican ranks. To my mind, "anti-Wilsonism" and the natural reaction following the war played almost as important parts in the election as any other one thing. Then, also, it must be taken into consideration that millions voted for Mr. Harding, following the advice of Taft, Hughes, Hoover, Root, and the rest of the "31," who predicted that with the Republicans in power the United States would enter the League. In this group were included that large body of voters who went Republican, not because of hostility towards joining the League at all, but on account of opposition to going in without adequate safeguards. Finally there were those reservationists, who, though realizing in spite of the "31" that a Republican administration would shelve the League, voted for Mr. Harding rather than to give their approval to the nation's entering without suitable reservations. With these facts in mind it is difficult to see how any fair-minded observer can say: "The League is a dead issue; it was settled in 1920." Suppose there had been a clear-cut issue between the irreconcilables and the reservationists aided by the non-reservationists. Suppose that the issue had been entering the League with the Lodge reservations or not at all. Would the people have rebuked the Senator from Massachusetts? Certainly not; for there is every reason to believe that a majority of the voters in 1920, all other issues disregarded, would have declared themselves in favor of this country's entering the League *with reservations.*

At the present time it seems plausible to go on the assumption that everyone who is not an irreconcilable is for this League either with or without reservations, and that very few who desire reservations wish to go beyond the Lodge proposals of 1919. The Association aims to unite all those who are not irreconcilables and all who can be won over from the irreconcilables. When such a combination has been effected, it will, I believe, be plain to the administration in power that the irreconcilable element is in the minority. There can be little doubt, however, that the country as a whole is against the United States joining the League *without reservations;* and that no administration within the next decade can bring about our entrance without reservations, unless there is an almost unbelievable reversal of popular feeling.

The part the 618 colleges and professional schools of the country can play in the carrying out of the purposes outlined above is a great one. If the colleges line up solidly in favor of the United States entering the League, the effects will be far-reaching. The very fact that the colleges are behind the movement will, of course, carry weight throughout the country just as the united appeal of labor or any other group of public opinion would be influential. This will be a direct effect. The indirect effects will perhaps be more important. In 1924, practically all students now in college above the present Freshman Class will be old enough to vote; by 1928 four more college classes will have become eligible. Knowledge of this will cause party headquarters to look up sharply, not only because of the votes these students will cast, but on account of the influence they will exert on other voters in their communities and various fields of activity.

Although the Division is essentially an undergraduate affair, no opportunity will be lost in enlisting the support of the members of the faculty and the graduate schools. In fact, in the branch recently established at Harvard the graduate schools are represented by two members on the Executive Council, while three faculty members are serving in an advisory capacity. The further technical details of the scheme I do not intend to discuss here, inasmuch as they have already been announced elsewhere.

I have not the space in this article to go deeply into the arguments for and against the United States entering the League. Nor is that the purpose of this essay. Rather than trying to prove conclusively any specific points, let me make a few self-evident observations.

The great tragedy of 1919 and 1920 was that the League question became the plaything of party politics. It never had a fair showing in the United States, misinterpreted and misrepresented by the politicians as it was. But this is 1923; and my plea is for all citizens of all parties to join now in repairing the mistakes of the past, whether Lodge or Wilson or both were in the wrong. Let the President, who as a Senator voted for the League with reservations in 1919, and the Republicans and Democrats of the Senate, a great many of whom did the same, reconsider, and if they want reservations, make them —but go in! That the League will accept reservations from this country there can be little question. For instance, let us study what Lord Robert Cecil said recently in regard to Article X: "Article X is an ill-drawn article and I never cared much for it. In practice it is doubtful if it could ever be brought into operation. Doubtless when the United States decides to enter the League, it will ask, reasonably and properly, that the article should either be struck out or redrafted, so as to make its real purpose unmistakable, and I do not imagine that there will be any serious opposition to that being done." But even with the Article X bogy eliminated and the "six votes to one" bogy answered in full by the President in his World Court defense, the irreconcilables can read into the League covenant numerous other objections which I am unable to include here.

Supporters of the League in this country have often been called impractical idealists. Let me simply call attention here to the present plight of the farmers in the Middle West. Why are they suffering so? The hard-headed business men of the country, to whom reasoning in facts is more familiar than to most of us, say that the primary cause is the lack of foreign markets. I can illustrate my point no better than by quoting from Mr. Bernard M. Baruch's address on "Agricultural Finance." He says in conclusion: "I affirm that there is nothing in the world that affects your credit so much as the shrinking of foreign markets for your products. There is nothing to which you can give your attention that is of greater moment to you in a practical way than the creation of the international relations that are a precedent to a re-establishment of those markets. I do not speak of our moral responsibility in the matter, nor of the great opportunity that America has to lead a stricken world into a finer and better order of things—an opportunity toward which the noble thoughts of all men urge them, though I do think this consideration the most compelling of all. . . . Rather, I dwell merely upon what enlightened selfishness or even just plain greedy selfishness demands—the necessity of keeping open and enlarging an ever-increasing market for the products of your hands and minds."

Of course there are those who wish to see the United States enter the League, not merely because such a step will aid our country materially, but also because it will help Europe and the world in general, because it will further the interests of world peace, because it will make this country greater in the eyes of its own and other peoples. Such sentiments may indeed be termed idealism, but combined as they are with common sense and practicability they express a kind of idealism of which we should be most proud. Impracticable idealism I decry; and it is just that sort of idealism, which I believe the bitter-enders uphold. They demand a perfect League, a perfect Treaty, and they will never obtain either. Of course the League has its grave faults, but what human document of its kind has not? I call it impracticable idealism of the plainest sort to oppose the United States' joining the League or the World Court, because these organizations are imperfect. Yet that is a fundamental part of the irreconcilables' doctrine. (Their other cry, for out-of-date "isolationism" based on an utter disregard of fact, is not worthy to be discussed.) And yet they have the effrontery—they who have grown morbidly sentimental over sentimentalism—to call their opponents political sentimentalists or impractical idealists.

It does not seem probable that these pages will be read by those whom I wish the most to reach. They are sitting back in contentment timorously meditating—if they meditate at all—on worn-out commonplaces,—certainly least of all things on politics. This is not Harvard indifference. It is the same throughout all the colleges of the country. Most of the students will live prosperous lives as bankers, lawyers, doctors, or what not. A courageous few will enter politics to struggle in an uphill battle against the sort of loose, timid, or wilfully perverted thinking that we see now on every hand in our government. I repeat the well-known statement that more college men must enter politics and that those who do not go in must, from the outside, take a keener interest. This must be if the United States is to attain the greatness of which it is capable. That is for the future. Even for the present every college student has a direct opportunity to use his influence in politics, to help make this America a greater nation at home and abroad—the opportunity of fighting, preferably but not necessarily as a member of the Non-Partisan Association, for the entrance of the United States into the League of Nations.

JUNE, 1923

Dudley Fitts, '25

1903–

Dudley Fitts, poet and translator, now teaches at Phillips Andover. Author of Poems 1929–1936, *he is best known for his translations from the Greek and the Spanish.*

TWO TRANSLATIONS IN SONNET FORM

I

Triste si veniens patruelis dicret umbra
Eja lugete, omnes! abscissit Maria crines . . .

NOVUM MARIALE. (11.921,930)

If from Elysion the inebriate ghost
Of my great-great granduncle Phineas
Had come to me and said "Ah, woe is us!
The Earth is flat, composed of buttered toast
And balanced in the heav'ns amid an host
Of pies and hot cross buns stelliferous—"
I'd have been shocked, no doubt; but even thus
I'd have observed "Well, fancy that!" at most.

But had he said to me, a week ago,
"Mary's just gone and bobbed her hair, you know,"
Then I'd have cried "Phantom, you utter lies!

Consociation with postmortem bliss
Has addled your perceptive sense: to Dis
  Return, and treat your astigmatic eyes."

II

I diss'n: "Lo palvro catto della vuostra quéra xia
Hat relitto chesta vista." et jò diss', "In pace sía!"
—CARMEN DÈ MARIÂ CALVULÂ

They said to me: "Your Aunt Priscilla's cat
  Is dead"; and I responded "*Requiem!*"
  They said: "By evil chance your Uncle Lem
Has caught the mumps." I sighed and said "That's that!"
They said: "Whilst dining in the Automat
  A misplaced bean cut off your Cousin Em."
  I dropped a silent tear and answered them:
"As God wills, be it done; Amen; *fiat!*"

They said: "Your house has burned down to the ground;
Your bank account has been attached"; no sound
  Of dole greeted this news with dolor rife.
They said: "Mary has bobbed her hair"; the cord
Of my endurance snapped; I cried "O Lord,
  It is enough—now take away my life."

MARCH, 1925

John Finley, '25

1904–

John Finley, now Eliot Professor of Greek at Harvard and master of Eliot House, was president of the ADVOCATE *while an undergraduate. Finley published* Thalia, *a long poem, in 1929. His* Thucydides *appeared in 1942, and he was one of the collaborators in Harvard's famous* General Education in a Free Society.

ELMER O. WILLIAMS, MANUFACTURER, PHILANTHROPIST, AND MAN

"*–And let the world say here was a man–*"

JULIUS CAESAR, II, 2.

"I WILL GIVE THE BEST THAT IS IN ME TO THE MUStard Plaster factory," said Elmer O. Williams when, after ten years of faithful and intelligent service in the factory, he was elected president. These words were but the reflection of his mood of the time, but to us coming later and examining into the fountain springs of his great nature, the words have a fuller significance. Indeed they give the key-note of the man. A constant willingness to pour out all his energies, to exert himself in ceaseless effort for any cause that he made his own are at once the foundation and the explanation of his great success. "Anything that is worth doing is worth doing well"

—that excellent proverb—Mr. Williams early made his rule of conduct, and when asked in the eighty-third and final year of his remarkably rich life whether he had ever been untrue to it, the great man replied with a note of his young vigour, "No, I never have." All men wondered at his constancy, his ability to see and pursue the right path, his thoroughness. He was wholehearted far beyond his associates and competitors, who in turn were forever despairing in their futile attempts to rival him whether in their own efficiency or that obtained from employees; for, as all knew, example is a great spur to endeavor. With his double facility, then, of accomplishing labor behind it there is little wonder that from its simple beginning the Mustard Plaster factory grew to that tremendous plant and system which all now link with the name Williams.

His boyhood spent in a small Ohio village named Fairview was one well fitted to lay the foundation stones of his future career. His parents were poor, and many were the duties about the house and yard which the little fellow had to perform. In addition to his other tasks, it fell to his lot as the youngest of the eleven children to secure and bring home his father's daily pail of beer. Speaking of this act in later years he often said, "I consider that the lessons I learned in punctuality by my father's affectionate, if rough, punishments for any tardiness have served me all my life." And this statement is equally true and equally applicable in respect to his other duties. Little Elmer early found that a task well done was its own reward. Many a time when he was sawing and piling wood or hoeing potatoes, he would pause in his work and return to correct some flaw in its execution. In fact, before he had come to his eighth year, the standard of his work became well known about the countryside. "As faithful as Williams' boy," is a quaint saying still found on the lips of the older inhabitants of Fairview. And since it is well known that the other ten children of the family were all girls, there can be no doubt that the reference is to

Elmer. We must not forget, however, in this brief sketch of his childhood the greatest factor or influence in it—his mother. A big, raw-boned woman of Irish extraction, she stood as ruler of that poor but singularly happy household. It was at her knee that Elmer learned his first lessons in the Bible and geography. And a glad picture it is to think of the child learning thus naturally the first lessons of life from one that was so suited to impart them. When asked many years later to what he attributed his success, the little fellow then grown into a great man said, very beautifully it was thought, "To my mother—God bless her."

It was at the age of fourteen that Elmer left Fairview to seek his fortune in the world. We can imagine the lad, fine and strong, starting out one spring to walk to the neighboring metropolis of Cleveland; for we must remember that he had not even the advantage of a railroad to bring him to his destination. And little did his good parents and his bevy of fluttering sisters suspect that when he was to return in twenty years the brass band would meet him at the depot and the town hall would be appropriately festooned with red, white, and blue, so inscrutable are the ways of Providence. Oddly enough, on reaching the city, he first paused beside the Mustard Plaster factory, then consisting of little more than a rambling two-storied building, located on the outskirts of the growing town. There it was, as he stopped to rest, that he experienced what he always spoke of later in awe. It seemed to him, that a voice spoke in his ear, saying to him, "My boy, some day you will own that factory." His senses quickened, and he looked up at the gaudy name painted across the front of the structure in appropriate mustard color. "By George, I shall," he said to himself, clenching his fist. "And you see I have," the great man was in the habit of concluding with a flash of that rare smile so well known in all countries, delineated as it was on the cover of each individual mustard plaster.

That day, then, when he heard the prophesying voice, young Williams applied for and received a position at the factory. At first, he worked with the common laborers, sorting over the tiny seeds shipped from so far and boiling them and spreading the paste formed on thin pieces of cloth. At that time he was a boy with the others, though he later said that even then he did not forget his first ambitions. Indeed it was told of him that he was one of the gayest hands at work, enlivening his fellow toilers by many merry jokes and quips. One of the happiest of these was later told by one of his old associates at the time of the presentation by the Elks of a gold medal having on one side a likeness of Mr. Williams and on the reverse a picture of Mercy giving a mustard plaster to a suffering world. The story went roughly like this. It appears that Elmer and his companions were engaged in spreading the paste on the cloths, in the process mentioned above. Now all were dispirited except Elmer, who, thinking to enliven the others by some fun, said, "By George, fellows, this is just like making peanut butter sandwiches." All rated this very amusing, though none went so far as to venture to taste one of these "sandwiches." It was not long, however, before he came under the eye of the officers of the company by reason of his application.

They noticed that he was studying methods of improvement at odd times and that he was so honest that, though he constantly brought ham sandwiches for his noon meal, he never took a single mustard seed to make his food more palatable. Young Elmer knew no compromise with evil. As a result of both of these qualifications and others that I have previously hinted at, he rapidly drew ahead of his fellows, occupying at first the position of overseer and later those of cashier, pay-master, treasurer, vice-president, and finally at the unripe age of twenty-four that of president. This rise so unprecedented in its rapidity was the cause of the nickname by which he was later known—the Meteor of the Middle West.

He was now president of a moderately profitable, though little known company, having by his own hands forged his way. Many a young fellow's ambitions and efforts would have stopped at that point, but not Elmer's. His whole future career was one of improving, building-up, and enlarging the factory. It did not content him to be the head of the largest Mustard Plaster factory in Cleveland (there was no other); his ambitions embraced higher thoughts. He wished to make his plant the largest in the world, receiving a warrant of success in this stupendous undertaking in very much the same fashion that he earlier did as he rested beside the old factory after his walk from Fairview. Nothing stood in his way in his impassioned efforts at building up the system to the position it now occupies. He recognized no obstacles. It was told of him that in the ten full years following his appointment as president he never left his office until after darkness had fallen and never took a holiday except on Christmas and the day of the Mason's annual parade. His first task was to systematize the office work and the book keeping, which he accomplished with great celerity and such a degree of permanence that even today in this efficient age the marks of his handiwork are discernible. Next he increased the plant until it outgrew the old building. He borrowed money to build a new factory of brick, this time entirely painted in the appropriate mustard color, and it was not more than six months after its completion that he was able to repay what was not his own, so great was the success that resulted from his feverish industry. Indeed, as he later observed with a touch of his quaint and compelling humor, it seemed then as if the whole world was wearing one of his plasters. The fame of Elmer O. Williams began to spread to far quarters. He had agents in all the large cities including New York, Pittsburg, Chicago, and even after some years in Paris and London. It was at this period that one first came to hear on the lips of so many people the name of Williams, The Mustard Plaster King.

We have followed this tremendous spirit in its upward battle to a position of fame and wealth, and now, leaving him the undisputed monarch of his trade, let us examine into his family life. He married at the age of twenty-eight the daughter of the former president and then Chairman of the Board of the company, feeling at the time, as he always continued to feel, that it was well to have every member of his family attached by no insecure bonds of sentiment and tradition to the old factory. She was a singularly attractive girl, large and ample in proportions, with a sweet smile and golden hair that glinted in the sun. "She reminds me of my mother," Williams used to say as he gazed musingly at his wife; or again, "They're an awful lot alike, those two." The marriage was blessed with six children, all boys, merry little rascals together in their youth and later firm, responsible citizens, a pride to their parents and their community. The eldest, now known as young Elmer (to distinguish him from his lamented father), is the present head of the Mustard Plaster concern. They were always a joy to their father, and many a time he would come home early from the office merely to join with them in their game. Never was there a more intimately companionable husband and father than he. Speaking of him after his untimely death in his eighty-third year, Mrs. Williams, who outlived him a small time, said with infinite sadness in her stricken face, "Elmer was always a good husband to me." And to this dutiful observation the children nodded sad assent.

Only space forbids the recounting of more traits of this loveable nature. He was a patron of art and progress, and to the end most active in all charitable endeavor. It was a beautiful sight to see this old gentleman with his long, white beard and habitual Prince Albert coat and tall hat dispensing food and money to those who in life had not been so fortunate as he. He was dearly loved by the poor of the city. "Father Elmer" they called him with almost reverent affection.

His funeral of May 18, 1911, was impressive and solemn, giving fitting tribute to that great nature. Many notables were present, among them one who was Mr. Williams' constant admirer and for whom a great destiny was in store, Warren G. Harding. The service was simple. The minister of the old church merely said a prayer and recited the old gentleman's favorite hymn, "Onward Christian Soldiers."

Surely Elmer O. Williams was a "Christian soldier."

MAY, 1923

Walter Edmonds, '26

1903–

Walter Edmonds was President of the ADVOCATE *following John Finley. Two of his best known novels are* Rome Haul *and* Drums Along the Mohawk.

BLACK MARIA

"HUH," SAID THE SKIPPER; AND HE PUT HIS TELEscope under his arm and asked me up to dinner.

The cottage was down the headland a way, stuck against the hillside, and through its windows shone the warm, cheerful gleam of a fire on the hearth. We walked up the narrow path, past the ancient dory, painted brightly green, with its vivid cargo of nasturtiums, and stepped on to the absurdly small porch with its pair of antique rockers.

"Belay aft," piped the skipper in invitation, as he held the screen door open for me. With a feeling of curiosity, I entered the snug little sitting room and looked about me. An angular woman, very sharp and bony, rose from a rocking chair, which she had been rocking very hard and which continued to rock for an incredibly long time after she had vacated it, as if in fear that she would return to torture it with her bony extremities the instant she saw it idle. The angular woman advanced directly toward me; she stopped in front of me with her hands firmly planted on her hips and her elbows jutting out port and starboard. I was a little taken aback at this uncompromising attitude; but fortunately the skipper entered at this precise moment and introduced me with his invariable formula, "Mr. E–, Mrs. Plunket: know each other!"

Mrs. Plunket placed her bony palm in mine and remarked mournfully that she was delighted to see me and that she was sure, she was certain, she was absolutely positive, in fact, that we were in for a particularly nasty spell of weather. My spirits thus dampened, she withdrew in bony solemnity to the kitchen.

"A fine figger of a woman, sir, a fine figger of a woman. You're young, I see, and conseq'ently immature, so I tell you, sir, when you come to matrimony, look about for a woman of bone. Yes, sir, they're th' kind that last; a good venture in a rough sea, they are, but mind, keep un 'tween-decks, well forrard, says I. Mrs. Plunket likes to take the wheel an' we have mutinies now an' again an' I have to look sharp since I've put up in drydock here, as it were. But she's a fine figger of a woman, now, ain't she?"

I agreed that she was beautifully bony, and the skipper smiled and winked at me in the most knowing manner in the world, as if to say that he had tried all sorts of bone, and that there wasn't one to compare with his spouse.

We were now as close as the oldest friends; I felt at liberty to examine the roundhouse, as the skipper called the parlor; and I did so fore and aft. The skipper followed hard in my wake, commenting on everything at preposterous length. We came to the sword of a sword-fish.

"Give me by Abe Mellows," explained the skipper, and he rambled into a long-winded narrative, in which he made as much headway as an old East-Indiaman trying to round the cape in the wrong season. The story was never finished. By this time I had come to the third corner, unsuspecting and in the best of humors, when a monstrosity leaped before my startled vision and gave my imagination a shock that caught me full amidships and layed me over on my beams' ends, until the skipper could come up to my aid.

"Lord!" I gasped. "What is it?"

"That," said the skipper, sententiously, "that is Black Mariar."

I had heard of Black Maria—a most remarkable creature, the pride of Pelmosset. Her name was a by-word among the nautical set of the town; the dock-hands swore by her; the retired sailors spoke of her over their games of checkers and cribbage—and, coupled with her name, I invariably heard that of Ebeneezer Plunket. My curiosity had been stirred by the name, but my social status would have been utterly ruined had I displayed my ignorance by asking questions. So I had addressed Plunket himself as he took his daily walk; all of which may be taken as the cause of the skipper's "Huh!", for he was a hospitable soul, and the invitation to dinner.

Thus Black Maria had been revealed to me. We were face to face. What dreams, in my ignorance, had I not had. First I had seen her as some exotic island beauty; then as some wild, buccaneering woman; and so on interminably—and now she, in her true form, was before me (what remained of her), and she gazed at me by means of two shoe-buttons, one that glinted oddly in the firelight, the other too rusty even to wink. The comb on her head was almost gone. Her legs—horrible objects! —had nearly left her; one, to be exact, was merely a mass of dust.

"Can this," I exclaimed, "can this be Black Maria?"

"As ever was," the skipper assured me.

"But I thought she saved your life in mid-ocean; that she made you what you are, the best sailing master on the coast, before you retired."

"Gospel—every word," said the skipper.

"But how in all creation could she, this chicken—this cross-grained *hen*—do that?"

It was too true. The Black Maria of coast-wise fame was a hen, presumably of Spanish Black extraction, and of enormous proportions. Before me were her shrivelled remains, as the skipper had mounted them. His knowledge of taxidermy was profoundly elemental, which, doubtless, accounted for the unmatched shoe-buttons, the forty-three remaining feathers, and the one leg.

"Why it was this-a-way," he said, "an' if you want to hear it, you an' me'll just settle down, an' with all drawin' free alow an' aloft, as nice as you please, we'll look into this-here."

He cut himself a fill of tobacco, ground it between his palms, and stuffed it into his pipe—and having thus cleared his decks for action, he began.

"It was way back," he said, "oh away back, before barommities an' such-like came to be a notion, an' a man tried to read th' weather by th' feel o' his bones, that I first put to sea as a foremast hand—not even as a crude A.B.; but, by th' great horned spoon, an' you can lay to that, in two years I was berthing aft, an' in four I was sailin' my own ship. Aye—an' it was all due to Black Mariar.

"She hust ha' been powerful young when she cut across my quarter, for she was with me nigh on twenty year—but she was a fine bird even then. The way she used to run close-hauled across th' poop, for all th' world like a clipper crowdin' sail afore th' trades, would do your heart good to see. She was th' pride of my heart, she was.

"Well I first put to sea before th' mast, I say, an' a pretty rough time I had of it. Th' cap'n an' mates couldn't see nothin' in me, an' they took pains to let me know it. But I commenced to learn pretty quick, after they'd started rope's-endin' me some, but I didn't like it at all an' stuck pretty much by myself, which wasn't so hard as th' whole ship-load o' us had a leanin' to drink. How we ever kept afloat's beyond me; it's all very well in port, says I, but at sea, no sir.

"We'd just put into Barbados an' out again, but th' skipper'd had time to get in a new lot o' gin for th' cabin an' to bring some poultry aboard her too. He put th' coops on th' foredeck an' of course we foremast hands'd kill one when th' afterguard was too far drunk to notice an' slip her to Hoe-Lee—he was the first yeller cook I ever saw—to be roasted. Well, it wasn't long before there was on'y one left, a big black one.

"That evenin' we were all pretty far gone. Hoe-Lee'd smuggled a case forrard. Th' officers was beyond hope, an' the rest of us were nigh as bad. I was sleepin' on th' foredeck—dead for all—an' all of a sudden it seemed like all Hell had hit us, an' I was over th' rail, holdin' on to Lord knows what not, an' th' scooner scuddin' away on her beams' ends before the squall. I wasn't much carin' then, but next mornin' I came round an' found I was floatin' in mid-ocean on a hen-coop; but it was a big one, six by eight, an' floated high an' dry. I heard a tarin' fuss at th' other end, an' there was that hen walkin' up an' down on the end an' squallin' like a Dutchman—just like th' old man used to.

"Then I looked closer an' seen she was walkin' back an' forth beside a big, fine egg an' admirin' it. Well, I got th' egg an' ate it an' gave her back th' shell, an' she ate that. So every mornin' for a week, she'd wake me up with her clackin' an' we'd do th' same, me eatin' th' egg, an' she peckin' up th' shell. We both got weaker an' weaker, but Black Mariar—I called her that now, after a dead aunt o' mine (th' 'Mariar' part of it, not th' 'Black')—an' she was game clear through, an' she lasted th' whole time, reg'lar every mornin', till we were picked up. She'd saved my life alright.

"I kept her with me after that—an' she went with me every trip. I was pretty smart an' I rose quick. You see that was before barommities an' such came into use, an' a skipper had to keep his weather eye pretty well open. But Black Mariar was as good as any barommity, an' better, as long as you knew how to read her; and I could, an' that was how I came up in the world, for th' cap'n, till I was master o' my own ship, an' then with me, would know way ahead what th' weather'd be. The people thought I was a prophet, or some such-like—but it was on'y Black Mariar.

"She'd lay an egg every mornin' we was to sea, never on shore, an' reg'lar as time too, right on th' foot o' my bunk, an' then she'd go out an' look at th' weather. If wind or rough water was comin', she's brustle up her feathers an' come in again as quiet as a nigger an' crawl under th' bunk—she used to get terrible sea-sick in a sea—and she'd lie there a-groanin' an' a-moanin' as loud as th' riggin'. But if th' weather was fine, she'd run out an' hop up th' larboard shrouds—always th' larboard, after she fell off th' others once—till she reached th' mizzen cross-trees, an' there she'd set, clackin' to all an' sundry, as pert as you please, till I'd fetch her down for dinner.

"So it all came through Black Mariar," concluded the skipper, looking fondly at the image.

I was about to make some appropriate remark, when Mrs. Plunket thrust a bony elbow through the door and announced dinner. We walked into the kitchen and sat down to a meal worthy even of Mrs. Plunket's bones, though I must say that the table cloth totally eclipsed the food, until my eyes grew slightly accustomed to its glaring red flowers. The skipper's consort offered us the dishes in a manner that reminded me of a chemist about to perform an intricate experiment. I always felt her eyes upon me as if she were tensely waiting a reaction of the utmost importance. As for her bones, they were everywhere. But the skipper beamed on everything with the utmost good-nature and whispered as she went over to the stove, "A fine figger of a woman, ain't she? You must say that, sir."

Mrs. Plunket returned with a plate of boiled eggs. The skipper looked doubtful. "These are fresh, Lizzie?"

"I should hope they would be," retorted his wife, belligerently running out her starboard elbow, and looking as if she hoped that a veritable army of chickens would fly from each egg and utterly confound us.

But the skipper never noticed her; he wore a dazed expression, one of complete bewilderment.

"Scupper my timbers," he said, getting the terms slightly mixed, "Shiver me else! I forgot all about it, an' it's the greatest thing she ever did."

"Who?" I asked.

"Black Mariar, you might guess it," sniffed Mrs. Plunket, her bony nose in the air.

"Tell it to me," I said to the skipper. I began to feel like another Boswell.

The skipper gulped down his coffee, discarded his prim little egg cup, and despite the frowns of the bony one, broke the egg into his cup. "Almost forgot it. Awful, ain't it? But she saved the ship, so she did, an' all hands, too, and they tell me she kept th' two countries out o' war.

"We were sailin' down around th' Gulf, tradin' as we could, when one day we put into an island—there was nothing on it but a few palms an' a spring—an' we were gettin' water an' layin' in to th' bay when into it from each side to once sailed two ships an' anchored on each side of us pretty handily for all that they looked like rotted wash tubs. I saw that they were men o' war of some sort an' that either one could make hash out o' us in no time, for we didn't carry any guns. Well, a boat put off from each one at the same time and put aboard us together. A man climbed up each side all rigged out in braid and finery, with a sword an' a big hat. One wore red and silver; t'other, green and gold. Me an' Black Mariar was standin' on th' quarter-deck.

" 'A hen,' says th' red one, twistin' his moustache.

" 'A hen,' says th' green one, 'A hen—A egg.'

" 'You're right,' says the red, still twistin' his moustache, 'what wouldn't I give for an egg!'

" 'I would blow this ship an' that tub o' yourn plum to Hell for an egg,' says green, clawin' his whisker; he turned to me, 'Signor, I shall come aboard tomorrow at eight for the egg—three minutes, please. Signor Gambuglio Arencia Vertucienza Parelzo De Bundrado, as admiral of my country, I shall take the egg by force of arms, if necessary, as I likewise,' he says to me, 'inform this honorable Signor.'

" 'Madre Dios,' says red, fierce-like, 'it would be a stain on the honor o' my nation. Signor Polgenza Dorasto Mostreador el Dyspepsia, (the skipper's memory had weakened and the last required great effort. Once he had mastered it, he smiled triumphantly and went on), an' you, Signor'—turnin' to me—'I shall be here tomorrow at eight for the egg, three minutes, prepared to fight if necessary.'

"They bowed to each other, to me, to everythin', an' then went back to their flag-ships. In a minute, each ran out the gun on th' side nearest me to cover th' schooner an' th' other. There was no way out. I called a council o' all hands aft. We argued pro an' against for more than an hour an' got nowhere.

" 'Huh,' says Mark Spoffin (he was mate), 'could she lay two to once?'

" 'Hell, no!' says Obadiah Bones, th' cook (we called him, 'Dead-an'-Gone'), 'Hell, no! Hens ain't built that way.'

" 'Couldn't we make 'er?' says Mark.

" 'Mark,' says I, cold-like, 'she don't lay but one a day, but,' says I, 'she does that regular, an' I don't, nor won't, ask more of any hen, let along Black Mariar.'

"Black Mariar'd been watchin' all this time. She walked up to me, an' I said to her, 'It's up to you, old lady. We leave it all to you.'

" 'Cluck-cluck,' says she winkin' at me an' goes below.

" 'Boys,' says I, 'we might as well give up. There ain't any chance. Pass 'er round; we'll go drunk an' in form.'

"We didn't come round until mornin'. Black Mariar was up early an' waked me an' went forrard to th' galley. I waked the crew an' 'Dead-an'-Gone' (Bones, you'll recollect) an' said somethin' was up with Black Mariar. She'd hopped up on th' stove an' settled in a fryin' pan. (The fire hadn't been lighted, you'll understand.) Black Mariar sets very still; an' we never moved.

" 'Stand back!' says 'Dead-an'-Gone' suddenly, 'Easy does it, mates.'

"Then there was a terrible cluckin', an' there was she, lookin' at th' biggest egg I ever saw.

" 'Is it, or ain't it?' says 'Dead-an'-Gone,' puttin' it to boil.

" 'What?' says Spoffin.

" 'It,' says th' cook.

" 'It what?' says Spoffin.

" 'Wait,' says th' cook.

"The two admirals layed us aboard right then, so I went up. They both bowed to me, an' I led 'em aft. We sat down.

" 'Breakfast, gen'lmen,' says I, 'will be here in a minute.'

" 'Good,' says green, 'I ain't seen an' egg in that long,' says he, 'that I'm dyin' for an egg.'

" 'Signor,' says red, 'since you must have the egg or die, you shall most certainly die. I shall eat th' egg, I, Gam. . . .'

"He started to wind up his names, but just then, faint an' feeble, I heard a cheer. In comes 'Dead-an'-Gone,' grinnin', an' sets a cup for each of 'em, an' in each cup was an egg, boiled three minutes by the ship's clock.

" '*What?*' says you.

" 'Why,' says I, 'it's simple—Black Mariar'd layed a double egg. Everything was fine; an' people say hens is fools.' "

The skipper wiped his eyes.

"And how did she come to die?" I asked, determined to have it all. We had finished dinner and Mrs. Plunket was out of hearing.

"Vindictiveness," whispered the skipper, looking anxiously over his shoulder. "The evils of vindictiveness is many, an' one got her; ain't it awful? She never would lay on land, you'll remember; it was against her principles. Lizzie had been on one of her matrimonial mutinies, an' knowin' this, in her vindictiveness, she fed Mariar 'Lay-or-Bust' while she was ashore. But Black Mariar was true to her principles, like me, an' she died—apoplexy, th' doctor said. So I set her up as you see her, sir, with Mark Spoffin to help—an' him bein' a bit wall-eyed, he didn't focus very good—but she looks natural, don't she? Struck a good pose. Her ballast pulls her a bit to starboard; but she's a fine figger of a he. . . ."

He checked himself in the nick of time.

"It don't apply," he mourned; then, catching a glimpse of Mrs. Plunket's bones, he went on, happily, "A fine figger of a woman, sir, ain't she?"

MAY, 1922

THE ABBOT SPEAKS

I'm dying—yes. I'll soon be dead, they say,
And then, good brother Francis, you will be
Their abbot in my place. It should agree
With you. Though you are young, the scattered gray
Above your ears tells how you work and pray.
You think that I am fat and lazily
Inclined to take my ease with Burgundy;
But I have heard the *aves* day by day
Creep under your cell-door at dawn when you

Have watched a whole night through in prayer upon
Your knees. The stones must have grown hard and cold—
Ugh! How I hate them!—I could feel them through
The sandals on my feet. Yes, when I've gone,
They'll surely make you shepherd of their fold.
Thanks, brother, thanks; my head rests better so,
A little raised, where I can see the light
Fall on my rosary, hanging like a bright,
Big ruby on that dull, gray wall. You know
Rubies are splendid—but pearls have a glow
Deep in them that moves softly, sometimes, quite
Like the stirring of a woman's breasts when fright
Of her first passion leaves her weak below
Her lover.—Don't start, brother—don't let what
I say disturb that pompous platitude
Of prayer to fit the kicking of my heels
With these smug, snivelling idiots have taught
You. You are one of this damned, holy brood;
But I'm your fat old abbot saying what he feels.
You're young to be an abbot, though a score
Of years have passed since you first came
To swell the holiness of this old abbey's fame.
You seem to feel religion's beauty more
Than I did when I passed the outer door
To steal a small salvation for my name.
And you will be an abbot without blame;
Where I, your predecessor, kept a whore.
Oh yes!—When I had washed away my fear
With fasting, the desire in me grew
To leave a seed of my new sanctity,
A planted thistle, growing rankly here,
Beside this smug, old gate-post.—No one knew:
The others prayed too busily to see.
Don't damn me, brother, with your hardened creed

Too suddenly. You can't; for there still lies
A misery of terror in your eyes.
It was a hellish scheme. The urge to breed,
You know, had ripened, and had gone to seed
From this restraint.–The rock-bound cedar tries
To sow itself in ranker soil.–The lies,
The meek hypocrisies had disagreed
With the starved fibres of my former life.
It seemed as if I must escape these stones,
Lichened unhealthily with scabs of heaven.
I went to her three times before the strife
Of my rebellion melted from my bones . . .
God pity me this hell I hoped to leaven!
She bore a son, and he was all I'd planned.
His name was cursed, before he disappeared,
By twenty houses in the town. Girls feared
And loved him for his beauty through the land.
He was a sin conceived beneath God's hand,
By me, God's instrument in sin. I steered
My sinful heart through stars which were unsphered.–
If you had seen her, you would understand:
She was small-hipped, and white. Her breasts
Were soft. On her left arm there was a mole
I used to kiss,–don't interrupt,–each brow
Joined each, a quiet arch . . . My son, it rests
With you. Long praying's needed for my soul.
. . . If she were here, I'd do it over now. . . .

NOVEMBER, 1925

James Gould Cozzens, '26

1903–

James Gould Cozzens, author of nine novels, received the Pulitzer Prize in 1949 for his Guard of Honor.

CONDOLENCE

How many times I've seen you, serious-eyed,
Regard me patient, toss that mist of hair,
Smooth thoughtfully the dark arm of your chair;–
"I like to hear you talk," you gravely lied.

What of the dawns, dance-weary, when you smiled,
And stroked my hand, and asked of fear and fate
And life beyond the grave and hope and hate,
And heard my folly, wide-eyed as a child.

What fluent folly, said of far-off things!
Then you could smile, and I could lightly tell
Of death as grateful sleep, say it was well,
And you could quite agree and twist your rings.

"But, O, he died in such a dreadful way"
You sob, and there is fear in your white face.

You look along the years to that dark place,
Where wintry night shall spill across your day.
And I, what can I say?

FEBRUARY, 1923

REMEMBER THE ROSE

THE AFTERNOON SUNLIGHT FELL IN SHAFTS BETWEEN the elms; hollyhocks along the brick wall stood like trophies and standards of August, bathed in golden glory. Above, the hills were settling into cool shadows and heights of sunny trees. A sky like unrippled blue silk came down to them and steep white clouds appeared with slow, adventurous intent along the crest.

There were cedars in one corner. The grass, a thick green tapestry reaching down from the wall by the road, hesitated, and gave way to warm, needle-soft openness about them, there was a faint perfume of cedars in the sun. A tea table was set here in the shadows with the tremble of breeze-stirred linen, the sheen of silver, and the fineness of pale porcelain.

Mrs. Bakewell, a contrast in her black silk and snowy hair, looked half smiling at a friend who had finished tea. The friend was a boy. He regarded abstracted the cigarette between his fingers and its slim straight column of smoke. You noticed first that he had that casual tan which comes from mornings on the links and the blaze of the tennis court. Afterwards you saw his hair was the color of old gold.

He broke the intimate silence at last, rousing himself and smiling a little; "I was in town this morning," he said, "I managed to get hold of that old book of Monsieur Hardy's." He produced a dingy volume from his pocket and laid it on the table beside her. "I thought you'd like it," he said.

"How very nice of you, Blair!" Mrs. Bakewell's smile carried you back to the days when she had been Nancy English and Joseph Ames had done her in oils, astounding the old Philadelphia Academy and making his own reputation. She looked at the battered gold lettering: *Un Fainéant dans la Roseraie.*

"I looked to see if this was the one in which he told about his work on the Damask roses," remarked the boy, "it's got a whole chapter on the Amanda Patenotte."

"It's been out of print for thirty years at least," Mrs. Bakewell turned the pages thoughtfully, "The love of roses, except for fanatics like you and me, died even longer ago. This had five editions in its day, and now it can't be bought."

Blair dropped the cigarette in the ash tray on his chair arm.

"Aren't the Duchess of Southerlands blooming yet, Mrs. Bakewell?"

"Oh, Blair, they are. I almost forgot. Shall we go and look at them?"

He arose and drew the chair away. Still bearing the book she led him through the round arch where the brick was lost under the green of the ramblers. It opened into a second walled garden with spacious gravel paths radiating from the steps and stone work of a sun dial in the center. They went down to the glossy leaved bed where the fresh buds of the Duchess of Southerlands had broken gently into crimson.

"It's really a triumph to have them blooming now," said Mrs. Bakewell, "it's because I pruned them so hard this spring. Thomas protested a great deal, but he found he couldn't do anything with me. He is really a good gardener in the sense that he keeps the paths so neat, but he will not learn about roses. I shall never forget his chagrin when he came that morning to tell me they had budded after all."

She and Blair passed down to the dial. The stone was softly

grey and graceful, the old bronze clear cut for all the long exposure, the rain and snow.

"I've always meant to look at that inscription," said Blair, bending before the metal plate set in the side. He read aloud the fine swash-letter script; 'Remember the Rose, how it doth fall.'

"Yes," smiled Mrs. Bakewell, "that dial was set up by my father and he had those lines put on it. A rebuke to youth, he called them. I can remember him so well on summer evenings walking the paths here in a yellow linen suit with a long cigar that trailed a delicious aroma, holding my brother's hand on one side and mine on the other. He would walk about and look at the roses and grumble over his problem of the moment —Verdier had sent him cuttings of his Souvenir de Malmaison, I remember one year, and he was trying to make them grow, refused to believe they were dead long after they really were —he would always end his stroll before the dial and read the words solemnly,—'Lines to take note of . . .' he would say, and thump off leaving us there to look at them. My brother used to make little parodies and father would be annoyed when we came out of the garden squealing with laughter."

They walked down toward the back. Those were the Phaloes, dusky over a faint flush of rose. So would Cleopatra's cheek have been, thought Blair. The Eugenie Jovins were like tinted foam. What could one call the Barbots? Blair thought of Watteau's fawns in a painted park.

Here were Eliza Sauvages, yellow like aged silk, and as thin and fine.

"You know," he said after a moment, "one can't say much of anything. I hate people who whisper 'ah, beautiful!' at everything from roses to Walter Pater."

"Some people can't say anything else, and they do mean it."

"I should think if they meant it they could say something else. They've spoiled a good word."

He paused among the musk roses. The Princess of Nassaus were in bud, golden.

"They are very white when they open," said Mrs. Bakewell, "it's like magic."

Beyond were the Eponines, true Persian roses, white as milk; Eponines, the slow drift of whose petals wise Omar hoped would soothe him in his grave. They stood in the gate presently.

"Such roses!" said Blair at last. "It's a dream, it really doesn't exist at all. You step through this gate into a dream garden which vanishes when your back is turned."

"Yes, but it always come back, when, like Peter Ibbetson, you dream true."

After he had left and a dusk was settling on the garden, dulling the rambling lines of the old white house, Mrs. Bakewell sat in the candle light at her desk waiting for dinner to be announced. She penned a fine script in a black bound book.

'My sixty-ninth birthday,' she wrote, 'I had a delightful tea with Blair and we looked at the roses afterwards. He and I, are I think, the last of the rosiéristes. . . .'

Her eye wandered to the book he had brought and from there the albums in the bottom of the book cases.

When Parke entered to tell Mrs. Bakewell dinner was served, he found her looking at the pages of faded letters; good wishes, congratulations and advice, written long ago by Vibert and Laffay and Hardy; the notes in the great Rivers' angular characters, the neat little lines from old Wood. Mr. English had known them all.

"Blair," said Mrs. Bakewell one afternoon as they left the garden, "would you care to come over for dinner Thursday night? My niece Millicent is going to spend a few weeks with me, and I would like very much to have you meet her."

"I'd love to," said Blair.

He rode John Halifax down to the village to get the mail

the next afternoon. The train was in, dark and compact along the open gravel platforms. He saw Mrs. Bakewell's carriage with the team of chestnuts waiting. John Halifax objected to trains, and pawing the air refused to go nearer. A girl appeared, laughing, followed by Mrs. Bakewell's man carrying bags. The train gathered strength with a tremendous burst of steam and iron roar, John Halifax backed away with desperate vigor, Mrs. Bakewell's carriage turned about. Blair went over to the post office steps and swung out of the saddle. As he lit a cigarette he saw the carriage disappear up the long maple arch of the road.

On the evening Blair was to come to dinner Millicent English had appeared in Mrs. Bakewell's rooms clad in heavenly blue over laid with silver, accepted Mrs. Bakewell's admiration with a happy smile, and gone downstairs. Mrs. Bakewell still stood by a window looking out over the gardens in the gathering twilight. The sound of Millicent at the piano reached her faintly and seemed to bring with it years very long ago. Late afternoons were perhaps more golden then, or better, a gold more soft. A certain magnificence had given way to cool efficiency; you saw it in the summer dusk, you saw it—Mrs. Bakewell half smiled—in Millicent's dress. She thought of the flowing gowns of those days, the billows and gorgeous mounds of lovely cloth. The evening clothes of today had none of the leisurely grace.

The pace of life had quickened. Men no longer wore such beautiful linen; their gloves and hats, the cut of their clothes, had sacrificed pleasant dignity and beauty. She thought of her husband with his curling mustachios, his graceful capes, the glitter of quiet gold, the cambrics no longer made, the rich folds of black satin. Such things had been relegated to a past which seemed now subtly better bred.

Her attention was taken by the appearance of Millicent and Blair strolling on the garden path. She saw thoughtfully the white of his shirt front, the cigarette in his hand. A gauze veil Millicent had slipped about her shoulders detached itself a little and floated after her in the light breeze. Across the sounds of summer evening her laugh came low and clear. Mrs. Bakewell turned away, went out of the room and down the wide cool stairs pensively.

The sound of horses hoofs died away on the road beyond the wall. The long shadows had sunk the tea table in coolness and quiet, and Mrs. Bakewell sat alone.

I'm glad they like each other so much, she thought. Blair and Millicent were always together, riding, or playing tennis, or paddling on the river. Only yesterday Millicent had brought home an armful of water lilies, wanly fragrant. There had been a dance or two in the village, dead dances, Blair had said, but they went none the less, laughing, and came back quite late still laughing.

Young people did things differently now. Millicent would come down in boyish riding clothes, flit into the breakfast room where the morning coolness yet remained, urge Parke to hurry and be out on horseback to ride away with Blair into the nine o'clock shadows, under breezy elms, up sunny slopes, untold miles into the summer country before she appeared dusty and breathless, late for lunch.

They had left now to ride over the hill road and see the sunset. Up there the long fields were yellow with golden rod; cardinal flowers and gentians grew in the hollows about the brooks, the asters, blue beneath the dust, thronged along the road. So Millicent said.

She had told Blair when they had finished tea a little while before that the Moirés were blooming at last. Once, she thought a little wistfully, he would have wanted to see them. Millicent had got up and gone toward the stables and he had followed, unreluctant.

It was late in September when Millicent left. The next afternoon Blair came in. He was very hurried.

"Thank you," he said. "I can't stay to tea, I've got lots of packing to do to get back to the University tomorrow."

"I'm sorry you're going, I haven't seen you at all lately, Blair; you and Millicent were so busy."

"She's very nice."

Mrs. Bakewell walked to the gate with him.

"The roses will soon be gone," she said.

"There will be more roses next spring," said Blair, and he smiled and turned down into the glory of the afternoon sunlight.

JUNE, 1923

Lincoln Kirstein, '29

1907–

Lincoln Kirstein, who founded Hound and Horn, *is the author of* Poems *(1935) and several books on ballet. He is at present director of the New York City Ballet Company.*

MARCH FROM THE RUINS OF ATHENS

1.

It's a pity she hasn't sense enough to grow old gracefully,
Ageing as she has in these last few years.
I know she dyes her hair, though her own grey's so pretty.
One can scarcely blame her . . . yet one might hope . . .
  Thus the ladies on Friday afternoon before the music:
  And thus the city gathers the dust of her lost bricks about
      her . . .
    I found Rome brick, and I left her—
    With a three inch veneer of Indiana limestone.
The plaster falls from doors and walls,
From hearths and houses old in story.
  But out of the brick dust, from rigid roots,
  Springs from a nest of steel, a new phoenix flight—
  (Including the new Statler, the new Ritz, and the Metro-
      politan Theater)

Splendor of scagiola, strict courtesy of ushers,
Prologue ballet, this week A Night in Venice,
Joseph Conrad in Lord Jim,
And a singsong with our wonder organist . . .
February melts the brown ice ruts for a little while,
Filling the marble halls for half a month.
Four new operas, complete with dancers, decor, and new dresses–
Direct from Chicago.
No–thanks. I shall not go.
I'll search my bureau drawers for yellow programs,
Remembering my lordkin, my lambkin, my Mordkin,
My beautiful ballay boy.
And Igor's archers and the faun's veil and Scheherazade,
So airy like, so fairy like, so very like
NIJINSKY.
Yes, I know. There are still the Pops, and the Ruskin Club,
And the old man who gives 'Personal Reminiscences of Liszt,'
And even the candle light and carols in Louisberg Square.
But lint piles up on the lids of Niobe, and the Ares Ludovici,
And on the plaster Praxiteles, with which our fathers filled the Athenaeum.
Though now we have a new wing, (Western Art, and early American.)
Change and decay about me all I see.

2.

Poplar leaves whirling in the few empty squares
Catch in the ruins of a cast iron balustrade.
The shutters are still up on the Avenue–
No, not yet returned.
(They usually go up to Grandmother's in New Hampshire, after Race Week.)

While feathery grass sings between the paving bricks
In front of their town houses.
They are sand-blasting the Touraine?
New lamps have been ordered for the Public Library?
Yes?
They tell me too. . . . The Manchus are bathed but twice;
At birth and then again at death.
Perhaps you're right,
You say we are not dying; dry rot is no sure sign of decay.
But little shops have driven the doctors further up Newbury Street
And there is a malady of apartments on the corners of Commonwealth.
It's catching, my dears, watch out.—We are only across a river.
You know how hard it is to burn, how easy to build a bridge.
Echoes have reached us, for the cord has never really been cut. . . .
Do we not ebb and flow,
With each unstaunching of the contractors' wounds?
O thou who changest not
Suffer us yet a little hour. What can another pebble matter
On the long grey breach?

3.

Yes, I do like modern music, but there is so much in Brahms
He has not played. Though I see what you mean.
We couldn't have all Brahms. That would be uninteresting.
But he played all Wagner just last year. . . .
Put on your gloves, fold up your program, slip the glasses back into your bag.
Hurry, the car is waiting, we mustn't block traffic.
It gets dark so early now, and colder too, these last few days

We shall soon be taking our furs out of storage;
Won't you come home to tea?
Winter will be upon us in no time.
Oh, thou who changest not, abide with me.

DECEMBER, 1926

James Agee, '32

1909–

James Agee was President of the ADVOCATE *in 1932. His book of poems,* Permit Me Voyage, *won the Yale Younger Poets Award in 1934. His latest book is* Let Us Now Praise Famous Men, *an experimental collaboration in which Agee has written text and Walker Evans supplied photographs.*

THE PASSIONATE POET TO HIS LOVE

Come live with me and be my love
Provided you think little of
Such stodge encumbrances as friends
Who keep their means for their own ends;

Granted we mutually agree
That yours was never a mother's knee,
Or, if the spiteful slime should bud,
Will nip the foetus while it's mud;

Provided you can smoothly be
Wife, mother or nonentity
As metamorphic moods require;
Provided, also, you admire

Nor ever dare to criticize
Each syllable that I devise,
And shall apprise me (though I know it)
Of my majority as a poet,

And, like four angels each with sword
Will guard the Inception of the Word—
If such persuasions aught can move,
Then live with me and be my love.

FEBRUARY, 1932

A POEM OF POETS

The harsh and profitable seasons pass
Bestowing each their own inestimable burdens,
Love its peculiar joy, love's end its proper grief,
Beauty its image, wisdom sought, its pain:
The mind so richly dowered, all withered are its guerdons;
Bloodless and sere and joyless, whose hour of green was brief,
They whisper deathly riddles to confused and dying grass.
Soon shall the mind be thoughtless and soon the autumn leaf
No more be bright memorial to the ancestral rain.

The mind is stunned, the tongue may find no word,
Nor in themselves may either find ever any thought
Beneath the awful instant of each high visitation,
Beneath the blinding and celestial fire,
Fit to do thankful honor to Him the fire Who wrought:
Wherefore with gilded praises and with false lamentation,
We sing into the darkening sky too tardily to be heard,
Who soon shall be brought low to earth and that humiliation
Which gluts the oak with pride and burns the poppy with
desire.

All seasons past, once more they swerve above,
Once more the mind is granted the living fire to breathe,
Once more with green and holly and far gathered leaves we
fashion,
Straitly implied with brief domestic flowers,
Pride, artifice, despair, our wild half hallowed wreath:—
To crown the mind with fame, and God with earth-bound
passion,
Flaw Truth with Beauty, make a holy whore of sickened love.
Once more, and now forever impends that immolation
Whence we shall rise to damn still other poets with half blind
powers.

APRIL, 1933

THE POETS' VALEDICTION

We, with our eyes impaled of fire,
We, with our flesh suffused of flame,
Our lips made purple with desire,
And our hearts dark with hooded shame:

Once in a young and evil hour
Ran foul of Beauty on the air
And since that time are in her power
To her delight and our despair;

Whence forth through all her weird ways
And devious incarnations, we
Have sought, whom guileless things amaze
With labyrinthine falsity,

That essence which is Beauty's life
Clothed in a myriad disguise
Which keenest thought nor shrewdest knife
Most swiftly urged may ever surprise.

When we were nearest her deceit
And she imperilled of her power
With windy grass she bound our feet
Or in a bright malignant shower

Involved our passage, and when these
Delusions served but to refresh,
In new dissemblance of dis-ease
She spun herself a gown of flesh:

Wherein she strolled athwart our way
Young, and irrationally wise,
And swift accomplished our dismay
With furious and gentle eyes.

Some time, as thoughtless as the air,
Remorseless and regardless quite
Of lost and further seeking, there
By love deceived and love's delight

We lingered in the simple joy
And operation of our lust;
Which that sweet texture did destroy
And sharply ravel toward the dust.

Then rose the mind in his despair
To kind obscene philosophy:
Superior to such repair
Love died of unsimplicity.

Half sure of finding, surer of
Solaceous ease if she were sped,
Rifling all various looms of love
We set corruption on each thread.

She was denatured out of flesh,
And was departed out of love,
And urged no summer wind to thresh
Music from no harmonious grove,

But from all bygone semblances
Which now were vulnerable of proof,
And every proof the heart assays
And soon destroys, she held aloof.

All these old seemings were become
Our properties, who exercised
Our wit and knowledge of their sum
And that familiar sum despised.

Out of that wealth which we despise
We fashioned various hymns to be
Sung in her worship, which, being lies,
Fractions of false totality,

As well we knew, whenever sung
Did but contaminate her name:
Men's praise and her own silence flung
Throughout our hearts the midnight's shame.

In self-despisal and despair
Alone and unobserv-ed each
Knelt and addressed to her a prayer
In broken undevis-ed speech:

And saw the hills resolve to their
Essential and primeval fire,
The shaken seas on air the air
Athwart ethereal space expire,

While through demolishment and smoke
And all creation set awry
Loud the ambiguous thunder spoke
Articulate along the sky

The lightnings wrote what none might read
The imperious patterned stars revolved
Their influence round the changing seed,
Despite which seed and stars dissolved.

The mad oracular din was quelled
All elemental stuffs unjointed
And all molecular mists dispelled
And all sure substance disappointed,

And down that spaceless disarray
Where now we waited undistressed
Where night concentralized with day
Beauty her Self made manifest.

Of that high Presence who shall prate,
Who from the black disanimate flame
And quiet whence all things emanate
Declared her mutiplicit name?

Silent we knelt and silent she
With never a need for any word
Proclaimed those verities which we
May find no speech for, who have heard,

While still we knelt, from out that space
Of holy nothingness exhaled
All things to their appointed place
And we to earth, whom speech has failed

Truly to make what we perceive
Identical with what we see:
Those guileful things which now amaze
With labyrinthine verity.

To the old quest we've fallen heir
Once more and to the ancient pain
And sick desire, who could not bear
For long the sight without the stain.

Wherefore with eyes impaled of fire
And with our flesh suffused of flame,
Our lips made lurid with desire
And our dark hearts destroyed by shame,

Silent henceforth we march toward
That silence which is Beauty's soul:
Be our oblivious reward
That some man tell of Beauty whole.

APRIL, 1933

Robert Fitzgerald, '33

1910–

Robert Fitzgerald published his Poems *in 1935. He has worked for* The Herald Tribune *and* Time. *Recently, Fitzgerald has published translations from the Greek, often in collaboration with Dudley Fitts.*

SYMPHONY ENDED

Say by what hale reverberance of music
Our lands lie borderless, unplumbed our main.
Jade time and crystal in a wrist-watch tick
Mental division to the falling grain,
And from the fire-thin sweet channeling
Which is our love and labyrinth of time,
Never ascends the distanceless pure wing
Drawn out of night in the undreamed to climb.
Never. O men and women of the world,
Hard shackled to the rock and the mind's blood
Ruinous, drink comfort from those lands
Whereto he only comes whose song is furled
White into silence, who has seen and stood
And taken to his lips the beggar's hands.

NOVEMBER, 1932

PARK AVENUE

Between dinner and death the crowds shadow the loom of
steel.
Engines dwell among the races; the tragic phrase
Falls soundless in the tune and tremble of them.
Spun beyond the sign of the virgin and bloomed with light
The globe leans into spring.
The daughter from the dead land returns.
Between the edges of her thighs desire and cruelty
Make their twin temples, whereof the columns sunder
In the reverberations of time past and to come.
A pestilence among us gives us life.
Sparks shot to the cylinders explode softly
Sheathing speed in sleep.

DECEMBER, 1932

SONG FOR SEPTEMBER

Respect the dreams of old men, said the cricket,
Summer behind the song, the streams falling
Ledge to ledge in the mountains where clouds come.

Attend the old men who wander, said the cricket.
Daylight and evening in the air grown cold
Time thins, leaving our will to wind and whispers.
The bells are swallowed gently underground.

Because in time the birds will leave this country
Waning south, not to appear again
Because light is a mad thing
And love falters without music

Because we walk in gardens among grasses
Touching the garments of the wind that passes
Dimming our eyes.

Give benches to the old men, said the cricket,
Listening by cool ways to the world that dies
Fainter than seas drawn off from mist and stone.

The rain that speaks at night is the prayer's answer.
What are dry phantoms to the old men
Lying at night alone?

They are not here whose gestures we have known:
Their hands in the dusk, the frail hair in the sun.

DECEMBER, 1932

James Laughlin, '36

1914–

James Laughlin was Pegasus of the ADVOCATE *as an undergraduate. He has been editor and publisher of New Directions since 1936, himself editing the annual anthologies of experimental writing. He has published a book of his own poems,* Some Natural Things. *"A Natural History," Laughlin's story here reprinted, was, together with a mild example of Henry Miller, the cause of the magazine's being banned from the mails in 1938.*

PIRATES PASS

Who sailed in violence the sea
whose waters as shed blood
as glint of gold the winds' caprice

Where now the northward flight
of pelicans is clear low music
above the oratory of waves

"A land so pleasing that a man. . .
"though he were melancholik. . .
"must change his humor"

And in the night as winds sigh
creak of sails where no ship
and echo of forgotten holy war

A lizard lies ensorcelled in the sun
that paints the palm's shape on the sand
(In an old dry book the mark of tears)

As ghosts reproaching previous death
ginbottles crabclaw stove-in waterkeg
make sorry wail along the beach

Temperately, then let us be judges
of time's passages reading in dreams
the meaning of lives lost deep in the sea

MAY, 1934

A CANON FOR BETROTHAL

Amaranthine
is our night
beloved

tender its darkness
and the sound of stars
in a caress

faithful beyond time
the chipped edges
of wedding china

thus in corners
forgotten laughter
as fine cobwebs

sunlight is bright
on photographs
at age 4 ys., 3 mos.

shadows reflecting
the cinematitudes
that flowers tell

and Olga the big Swede
coeval to our
sweet immodesties

Amaranthine are we
as on the pillow
the silent skull

JUNE, 1934

A NATURAL HISTORY

WELL THEY WERE REAL TRACKS THIS TIME, NOT LIKE the ones Hank and Gussy had made the week before to fool Helena, and we followed them up the beach and found the turtle high in the dry sand, where the warmth of the sun hatches the eggs, already popping them. It was a big old bitch and she was half backed down into the hole she'd dug, dropping about two eggs a minute as near as I could time it. Helena started giggling, she hadn't ever seen one laying before, and we'd come out a week before, too early, because she was so het up about it and wanted to see one before she had to go up back north again, and there hadn't been any, they hardly ever start coming up out of the sea before the end of May, so Gussy and Hank faked up a flipper track with their elbows while I kept Helena busy up the beach, and then they came running up the beach shouting that they'd just seen a big one going back into the water, the idea was to try to get Helena to dig for the eggs where there weren't any, but it didn't work because she caught on because Gussy had put his foot down a couple of times when they were making the track and the pattern of the sole showed on the sand, but Helena hadn't had to go north so soon after all because her old man, who is drunk almost all the time, had the d-t's just the night before they were going to start driving back to Illinois, and they'd had to take him down to Miami to the hospital to get over them, so she could stay on longer and we'd come out again when the moon got full because the old nigger who cuts the lawn for Senator Blossom says that's what gives the turtles the signal to come up out of the sea. Helena started giggling, and Hank slapped her fanny and said something I didn't catch that made her awful sore. "That ain't one bit funny, Hank," said Georgia. I could see, with the big moon, that Georgia wasn't liking it much, but Elsy was eating it right up. She got down in the sand to look into the hole. You could hear the eggs landing as they fell, plip . . . plep . . . plip, like that, like the slow drip of a faucet into a drain tub. "Wouldya lookit the way they bounce!" said Elsy. Georgia was looking like she was going to be sick any minute and Gussy said, "Isn't that cute the way nature makes them sorta soft so they can bounce like that and not get broke?" Georgia sat down in the sand and looked the other way; "Come on be a sport," said Helena, "You knowya wanted to come 'n you said how you came last year 'n what a laugh it was." Georgia didn't say anything. Plip . . . plep . . . plip . . . I was wondering how that poor goddam turtle must feel. She knew we were there all right, she'd pulled in her head under the shell, but once they get started laying they can't get themselves stopped, and there she had to go on with it knowing all the time that we'd cop the eggs just as soon as she got them dropped. Gussy was starting to fish some of them out of the hole already while she was still working. He gave one to Elsy and she turned it over in her fingers, fascinated with the way the air dent rolled around the shell as she moved it. "Look Gussy," I said, "Why don't you just put the basket down inside the hole? Save a lot of work." He tried it, scooping away some sand to get it down, but trying to work it under the turtle he must have scraped her behind because she struck out at him, quick as lightning, with her back foot and ripped a long bloody scratch down his wrist and hand. He swore at the turtle and gave it a kick which only hurt his toe. His hand was bleeding some and the girls clustered round. He was starting to suck at the cut but Helena said not to. Elsy asked him if it hurt bad, Georgia couldn't take her eyes off it. "Wash it in the salt water," said Helena, "Salt's just as good as iodine." They went down to the water and I stood watching the turtle. Hank fetched back the basket that Gussy had slung away in his anger. Plip . . . plep . . . plip, the hole was nearly full now and the eggs seemed to be coming a little quicker. The turtle edged her head out cautiously from under the shell and jerked it back in again when she saw me. "How would you be feeling if you was this turtle?" I asked Hank. "I don' getcha," said Hank. "Well, having all your eggs swiped from you after you'd worked so damn hard to lay 'em." "Oh," said Hank, "Oh yeah, well I guess I'd be perty sore, I guess . . . hell, I didn't never think nothin' about it, I ain't no damn turtle." Gussy and the girls came back up the beach from the water, they'd tied a couple of handkerchiefs around his wrist. "Hey look," said Elsy, "She's going to fill up the hole." The turtle had finished laying and was turned around pushing sand into the hole with her flippers. Whether or not we were there waiting to steal her eggs she was going to finish up her job the way her instinct made her. She filled up her hole to the level of the beach and then hit right out for the water. And turtles aren't so slow either, she went right along with a quick jerking movement, the flippers pulling in front and the feet pushing from behind. Hank picked up Elsy to put her on the turtle's back, we'd filled the girls up with stories about how you could ride on the turtle's backs, how on real hot nights they ran a regular taxi service up and down the beach, how you could have races on them, but Elsy'd seen what that turtle had done to Gussy and she wasn't going to get herself within reach of it. Hank was carrying her along behind the turtle, trying to sit her down on its back, but she grabbed hold of his hair, he has long hair, when he combs it down the wrong way he can chew the ends of it, and pulled until he had to dump her or lose two handfuls of it. I followed the turtle as she scrambled down the beach, and the way she was going it looked as though once she got back in the water she'd never more come out again. A big wave hit her as she went into the surf, it rolled her on her side, but she flopped down again and pushed on out into deep water. For a little while I could see her swimming along the surface but then she dove under and disappeared. I watched for a while to see if she would come up again further out but she didn't. The moon on the water was something marvellous, like some sort of silver fire if there ever was such a thing. I stood there just watching it, it was so wonderful, and Helena came up behind me and leaned against me, rubbing her chin against my shoulder. "What'you think of that?" I said, "Ever see anything like that up in Illinois?" She rubbed her chin on the side of my neck and put a hand on my arm, I could feel her breath on my cheek and the softness of her pressing against my back. "Y'know I wish I weren't never going back home at all, I wish I was just always going to stay here with. . ." "Sure," I said quickly, "That'd be great, Hel, but y'know it gets awful hot down here in summer, it gets terrible hot, I think you'd pretty soon get fed with it down here in summer." She moved away from me and kicked at something in the sand. "Come on," I said. "We've got to tote those eggs up to the car." She followed me up the beach without speaking.

Well, we got this stuff from a guy with a truck who'd killed a big turtle and couldn't get it up from the beach to the road it was so heavy. It's against the law to kill them but bootlegging them is worthwhile because the niggers love the meat, they eat everything but the shell, and one of those big ones, two or three hundred pounds of turtle, will feed a lot of niggers. This guy had come down from Stuart with his truck, and he'd located a whopping big turtle and been able to kill it by getting it turned over on its back with a crowbar and then taking an axe to it, but even at that it wasn't clean dead, a turtle is such a tough old bastard that you can't really call it dead till you've cut it in pieces, because as long as two pieces are still together they can manage to wiggle, I know because Hank tried to kill one one day, just a small one, and it took him over an hour with a meat knife and a hammer and screwdriver, its legs kept twitching after he had all the insides cut out of the shell, and the heart went on beating for about two hours after he'd cut it out and there wasn't any blood left in it, it just seemed to be beating on air, and when you'd poke it with a finger it would take on a spurt and beat faster for a while and then gradually quiet down again. Well we found this guy sitting on the fender of Gussy's car when we got back to the road with the eggs in a basket, and he asked would we give him a hand with his turtle. We had quite a job dragging it up to the road even though there were four of us because it was so big around there was no way you could get ahold of it, you couldn't get a grip on the smooth edge of the shell and nobody wanted to grab it by the feet because they were still jerking in spite of how its head was all mashed to hell and blood dripping over the sand. Finally Gussy got an idea, he remembered he had an old pair of chains under the seat of his car left over from the time when it was new and he used to drive people from the Beach out into the Glades to shoot. We got a hitch around the shell with the chains and that gave us something to haul on. Just the same it was some job to get it up that bank to the road, and while we were resting in the middle this guy brought down a big jug of this stuff from his truck and passed it around. And then when we'd gotten the turtle into the truck he'd brought along planks for that so it wasn't so hard, we had another round from the jug and he filled a quart bottle from it and give it to us to take along home. I don't know whatever this stuff could have been, it tasted something godawful, but it went down like a hurricane and hit like a landslide. It did the job all right, and by the time we got back to the beginning of West Palm we were feeling just fine and dandy and plenty left over to spare. Gussy had the old wreck wide open, you could have heard it a mile away, and we went down the boulevard like an itchy snake trying to scratch its back on both sides of the street at once. We were all feeling happy, hollering and singing and almost falling out of the car, and Elsy started throwing eggs at the cars parked along the sidewalk. Georgia tried to stop her, she hadn't kept up with the rest of us, but we all pretty soon forgot that we'd gotten the eggs to eat when we saw the way they splattered all over the cars as they broke. That was some ride I can tell you, and I guess there weren't two cars in twenty blocks that didn't get messed up the way we were slinging those turtle eggs. Then somebody thought of niggertown and it caught like a light, we were all yelling "Get those goddam niggers!" as we bumped over the tracks into Blackland. It was Saturday night and they were all still outside standing under the streetlights and sitting in front of their shacks. Gussy slowed down the car and we stood up and let 'em have it, all of us firing at once except Georgia who was sore and getting scared. We went down that old street like a mowing machine potting those damn niggers on both sides and you shoulda heard them swear and holler. A couple of them ran out and tried to hop our running board but Hank and I had a wrench and jack-handle ready and we let 'em have it right in the snoot. The rest of them all beat it back into their shacks but we went up and down a couple more times just decorating their windows. Then we heard a siren across the tracks, some nigger must have telephoned to the cops, so we scrammed out the back end of the street and beat it for home. When we pulled into Gussy's garage we were just too drunk tired to get out and go home so we lay there in the car, all but Georgia who went off by herself and left us. I was lying in the back seat, looking at the dark while the inside of my head rolled round and round in my skull, and Helena rolled over on top of me and started sucking my ear with her teeth the way she does. She was all set for it I could tell but I didn't try to get anywhere at all, I was so marvellously sleepy with the likker slowly wearing off, and we just lay there tight together feeling real hot and sleepy and good.

SEPTEMBER, 1935

Peter Viereck, '37

1916–

Peter Viereck received his M.A. in 1937 and his Ph.D. in 1942. He is the author of two historical works, Metapolitics *and* Conservatism Revisited, *and two books of verse,* Terror and Decorum, *which won the Pulitzer Prize in 1949, and* Strike Through the Mask. *"Dies Irae, Dies Illa," was one of a group of poems for which Viereck was awarded the Lloyd McKim Garrison Prize for Poetry at Harvard. Viereck now teaches at Mt. Holyoke.*

"DIES IRAE, DIES ILLA"

Everywhere
Awareness lurks aloof behind earth's blendings,
Shudders even in spring's greenest oases
At hard-riding portents saddled like thistledown
On breezes that have strayed in many places,
Seen many forgotten beginnings and thrown
The dust of many great and little endings
Into the air.

Even from the air
Death like a perfume goads our breath. Death,
Like a run-away outlaw nerve, goads our brain-cells with

Awareness: though the leaves, the leaves are still green,
There is danger of death in sunny fields and soothing waters,
Rapid, shadowless, not to be foreseen,
  Though we search and stare.

  And death's own stare
Meets ours from every thicket, austere, unblinking.
My dear, my dear, we have come to an enchanted place
Where sun-flowers have eyes that follow us.
Take care lest twilight yawn and swallow us.
Let us hurry; we are watched by a cloud with a crafty face.
Let us hurry, for the sun is sinking
  And clutches your hair,

  And drags you beneath by your hair.
Oh, hold me closer; I will never let you go.
And Because I will never let you go,
Because this "Because" is the grim silent compact of love,
You are freed again. Because I won't let you go,
Your hair is freed from all the clutch of things. Now I know
That all things—except one—have compassion for love,
  That all except one will spare.

  And Because death will not spare, sickly
And shameful would it be for our love to greet him
Hostage-like before we meet him, and paltry for us
To meet him while each spring blind weeds still cheat him.
Let love not die alone, let all things die,
The world and we, in one startled unfinished cry.
Through our window, as we sleep tonight, let death explore
    us,
  Settling mist-like, thickly,

Crushing the earth like a fog pressing thickly.
Then if—who knows, who knows?—if this old world ends tonight,
You will cling to me amid fire and all the thunder,
Cling and feel safe as when you dreamed such things,
Till, floodlike, hell subsides, and—strangest of awakenings—
Outside your window angel-clamor, dawn-frenzied, hails the newborn light. . .
You will rub your eyes and listen with young wonder
And wake me quickly.

SEPTEMBER, 1936

Arthur Schlesinger, Jr., '38

1917–

Arthur Schlesinger, Jr., who was a member of Harvard's Society of Fellows for three years after his graduation, received the Pulitzer Prize for his Age of Jackson. *His most recent book is* The Vital Center.

HARVARD TODAY

A THOUSAND DIFFERENT EXPERTS HAVE DEFINED THE purpose of education in a thousand different ways. You are told that the aim of education is the aim of living—which leaves the problem with the philosophers; or that it is to produce a good community by adjusting the individual to his environment—which delivers it to the sociologists. To Milton it is "to fit a man to perform justly, skillfully and magnanimously all the offices, both private and public, of peace and war"; to Emerson the purpose is "to teach self-trust"; and to Whitehead, "Education is the acquisition of the art of utilization of knowledge." But if you look carefuly at these definitions, you see that they name the goal without telling how it is to be reached. They describe amiably enough the purpose of education, but they don't mention its function. To define education in terms of its ultimate end is to contemplate pie in the sky: the reward is so distant and celestial that knowing it doesn't help the ordinary man. If we are to benefit from knowing the aim of education, it must be described in terms of its more immediate effects. The important immediate effect of education, I take it, is to endow man's appetites with discrimination. Education is the instruction and nourishment of desires. It furnishes means and methods; it cannot prescribe goals and ultimate ideals, but it can criticize and clarify them. Man is a creature of desire, and education gives him a sense of what is important.

If education's aim is to instill discrimination and thus to produce mature conduct, blue books provide no adequate test of its success; and the university must include a great deal more than courses, professors and buildings. The student at Harvard exposes himself to many influences besides teachers, test-tubes and reading assignments. People doubt sometimes whether study does much to develop the individual, but no one doubts the influence of non-scholastic activities. They are undertaken by choice, which means they matter to the student, while he ordinarily looks on courses as a disagreeable necessity, like tuition. Harvard is equal to the sum of its parts: its parts include Soldiers' Field, Boston debutante parties and the *Lampoon* as well as the Widener Library, Mallinckrodt Laboratory, and Professor Lowes.

Students acquire by osmosis and imitation the variety of ideas, attitudes and poses which somehow add up to a Harvard education. In earlier and simpler days Harvard produced a definite type often enough to stamp the country with the typical Harvard man. "You can always tell a Harvard man, but you can't tell him much," became a legend; and another popular maxim pigeonholed the ambition of the Harvard gentleman with stinging exactness, "Three C's and a D, and keep out of the newspapers." In the remoter sections of the country, this picture probably survives unchanged; but its original is fast fading. The factors in a Harvard education have multiplied, and the possible products have increased by geometrical progression. The invasion of the Middle Westerners, the newer immigrants and the public school men has changed radically the complexion of the college. People who send their sons to Cambridge in smiling confidence that four years will return to them a suave and elegant young man with a casual air and a sesamic entree to Park Avenue and the Union League Club are asking for disappointment. Twentieth century Harvard is quite bewildering. It has a growing resemblance to a slot machine: you can put your nickel in, but God knows what is likely to come out. And the odds are lengthening that it will not be the Harvard gentleman.

Many people are horrified by the crumbling of the homogeneity which spawned the Harvard gentleman. They cringe from the new diversity with the lowered social standards they feel it brings: a Harvard degree no longer guarantees that a man will be a fit business associate or son-in-law. The cry to keep out the Jews has come largely from this class. Its strongholds are the final clubs; and the chief target of its attack is the cross-section plan in the House system. To others, the increasing diversity is wholly natural and healthful. The homogeneous Harvard, they think, was going stale; and "Three C's and a D, and keep out of the newspapers" seemed hardly an ideal definition of the good life. These people welcome recent innovations which break with tradition: the tutorial system; the House plan, a shameless attempt to enforce diversity; and the Prize scholarships with their implication that the future of Harvard lies with the Middle West.

This inquiry intends to examine the chief influences which make up the heterogeneous Harvard of today. And it hopes to give some sort of answer to the vital question of the Tercentenary year: is there much to celebrate in the Harvard of 1936?

I. THE CLUBS AND THE HOUSES

Next to the tutorial system, the House plan is undoubtedly the greatest educational reform at Harvard in twenty-five years. Before Harkness, student life was divided among dormitories, lodging houses and clubs; the last gave their members real advantages in comfort and in social prestige. The clubs gained a genuine social dominance from their tendency to attract the superior men, though they seldom chose to formalize it by the political manipulation which insures the power of the Dartmouth or Michigan fraternities. This saved them from the inevitable reaction against an organized overlordship. Yet the superiority which they assumed so casually proved in the end as effective as any systematic management of undergraduate politics might have. Few challenged the assumption of social primacy because it affected no one except the aspirants to the clubs—and they rushed to acknowledge it. The rest of the students could preserve an impenetrable indifference to the clubs, and most of them did. But the clubs, with their belief that they were the reservoir of all that was desirable at Harvard, still stood supreme, even if their prestige sank as the stature of the men from Groton and Lawrenceville lessened in the eyes of an increasingly democratic college.

At this moment Harkness rebounded from the inhospitable offices of Yale to tug at President Lowell's hanging latchstring; and Lowell, a discriminating Anglophile, outlined his discreet adaptation of the English scheme of small colleges within the university. The result was the erection of seven Houses in three years and the installation of so-called social regimentation at Harvard.

The House plan dealt a solar-plexus blow to the clubs. It set up a way of life which beat anything the clubs had ever known in comfort, convenience and general amplitude. With a wave of Harkness's wand, their chief excuse for existence—

the pleasant living they provided—vanished. In the first shock they suffered greatly, and alumni freely predicted that the House plan would ruin the college. But the springs of 1935 and 1936 were more heartening. Each saw an exodus of sophomores from the Houses to Mt. Auburn Street. Diehard clubmen declared this return to the promised land to be an unassailable verification of their compact with the Lord; but it really proved little or nothing except that the more sensitive men choked at the recurrence of lamb stews on House menus or didn't like to look at the obnoxious outlander who might live across the hall.

The best type of clubman—the one with a wide range of activities and friends—has remained in the Houses. In his eyes the club has shrunk into a place for an occasional lunch. It is only the man who finds nothing at Harvard beyond his club that moves to the Mt. Auburn Street clubhouse after his sophomore year and seals himself into the vacuum of its life. The clubman, old style, is archaic: he represents the last stand of the gentleman of thirty years ago whose name lingers in the epithet attached to C—"the gentleman's grade." The clubs will probably persist, vain and exclusive little organisms, sustained by sons who join the clubs of their fathers, looking from within like the distillations of the best in Harvard life but from without like fragile soda water bubbles; yet the day is in sight when they will stop being very important even to the five per cent who now turn to them for refuge.

The irreconcilables who won't follow their more reasonable associates to Eliot and Dunster Houses are responsible for a growing spirit of intolerance which is new to Harvard. It generally takes the form of the conviction that activity directed to earnest public purposes is immoral and should be discouraged. The mental complex which produces this singular doctrine defies analysis; but there seems roughly to be an interrelationship among the diehards' dislike for serious action, their distaste for the people (generally Middle Westerners, middle class Easterners or Jews) who take part in serious activities, their resentment for a Harvard which centers about these strange activities rather than themselves, and the more subtle fact that most of the activities strike, by implication, at least, at the source of their fathers' incomes. Without stirring from their Mount Auburn Street trenches, they are wonderfully able to combat the people who want Browder for president, or the ones who go out on preposterous strikes for peace, or those whose mere presence helps engulf the Harvard gentleman. They parade their social prejudices as verities; and the prejudices seep down from them into the hangers-on and then to the student body. Anti-pacifism, anti-radicalism, anti-Semitism, all were born in the clubs.

Occasionally these sentiments have boiled into actual violence: the Michael Mullins Chowder and Marching Club is a notorious example, and the furtive destruction of the rooms of conspicuous radicals is another. The clubmen are ordinarily not to blame for the violence. They are too well bred to insult a person to his face; and to shave a Communist's head, in the M. I. T. fashion, or throw him into the lake, as they do at Wisconsin, is to show somewhat too obviously that you don't like him. The clubs are unlikely to start pogroms against the radicals; but the aspirants to clubs, who ape the sneers and poses of the members, but not their good manners, are excellent material for a mob. This new attitude among the clubs shows that, feeling the shift of the center of gravity, they are going to fight to retain their importance.

At his best, the clubman has given Harvard interesting opinions, grounded, no doubt, on taste—and the taste was often good—and on intuitions—and the intuitions were often keen. His contribution here is by no means inconsiderable. Harvard indifference—that item of college faith which permits every one to be himself—passed from the clubs into the Harvard spirit. It is evidence of their decline that the diehard clubmen are beginning to hedge on Harvard indifference now that it means liberty to people they dislike. And today the best clubmen are virtually indistinguishable from the best non-clubmen. The House plan has probably ended any really useful role for the clubs in Harvard life.

In these few years the Houses have become integral parts of Harvard. Students today can't conceive the college without them. They fulfilled a need which apparently few knew existed; and by balancing delicately between Harvard indifference and communal comfort they have organized social life without cramping the individual. Yet their future is no matter of natural evolution. The cross-section, a device invented by the Central Committee to make sure that all Boston Latin men won't go to Winthrop, all New Yorkers to Dunster and all Blue Book men to Kirkland, has provoked some of the Masters whose Houses are overapplied to a singular ferocity. They want to select what students they please, and they see no reason to send desirable men down the river to Leverett because of the vexing injunctions of the Central Committee. But the other Houses, saved by the cross-section from turning into barracks for grinds or basketball players, rely on it practically for their existence.

In actual fact the cross-section works imperfectly. Winthrop has each year most of the football team, Eliot many of the concentrators in classics, Adams more than its share of the concentrators in history. But to end it completely would be to transform the House system into a large-scale variant on the old club system. There would be superior Houses and inferior Houses, desirable Houses and undesirable Houses; and Harvard's present diversity would settle into a caste system more vicious—because more inclusive—than the clubs. To do away with the cross-section would be to contradict the House plan in theory, by discarding the diversity it tries to enforce; and to wreck it in practice, by making snobbery the criterion of selection. Nevertheless, a few Masters who try to sabotage the House plan are powerful enough to make its future highly uncertain. Eliot House's recent Gaudy shows the savagery of the feeling in some quarters toward the cross-section. But President Conant evidently still believes it necessary for the correct working of the House system.

The foes of the cross-section want substantially to make the Houses the heirs of the snobbery of the clubs by giving each House a grade in the scale of social acceptability. The cross-section, though it has frequently fumbled in distributing the students, has on the whole kept the Houses too much alike to give excuse for students to discriminate very much in their choice. The accidents of apportionment may color a House with one shade for one year, but it is unlikely that four years later will find the shade the same. Fashions in Houses change like fashions in clothes: the rise of Kirkland from "a social oasis," as the Crimson labelled it three years ago, to a minor-league Eliot shows how quickly bad reputations fade when the people who caused them graduate. Under the present set-up the popularity of each House will fluctuate, and the kind of students it attracts vary.

There is, of course, no deadly similarity among the Houses. No one would confound Lowell with Dunster, or Winthrop with Leverett; but the trouble seems to be that the Lowell of 1940 will probably not be much like the Lowell of 1936. Yet a few characteristics have developed which appear to be permanent. The make-up of the tutorial staffs may generate a degree of individuality. Working within the limits of the cross-section, Ferry of Winthrop and Baxter of Adams have done much, by a calculated choice of tutors and students, to point the interests of their Houses in special directions. And there are characteristics dictated by the architecture or location of the Houses. The riverbank sites of Eliot and Dunster, for instance, drawing most of the men who would have lived in clubs before the House plan, have gained for these Houses most of the elusive flavors which made the clubs attractive. But all of these distinguishing marks are somewhat capricious; and they conform to no comprehensible pattern. Every House has its fragments of individuality, but they jut out at different angles and on different planes so that orderly comparison is impossible. And the absence of a smooth and regular table of differences minimizes the importance of snobbery in choosing a House.

The champions of individuality argue chiefly by appeal to the example of Balliol and Corpus Christi. But the relevance of Oxford is at best highly doubtful; and the analogy is absurd. If the House plan is to continue as Lowell, Harkness and Conant conceive it, one House cannot be set aside for Roman Catholics and another for graduates of Groton. Continuity in House reputations may fit in nicely with the manufacture of college traditions. It is more important, however, to educate the young than to entertain the old; and, though the cross-section may displease the sentimentalists who want to find their House exactly the same at their twenty-fifth reunion as it was at their first, without the cross-section the bottom would fall out of the House plan.

What has the House system given to Harvard life? It is probably Harvard's most potent tool in the development of mature conduct—that is, in education. By throwing together men from different places, social and geographic, it has broadened and refined the scale of values which college inevitably leaves with its students. By furnishing college life with the one indispensable thing the clubs had given, it has drained of its importance a system which put a premium on social snobbishness and artificial distinctions. By encouraging students and tutors to eat together, talk together and play together, it has gone far to banish the viewpoints and conduct of the prep school. And by recognizing that the pre-war homogeneity is now hopelessly lost, it has kept the theory of Harvard life in harmony with the facts. Briefly, the House plan has become tremendously significant in a Harvard education because the mature environment it provides has gone far to produce that discrimination which underlies mature conduct.

II. FACULTY AND COURSES

The American university evidently decided that book-learning was the best way of giving an education. A college can exist without buildings or grounds; it can exist even without a football team or a glee club or a cocktail shaker; but it can't exist without teachers and a curriculum. Driving book-knowledge into the heads of its students: this is the one technique the college finds essential in education. The situation, after all, is easily understood. Universities depend on this technique because it is the only one tangible enough to be handled by most of the men on their faculties. There are a million Gradgrinds while there is one Socrates. The inculcation of book knowledge is a pretty concrete method. It is easily mastered, and its results are quickly measured. You can't rate objectively the educational effects of the Deutches Verein or the Fly Club; but it is plausible to assume that blue-books rate objectively the degree that students have memorized the information contained in Government 6 or Mathematics 24.

But reliance on book learning, however convenient it is for the teachers, is ruinous for the universities; for it is a great cause of their failure to educate. The professor may hammer in facts and ideas, but he rarely hammers in the conviction that they should be used except to pass examinations. Students accumulate vast piles of knowledge, most of which might be relevant to their daily lives; but they carry on their daily lives without reference to this knowledge. There is a strange compartmentalization in the minds of the college students. In one section they store the information they get in courses and label it, "For exams." Elsewhere the notions they picked up from their fathers and their newspapers and their clubs flourish, quite unaffected by the book knowledge. There may be, and usually is, a contradiction between the two bodies of information; but there is infrequently any conflict, because few think of applying book-learning to everyday life. American universities run on the assumption that the knowledge they dole out comes in a bottle with directions for its use. The assumption is false. Students may swallow great doses of ideas and facts, but they rarely digest them. They usually vomit them up into their last exam. The theory to which the universities cling is that education is the end of book learning. In actuality, the end is examinations.

Almost the only person who uses the ideas and facts he learns in his courses is the one headed for a professional life—in other words, the one who expects to earn his living by them. If a man intends to teach history, he has generally assimilated enough history so that he instinctively guides much of his conduct by it. But the concentrator in history who goes into engineering or professional athletics will, say, vote the Republican ticket just as if he had never heard of Harding and Hoover. The man who seeks his life career in economics will pay some attention to its precepts, but the man who leaves his college economics to become a broker will demand a protective tariff. The man who hopes to teach English will line his study walls with Dryden and Whitman; but ask the English concentrator who goes on to the law what he has read in the years since his commencement, and you will get a list of magazines and detective stories. The student absorbs book learning who will find it valuable professionally. But he is very much in the minority at Harvard as at any college. Most Harvard students shed the information they get from courses without even noticing it. They might as well spend their four years at Harvard and not enter a class room or open a book.

Nevertheless, for the few who have the desire and the ability to take advantage of it, Harvard offers a program of courses which for variety and quality is unequalled on this continent. Embree gave Harvard first place in his list of American universities, rating 22 out of 24 departments "distinguished." The mathematical and science departments are rivalled, outside of the technical schools, only by Chicago and California. The philosophy department has perhaps the one first-rank philosopher thus far of the century. The English department, now that the cold philological hand of Kittredge has been removed, should take again a leading position, though in losing De Voto, it lost its best teacher of composition and one of the few men in the department to consider literature as much a branch of social history as of aesthetics or linguistics. The economics department, much less disfigured by dogmatic standpatters than is usual in colleges today, has to admit equality only with Chicago and Columbia. Indeed, in practically every field except the two noted by Embree as the weakest—sociology and engineering—Harvard has the best or very nearly the best men in the United States.

President Conant has shown his anxiety to make Harvard the foremost center of science and learning in the world. But this ambition has brought him a good deal of thoughtless criticism, much of it by alumni, some by students. The criticism is focused on the alleged preoccupation of the faculty with original contributions to knowledge. "Productive scholarship," a convenient epithet since its meaning is always dark, has been loudly proclaimed the villain in the new Harvard.

The graduates, remembering the gods who walked the Yard in their day, look on the decline of great personalities and the rise of specialists as another evidence that Harvard is going to the dogs. Actually, of course, the demand for professional scholars is symptomatic of a great change in the temper of college life. The students of today are much too skeptical ever to set up a pantheon of campus gods. One man alone gets wide reverence, Whitehead; and he deserves it more than a carload of the pleasant second-raters who seem to have been worshipped by the Harvard of a generation ago. If the students of today faced the faculty of 1906, they would pay homage to the James's, Taussigs and the Richardses, not the Wendells and Copelands.

The age of the campus big shots meant less an age of heroes than one of hero worship. It reflected an adolescent state-of-mind. The tutorial system and the general examinations have forced the student to grow up. He no longer looks to courses as ends in themselves, simply to be passed and added to a list of credit-hours. They are now important primarily in their relation to a greater end—the general examination. Slovenly teaching got by when a course's usefulness ended with the day of its final exam. But now a student expects most of his courses to prepare him for portions of this last comprehensive test. He can't, like his fellow of thirty years ago, accept bad courses gratefully as "snaps." He scrutinizes every professor closely and requires a great deal from him, much more than he would if each course were the be-all and end-all, an isolated unit, existing pretty much in a vacuum and taken only for itself. And the tutorial system not only makes the general examination possible by filling in gaps in the student's knowledge but, by fostering personal contact between instructors and students, has reduced the need for compelling personalities on the lecture platforms.

It is idle to condemn the present faculty because the students are unlikely to organize a memorial association for any of its members. The critical attitude axiomatic at the Harvard of 1936 is surely healthier than the hopelessly uncritical devotion commanded by the "great" men of the last generation, men whose reputations have barely survived their retirement. The student today picks his idols cautiously and never concedes them infallibility. Almost without exception the professor who gets the enthusiasm of his classes bases his histrionic appeal on a sound and stubborn scholarship. Harvard would appreciate Haskins, Santayana and Lowell today. The teachers' magnetism may not be as strong now as it was in the early days, though men like Langer, Demos and Schumpeter seem to cast a spell on their students; yet "the examined life" is certainly as much to be preferred now as it was in the time of Plato.

The student who criticizes the administration for its emphasis on productive scholarship is as far off the mark as the alumnus. You hear in outraged tones that the teacher is being succeeded by the scholar; that the chief interest of the Harvard professor is no longer his class but infertile research. If a genial section man or tutor misses reappointment because he fails to write learned articles, then he is another martyr to productive scholarship and students complain that they are being forgotten in this mad race which can end only in sterility.

Productive scholarship is not a witless discipline; and the pedantry it is supposed to bring will never exist long in an environment filled with the acid of criticism and the explosive salts of genius. Harvard is not a dust-bowl. Until it becomes one, "dry-as-dust" pedantry is as insubstantial a bogey as the Loch Ness monster. Productive scholarship may cause a few instructors to be dropped by the wayside; but it is no more a danger to effective teaching than it is a destroyer of campus personalities.

The Cambridge environment is peculiarly kind to scholarship. It is exceedingly unfortunate that so few students should make profitable use of Harvard's superb equipment for intellectual endeavor. Probably more do than at any other American college. Yet to most students the faculty is only an official cramming school whose primary function is to help them in passing examinations. This tragic conception of a university reveals in a lightning flash the failure of education in the United States.

SEPTEMBER, 1936

Leonard Bernstein, '39

1918–

Leonard Bernstein, pianist, conductor, and composer, has recently been musical director of the Israel Philharmonic Orchestra. Bernstein's music column is here included, though it has lost its immediate topical significance, as an example of the way an ADVOCATE *feature is handled.*

MUSIC

WHAT WITH T. S. ELIOT NUMBERS OF THE ADVOCATE and the like, it has been a long time since music was last hashed over between you and me. In the interim recordings have been pouring out thick and fast—and so many worth consideration that this column will have to be purely discological.

There have been four top-notchers in the last few months—musical musts. Give the credit for one to Columbia—the Schubert Cello Sonata in A minor (Set 346) played by the great Feuermann. And played incomparably. The ease, charm, and flawless musicianship of the performance is incredible. You play each movement over and over to make sure you were not just imagining. The tone throughout might be that of a viola (if it didn't descend an extra octave) so unforced and sure is Feuermann's bowing. And his sexiest sliding—which makes you gasp—is never cheap. The tempi are psychologically perfect, the dynamics just right, the movements (thank heaven) unusually short for Schubert, the music itself charming, the accompaniment by Gerald Moore never obtrusive, and the actual recording excellent. It just goes over the top.

The other three highspots are Victor products. Two of them owe their success to Koussevitzky and his phenomenal Boston orchestra: the Fifth Symphony of Sibelius (M-474) and Haydn's 102nd Symphony (M-529). The third is the delightful Third Quartet of Hindemith (M-524) played with justly supreme authority by the Coolidge Quartet. Of the Sibelius the least that can be said is that this is the definitive performance of a great work of art. The first movement, especially, would be pure Elysium if only the French horns had disappointed us by *not* sounding in one place like a boy whose voice is changing.

The Haydn Symphony is not just another Haydn symphony. With all its good humor it has great power and breadth, almost in the Beethoven manner; it is the kind of thing that will close a program as successfully as it will open one. Of course, Koussevitzky takes the final Rondo at a pace that puts you on horseback; but somehow in this work it is far less objectionable than usual. Besides, you are perfectly confident that the orchestra could do it twice as fast.

Everyone—even anti-modernists—will like the Hindemith quartet. It has five short, direct, significant and satisfying movements, which are all played with unfailing taste and appeal. It would be both appropriate and encouraging to see this on Victor's list of "Ten Victor Records That Should Be in Every Home."

End of top-notchers.

* * * *

Columbia has done some fine things in recent months, like the first volume of Debussy preludes played magnificently by

Gieseking (Set 352), the Roussel Quartet in D played by the Roth (Set 339–for rather subdued Roussel), Bach's Second Sonata for viola da gamba and harpsichord (X-111, and fine Bach), and the Brahms Variations on a theme of Handel (Set 345) played with verve and understanding by Egon Petri (this just falls short of the top-notch list). But we cannot forgive the pressing of Deems Taylor's "Through the Looking-Glass" (Set 350). Now Taylor is a fine man: a sound and sensible musician, an expert informal orator, and a competent, likeable person. But he is not a great, nor a significant, nor even an interesting composer. Alice does seem so unhappy embedded in all this ill-concealed Franck and Wagner with Debussy dressing. True, it is cleverly orchestrated and neatly written, but that doesn't atone for the fact that if "modern" American music were going to be recorded, Columbia could have made it worth while. I do not want to be unfair to Columbia; she has released perhaps more American music than any other single commercial organization. And if the Looking-Glass pleases some listeners, well and good; recordings must be representative. But think of all that wax that might have been used for Copland's Ode or William Schuman's Second Symphony!

End of tirade.

* * * *

For the rest, Columbia and Victor share about equal credit and discredit. To Columbia, many thanks for the new Weingartner recording of Brahms' Third Symphony (Set 353) which would be fine if the strings were more precise, if Weingartner's phrasings were not so overdone that each melodic fragment ends in a hiccough, and if the chords did not waver so. (It is possible that the holes are punched off-center. This should be remedied.) More thanks for Margaret Roesgen-Champion's delightful performance of the Haydn Piano Concerto (Set X-118), but not so many for a rather unclear recording of the Franck Piano Quintet, played somewhat stodgily by E. Robert Schmitz and the Roth Quartet (Set 334).

To Victor, thanks for Stokowski's playing of his synthesis from "Tristan" (M-508). If you like your Tristan with much Weltschmerz and passion (and there is no reason why you shouldn't) this is your best bet. The Liebesnacht, in fact, is something of a challenge.

There is much Gershwin: a Memorial Album (C-29) which is good for its hits of ancient days, but not for things like numbers from "Porgy" which it cuts to shreds. The two Iturbis do a "Rhapsody in Blue" (M-517) which is almost occult in its perfection of ensemble, but is lacking in the jazz feeling.

Schnabel, but for his Viennese conception of fugue-rhythms, plays the C minor and D major Toccatas of Bach (M-532) as well as is possible on the modern piano. And a special acknowledgment of Alexander Kipnis' remarkable bass voice singing a fat album of Brahms' songs (M-522). It is wonderful to hear his versatility of rendition: the lightness with which he does the "Vergebliches Ständchen" contrasts amazingly with the ponderousness of the "Four Serious Songs." The latter, by the way, for their rarity of performance and grandeur of sound are well worth the whole album.

And please read Aaron Copland's new book "How to Listen to Music." It is worth anybody's time. If you don't know much about music you will learn easily and enjoyably; if you do know much you will learn more; and if you simply don't care, you soon will. Let this be our final will at the great noon-tide. Thus Spake Zarathustra.

MARCH, 1939

Dunstan Thompson, '40

1918–

Dunstan Thompson is author of Poems *and* Lament for the Sleepwalkers.

MEMORARE

Remember, at this moment, O somewhere
The plane falls through the indifferent air,
No longer flying the about to be dying
Pilot to any over-the-border disaster, but lying
Like the boyhood toy, by bad luck destroyed.
The lost lads are gone
God grace them

Remember how, even now, when the ship sinks,
The sailor, paler than a pearl, only thinks,
Diving through destiny to be invested with coral,
Of himself—saved from the sea caves where no laurel
Lives—and so gives up a gay ghost at land's end.
The lost lads are gone
God grace them

Remember, also, as the soldier in amber fires
Too late, his nerves, swerving on exploded tires,

Plunge through the past to exhaust their history
In the silent, never again to be violent mystery,
Which the womb worshiped more than the hero's tomb.
The lost lads are gone
God grace them

Remember—do not forget—the numbered, anonymous spy's
Suddenly surprised, not quite clever enough disguise,
And see him, neither gallant nor grim, obeying
The code, sans cipher, of the classroom saying:
O happy and hallowed to die for a flag.
The lost lads are gone
God grace them

Remember the enemy, always remembering you,
Whose heartbreaks heartbeat defeats, who too,
Shedding tears during prayers for the dead, discovers
Himself forever alone, the last of his lovers
Laid low for love, and, O at your mercy, murdered.
The lost lads are gone
God grace them

NOVEMBER, 1941

WHERE IS THE CLOCK TO TELL MY TIME OF TEARS

Where is the clock to tell my time of tears,
That strikes like midnight when love's hands are noon?
Or where, while diastolic tide of fears
Flows over me, find out the utter ice-floe moon?

Now I am serviced by a pageboy smile
As doors revolve me through a lounge of brass
Who passed for millionaire across the pile,
So soft my mirror fell into a snow of glass.

Happy I was but happy shall not be,
Outfaced by luck as fancy as a tart.
Nor may I go to bed today and see
Tomorrow less like sorrow break the heart;
Since what was more exciting than a football game,
No longer watched with love, is not for me the same.

APRIL, 1942

Harry Brown, '40

1917–

Harry Brown, one time Pegasus of the ADVOCATE, *has worked on* Time, The New Yorker, *and* Yank. *He is author of a play, four books of verse,* Artie Greengroin, Pfc., *and his best known book, the novel,* A Walk in the Sun. *He is now in Hollywood, writing for Cagney Productions.*

ELEGY ON THE DEATH OF YEATS

Now Lear has moved across the broken plain,
And the lightnings are departed. In that region
After the storms the sun comes, bursting full
Out of the morning. In that place the rain
Succumbs. In that calm quarter of the world
The marble statues breathe and moan:
They are moved by love, their own love moves them.

What is this place, what region? This is the country
Where the devout, tall passes of the mind
Are taken by lone travellers, this the land
Of last ascent, where the small stones babbling murmur,
The fierce oaks threaten the sky, the water whispers;
Intellect's outpost, this, and those who reach it,
Prophets and madmen, neither live nor die.

Man in his gyre goes upward, ever rising
In love to love; and he has picked for guides
Those who, gray-headed, bent, and full of state,
Have opened for a moment nature's door,
Have gasped to see a wonder, and have reached
Desperately up; then dropped back, weeping, knowing
They had found the absolute and almost held it.

MARCH, 1939

AN ODE FOR RICHARD EBERHART

You in the country, Richard, I in Cambridge,
Surveyors of the passage of sun and seasons,
Observers of animals, sudden dialecticians,
Each pursuing a fiction, each a world,
          Are uneasy mimics,
The nervous pupils of a passing art.

Sprung from a tight tradition of historians,
We wander through the Asias of the mind,
Describing fields and forests and the contours
Of the immense plateaus of human order,
          Where the distraught
Go mad for loss and love, and humbly die.

Servants of poetry, soul's topographers,
We move in the sudden decades, when the air
Is filled with murmurs; and, though insecure
Among the raucous continents, pursue
          The plans bequeathed
By centuries that moved amazed through time.

Think, then, on William Blake, that violent man
Who murdered the moral dimensions, made his own,
And chased throughout life the Furies, not they him:
He thought himself Isaiah born out of age,
          Whose turgid body was
Stabbed into truth with Saint Theresa's arrow.

Gentle geographer, lulling the sultry land
With his bright, unmanned borders, Wordsworth sped:
Shakespeare, as proud as Adam, loose with art,
Knew the uncertainties of style, and fell
          Prey to a throne,
And put its weight of ardor on his back.

The opposition of our previous masters,
Dante gone furious, Hopkins heavy with God,
And Poe and Coleridge deceived by dreams–
All the above must turn our innocence
          To an attack
That, if no more, will set a course for love.

Wherever the wild horse grazes is our country,
Wherever the free man muses are our people,
We possess Nature, wonders are worked for us
Wherever our eyes rest; spring and golden fall
          Resound with wisdom,
The just and ceaseless circle of the seasons.

Yet the unhindered holds us. Man's despair
Springs of itself, scatters its secret seeds
Upon the highway or within the porches
Of the devout; no place is sealed, no hollow
          So wisely harrowed
As to escape the flying of the chaff.

O, the gates must be opened, the doors unlocked,
And the silent prisoners escape the squad,
The records altered, and our quick resignation
Broken. The skies hold astrologic omens.
We must stand up
And speak directly to the ears of men.

You in the country, Richard, I in Cambridge,
Owning no more than some small sense of words,
Must weld them to a history, must possess
Passion resigned to reason, must bring down
With our poor eager power
An age in agitation, the doors of death.

NOVEMBER, 1940

THE BRIEF, UNFINISHED HISTORY OF JOHN CUDLOW

IT WASN'T THE ALARM-CLOCK OR HIS WIFE'S VOICE or anything like that; nothing as abstract as sound. No, it was something solid. Mr. Cudlow could feel it pressing against the small of his back—and digging in deeply, too. He lay there, half-asleep, wondering what it was. In the first place, it wasn't Mrs. Cudlow or any part of her, for he could hear her in the kitchenette, getting his breakfast ready. Unless there was a burglar in the kitchenette. He closed one eye and, turning his head sharply, focused the other on his wife's bed, six feet from his own. It was empty. Mr. Cudlow decided that his wife, and not a burglar, was in the kitchenette.

But that didn't solve the mystery of what was pressing into his flesh, the thing that had awakened him—he cocked an eye at the alarm-clock on the night table—eight minutes before the usual time. No, that solved absolutely nothing. It would be a good plan to roll half-over on his side, slip an arm underneath the sheets, and drag it out. He was about to go through with this procedure when the idea came to him that the object might be a dead rat. There was no reason for thinking it *was* a dead rat; but on the other hand there was no reason for thinking it wasn't. The longer he lay there and considered the situation, the surer he became that it was. Suddenly, with the speed of a rabbit in distress, seized with horror at the thought of a dead rat for a sleeping companion, Mr. Cudlow leaped from the bed. With a single sweeping motion he yanked down the blankets.

What he uncovered made his eyes nearly burst from his head. For the object, which had so disrupted the last passages of his sleep, was an egg. A golden egg. A lovely, oval golden egg.

For almost a minute he stood there, staring at its dull, reddish-yellow surface. Finally he picked it up and turned it over and over in his hands. It was gold, all right. He compared it to his wedding ring. Yes, it was gold and, as well as he could judge, pretty high quality gold at that. His hands began to shake violently, so violently that the egg slipped from them and rolled on the bed. "Martha," he called in a weak voice, "Martha!"

Mrs. Cudlow came in from the kitchenette, wearing a dressing gown and slippers, her hair in braids. She stood, hands on hips, in the doorway, staring glumly at her husband's back. "Well, John," she said, "for once you were up before the alarm. You must be sick. I—" Here she stopped, for Mr. Cudlow had turned around and he certainly did not look well. The shaking had progressed from his hands to the rest of his body. Mrs. Cudlow immediately became solicitous.

She crossed over to him. "You're *not* sick, are you, John?" she asked, placing her hand on his forehead.

"No," Mr. Cudlow said desperately, "no, I'm not."

"Then for goodness' sake," said his wife, a note of pique in her voice, "why are you carrying on like this?"

Mr. Cudlow gained control of himself briefly. "Look," he said, pointing to the object on the bed.

Mrs. Cudlow picked it up and her eyes took on a puzzled expression. "What is it?" she wanted to know.

"It's an egg," said Mr. Cudlow.

"Heaviest egg I ever saw," said his wife.

"It's a golden egg," said Mr. Cudlow. He began to shake again.

His wife almost dropped it in her surprise. "Where did you get it?" she asked. She sounded hoarse, as though she had suddenly developed a heavy cold.

Once more Mr. Cudlow pointed to the bed. "In there," he said. Mrs. Cudlow followed the line of his finger and then turned back to him, carefully searching his eyes. "John–." Hesitation and doubt were in the word.

"What?"

"John–you didn't steal it, did you, John?"

Mr. Cudlow stopped shaking. "I did not," he said firmly.

His wife was a persistent woman. "Then where did you get it? And don't try to lie, either. These things don't grow on trees, you know."

"I told you I found it in bed. That bed, *My* bed. This morning."

"And just *how* did a golden egg get in your bed?"

"How in the devil do I know?" Mr. Cudlow exclaimed. He was getting angry. After all, was it his fault if he woke up and found a golden egg in his bed? No. And *how* was he to explain how it got there? Answer: he wasn't. What did the woman expect, anyway? "My word," he began, "do you think I la–." Here he stopped abruptly and sat down heavily on the bed. "Merciful heavens," he said.

His wife sat down beside him, the egg still in her hand. "For goodness' sake, John," she said, "what's the matter?"

"Merciful heavens," Mr. Cudlow said again, "I must have laid that egg myself."

"Merciful heavens," echoed Mrs. Cudlow. She began to weep softly.

Her husband watched a large, round tear roll down her left cheek. "Well, after all–" he said. Then: "What are you bawling about?"

"You," said Mrs. Cudlow. She continued to cry, her sobs increasing in volume. Mr. Cudlow began to feel uneasy. "There's no sense in yelling your head off," he said. "This egg here"–and he took it from her limp palm–"is probably worth a good deal of money."

"It's not that," his wife said, bringing the back of one hand across her eyes, "it's just what people will say."

Mr. Cudlow's feeling of uneasiness wore off and was supplanted by a vague sense of opulence. He was beginning to be more than a little proud of himself. "And just what," he asked, "will people say?" While he waited for her answer he amused himself by tossing the egg in the air and catching it.

For a moment Mrs. Cudlow managed to gain the upper hand over her emotions. "They'll say," she said, "that my husband is a–a monster who lays golden eggs." Rising rage held back her tears. "It'll be a fine thing," she went on, "to have people point me out on the street and say 'There goes Martha Cudlow. Her husband's the one that lays the eggs.' And what will the girls at the Bridge Club say when they hear about it?" Having delivered herself of this personal interest in the matter, Mrs. Cudlow went on with her weeping.

"Oh, dear," said Mr. Cudlow, his air of being pleased with himself thoroughly quashed, "I never thought of that."

"No," said his wife, "no, *you* wouldn't."

There were a few seconds of silence, broken only by the

sound of Mrs. Cudlow's very competent tears. At last Mr. Cudlow stood up. "You know," he said, his eyes fixed on vacancy, "when you come right down to it, it *is* a pretty unnatural thing." He sniffed at the air. "I think the toast is burning, my sweet," he added calmly.

Mrs. Cudlow, tears and all, rose and dashed into the kitchenette, followed by her husband. The toast was burned—completely burned—and the kitchenette was full of rich black smoke that was slowly making its way through the entire flat. "I think," said Mr. Cudlow as he opened a window, "that it would be better if neither of us said anything about this."

Almost simultaneously Mrs. Cudlow's arms were around him. "Oh, John," she cried, "do you promise?"

"I promise," said Mr. Cudlow, gently removing her arms from about his neck. "After all, it wouldn't be a very pleasant future to be compared to a duck."

"And what shall we do with the egg?" asked Mrs. Cudlow as she put fresh toast in the toaster.

Mr. Cudlow was on his way back to the bedroom. "I don't know," he said. "We'd better keep it around, though. It might come in handy someday."

The next morning he was awakened by the hand of Mrs. Cudlow on his shoulder. As he turned sleepily to see what she wanted, his third rib encountered a familiar object in the bed. Before he had time to say anything about it, however, the sound of his wife's voice came in on his half-conscious thoughts. "Are you all right this morning, John?" she was asking. "Are you all right this morning?"

Mr. Cudlow dragged himself up to a sitting position. "No," he said shortly.

"Another one?" Mrs. Cudlow said, her face falling.

"Yes," Mr. Cudlow said, "another one." He reached under the covers and brought it out into the light. It was, if anything, bigger than the previous egg, with a definitely richer glow.

"Oh, John," said Mrs. Cudlow sitting down on the bed, "I've been *so* worried. I haven't been able to sleep a wink all night, thinking of you and these terrible eggs."

"They're not so terrible," said Mr. Cudlow, pushing her aside in order to slip his feet from under the covers and put them on the floor. "At least, it doesn't hurt."

"I know," his wife said. "You didn't make a sound or movement all night long."

"Didn't I?" Mr. Cudlow asked dispassionately. "Well, well." He put his feet into his slippers and started to stand up.

"John—." Mrs. Cudlow put up a restraining hand.

"What is it now?"

"John, something's got to be done."

He placed the egg on the night-table and got into his bathrobe. "Something's got to be done about what?" he wanted to know.

"You," said his wife, rising, "you, and these horrible eggs."

Mr. Cudlow went over to the window and looked out at the Murphys' wash. "What would you advise?" he said.

"You've got to go to the doctor."

"But I don't *want* to go to the doctor."

"You've got to go," Mrs. Cudlow said doggedly. "You're ill."

"I *am not* ill." After all, why should a man be considered ill, just because he lays a golden egg or two? Jealousy, that's what it was, downright jealousy.

"You *are* ill," Mrs. Cudlow said. "Anyone who lays an egg —and a man especially—must be ill."

Mr. Cudlow was taking inventory of the Murphys' wash. Two cotton dresses, six pairs of drawers, one set of B. V. D.'s (Mr. Murphy must be rather dirty, he thought), four sheets. "Why must he be ill?" he asked absently.

"Why—why, he must be," stammered Mrs. Cudlow. "It's—it's—it's against *Nature!*" she finished triumphantly.

"You said yesterday," continued Mr. Cudlow, as though he had not heard her, "that you didn't want anyone to know about it."

"I know I did," his wife said, "and I *don't* want anybody to know about it. But doctors are different. Doctors are—"

"Different," said Mr. Cudlow.

"Yes," said his wife.

"All right," he said, his survey of the wash completed, "I'll go to a doctor. I don't feel like working today, anyway."

Mrs. Cudlow looked relieved. "I'll call the office this minute," she said, "and tell them that you're ill and can't come in today. That is if anyone's there yet."

"Tell them I've got leprosy," said Mr. Cudlow as she started for the phone. "Ripe, galloping leprosy," he called after her.

As he started to dress he heard his wife talking to someone at the office. "I'm terribly sorry, but Mr. Cudlow can't come in this morning. Yes, he's ill. No, nothing serious—a little cold. Yes, better to keep him at home and play safe. Yes. Yes. Goodbye. Goodbye."

"The doctor will see you now," said the nurse at the desk.

"Thank you," said Mrs. Cudlow, rising. "Come, John."

"I'm coming, I'm coming," her husband muttered under his breath. Who did the woman think she was, anyway, leading him around like a monkey on a string. Just who did she think she was. Who's laying these eggs? I am, by George.

The doctor met them at the door of his inner office. He held out his hand. "Mrs.—?" he said.

"Cudlow," said Mrs. Cudlow. "And this is my husband, Mr. Cudlow."

"Come in, Mrs. Cudlow, come in, Mr. Cudlow," said the

doctor. He closed the door behind them. "Now you sit here, Mrs. Cudlow. And you here, Mr. Cudlow."

They all sat down. "Now," said the doctor, "just what is the matter, Mrs. Cudlow?"

Mrs. Cudlow blushed. "It's my husband, doctor. You tell him, John."

"Well, doctor," said the addressed, "I have a trouble."

"That's too bad," said the doctor. "And just what is this trouble?"

"Well, doctor, it's hard to say–"

"Really?" said the doctor. "That's bad."

"That's what my wife thinks," Mr. Cudlow said. "It doesn't bother me at all."

The doctor picked up a paperweight from his desk, turned it upside down, and set it back. "Just what *is* this trouble?" he asked again.

"Well, doctor," said Mr. Cudlow, "it's hard to say."

"Oh, for goodness' sake, John," said his wife. She turned to the doctor. "I'll tell you," she said. Her voice fell to a whisper. "He lays eggs. Golden eggs."

The doctor leaned back in his chair and looked at her in a peculiar way. Then he shook his head. "So early in the morning, too," he said.

"Well, it's true," said Mrs. Cudlow. "He does."

"That's right," her husband agreed, not without pride.

"Look," the doctor began, "I'm a very busy man–"

"Yes, doctor, we know," Mrs. Cudlow said, fumbling in her purse.

"And I can't be bothered–"

"Yes, doctor, we know." The purse snapped shut. "Here." And she held something out to the doctor.

It was the second egg.

The doctor took it carelessly and turned it over and over in his hands. As he did so he lost his air of carelessness and his face took on, by degrees, the color of ashes. At last he raised his head slowly and looked directly at Mr. Cudlow. "My God," he said.

Mrs. Cudlow nodded agreement. "It's terrible, isn't it, doctor?"

The doctor ignored her. "How long has this been going on?" he asked her husband.

"Not long," said Mr. Cudlow in an off-hand manner. "Two days, two eggs."

"My God," the doctor said again.

"Can you do something for him?" asked Mrs. Cudlow.

The doctor shook his head violently, as though making sure he was not dreaming. Then he rose to his feet. "Why?" he said.

"Why what?" said Mrs. Cudlow blankly.

"Why do something for him?" The doctor's attention was once more on the egg.

Mrs. Cudlow, too, stood up. "Why do something for him?" she repeated in a strained voice. "It's against Nature, that's why. I mean his laying eggs," she finished lamely.

The doctor handed the egg back to her. "Oh, yes, against Nature," he said. "So it is, so it is. But I can't do anything for him. He can go on laying eggs till Doomsday for all of me. I can give him an X-ray, that's all."

"That will be fine," Mrs. Cudlow said, reseating herself.

The doctor had regained his composure. Once more he picked up the paperweight and dandled it lightly. "Yes," he said, "an X-ray. Perhaps even more. Quite possibly more. Oh, quite possibly more." He turned to Mrs. Cudlow. "I suppose, Madam, that you are leaving your husband completely in my hands."

"Certainly, doctor," Mrs. Cudlow said. "I do hope it's nothing serious."

"It could be, it could be," the doctor said. "He may even have to go away for awhile."

"Oh, dear," Mrs. Cudlow said.

"I run a little place up in the mountains," the doctor went on. "He'll be quiet there. Of course, only if it's absolutely necessary."

"Of course," murmured Mrs. Cudlow.

The doctor put down the paperweight. "Well, then, now for that X-ray," he said, "Come along, old man." He crossed the room and opened a small door at the further end. "It may take quite a while. Perhaps you'd better go home, Mrs. Cudlow. You don't mind, do you?"

"Not at all," she said, beaming at him, "not at all."

Mr. Cudlow rose and walked through the door. As he passed through it the doctor clapped him heavily on the shoulder. "*Well*, Mr. Cudlow," he said.

SEPTEMBER, 1941

William Abrahams, '41

1919–

William Abrahams is the author of two short novels, Interval in Carolina *and* By the Beautiful Sea.

GARGOYLE IN A PERAMBULATOR

FOR RIMBAUD

Where is the infant-child with rosy cheeks,
That like a chessy cat, lolled in his carriage,
And was worshipped by his parents for several weeks,
Symbolic of their happy, happy marriage.

Where is the infant-child, rosy and gay,
Who tickled the fancy of matrons out for walks,
And brightened up the sulky tradesman's day,
And gave his mother subjects for telephone talks.

Yesterday he lolled like a chessy cat,
Sleek and cozy, dreaming of warm dark shells,
But today he has sprouted the wings of a bat,
And in his drunken eyes a daemon dwells.

He squeaks, pontificates, disowns his past,
Worships Pan, and tries to rape his nurse,

And mocks his mother and father who pray and fast
And hope by ritual to end his curse.

MAY, 1940

DOMESDAY

The almanac reveals our terrors, new
Discovered names mark out the zones of death,
And in a world that guns proliferate,
We are aware of nightmares withering.

Strange that once we lived in pantomime,
Deaf to the incantations of other cities,
Knowing only the accustomed suburbs, where
Cosmos lodged in a solarium.

Now, like gongs gone mad from strident hammers,
New names explode, new places, new networks,
And toy countries on toy maps parade
Through comic strips to shout their messages.

JUNE, 1940

Howard Nemerov, '41

1920–

Howard Nemerov, who teaches at Bennington College, is the author of a novel and two books of verse. An editor of Furioso, *Nemerov's most recent book is* Guide to the Ruins *(1950).*

INVENTORY AND STATEMENT: A DECLAMATION

50 beautiful girls count 'em 50, are dying,
all together and slowly. Their hearts
beat one-two-three-four, they've worked
together all their lives and given you
good entertainment: and the young clerk
with the hot pants, in the third row center,
was perhaps the least of the sinners among you.

Plato dreamed of a surpassing love
bound up beyond the moving spheres: and Ziegfeld
dreamed of fifty beautiful girls fifty,
who are dying.
The private citizen talks Babylon,
and has a righteous tea with the pastor,
and lusts in his heart; while my landlady

threw Alice out on the street and read Paris Nights.
Plato is dead, and Ziegfeld no less dead:
for I have given you here a thread of mine own life,
or that for which I lived.

What shall you do when winter is on the world,
and time comes out of the cliff to dine among you:
and the strumpet has none to love with her legs,
and the bride goes to an empty bed,
and the lover lies in the hasty grave
the earthworms dug under him?
Why, then you will set alarm clocks,
and whisper the time in restaurants;
there will be learned discussions, there will be
symposia; and the newsreels will picture
decay in the organism, newspapers will devote columns
to the death of a leaf.

Enforce the censorship: excise the merely
heterosexual: and show instead
defecation, masturbation, and a new
all-color version of Les Cent-Vingt Jours
—let the people learn the fashionable
technic from Alcibiades, and let
the newsboys peddle pictures of the Marquis
performing a subtle experiment.

For the fifty fair are dead, and godhead gone:
Brightness is dust, and through these portals pass
Plato, Ziegfeld, and all loveliness.

MARCH, 1940

POEM

From the cold streets of Cambridge
The lapis and basalt of St. Paul's
Makes disturbing division, a golden
And Byzantine disarray. Hath not
Some golden Paleologus of the City Council
Ordained this disorderly splendor?
Jumbled adornment we have seen before
In the rocky palaces of pagan men,
In excavations of the rotogravure.

Perhaps if the people of this city
Were possessed of a warmer temperament,
If the sun stood more hotly over us,
Being of one faith a bell to the faithful
And a usurer to those more penurious of themselves—

I tell you, in the old days
It would not have been countenanced. And even now
Many worshipers are worried by the old
Bronze and singing gods that in the shadows
Preen and pout and trill,
Making themselves at home, and tend to pluck
By the hair what children wander from
The clear ghastly light of the nave.

MARCH, 1941

THE NATIVE IN THE WORLD

THE CLIMB FROM SLEEP WAS DIFFICULT, A STRUGGLE up a staircase of soft pillows into which he sank again and again, drowsily defeated, from which he clumsily climbed again to a sight of the room that, seen in the equivocal wisdom of sleep, seemed to him any room, or all the rooms, in which he had ever slept, or ever been at home. Perhaps (an instant afterward he could no longer remember)—perhaps the phrase 'at home' struck the first tone of clarity in his mind, for about it the room began to arrange itself, to become again the familiar fashion of his circumstance, rising and composing to his own composition of its features. One thing—the overturned chair by the desk, with his clothes crushed under it—remained obstinately unfamiliar; when had he done that? He searched his memory, but the incident had sunk under sleep; he could readily imagine himself coming in drunk and knocking the chair down in the effort to hang his clothes over it, but actually to remember doing it—that was a different thing.

He got out of bed, and as he stood up felt pain protest harshly in his forehead, making him dizzy with the angry sleep that would not readily dissolve. The clock said ten more or less exactly and it was dark outside. That meant twenty hours sleep; since two Tuesday morning. The dizziness surged higher as he bent in a methodical stupor to set the chair right and get his clothes. Going into the next room he started the phonograph and put on the Ricercare of the Musikalisches Opfer; then settled back in the darkness of a far corner. The one voice strode through his mind with a more or less plaintive confidence that another would follow, and soon another did, then one more and another, and the rest were sunken in the ensemble and the scratch of the needle. He closed his eyes, and as if his consciousness rested on quicksand he was irresistibly sucked back toward sleep, his eyelids grew heavy in a sort of undertow that he could feel heavily about his head. A dream, some frightening and fast forgotten dream, jarred him out of sleep; he had a vague impression of fear, something was being thrown at him. He turned on the light, changed over the record and picked up a book that was lying on the couch:

Alcohol the Friend of Man. It was a reassuring volume by a doctor of unspecified repute; one must, he thought, turning over the pages, combine theory with practice. It seemed to him, as he had so often said, that there was a way to drink seriously, and a way not to drink seriously. Of three years at Harvard he had spent the last two learning the former, and was glad to distinguish himself from many of his acquaintances whose drinking was of the rowdy-up-and-puke sort. If a man wish to drink himself into insensibility, he phrased it pedantically, that is his own business; but equally he should not become a charge on his fellow-beings, and there is no excuse for forgetting manners one instant before passing out.

The record was over, and he walked across the room to change it, a strange figure in white pajamas, barefoot, head slightly too large for his excessively small frail body. He already had on his silver-rimmed reading glasses; he must have picked them up from the desk without thinking. He came from the Middle West, but one would unhesitatingly have called him a Yankee, judging by his pedantic contemptuous manner, his manners so civil as to be rude whenever he gave a cutting edge to his voice. His own estimate of himself was quite accurate: that his aloofness was respected, also his enormous and casual erudition; that even full professors were chary of a too great freedom with him or with his papers; that it was generally said of him that he would go far if he did not drink himself to death; that his paper on Augustinianism in the 17th century would no doubt put him in line for a fellowship; and at last, that he was drinking himself to death, or near to it—a state which he conceived of dubiously as a slight chill in his personal weather, as though a cloud should slide over a hill on which he was sunning himself. As to his reasons—if a man wish to drink himself into insensibility, he thought again . . . and perhaps it is not even his own business, or perhaps it is a shady transaction in that business, into which he does well not to inquire too far; look what happened to Oedipus.

He had put on the Ricercare again, but now he turned it off in the middle and called Rico's number. He listened apprehensively to the empty buzz of the phone, three, four, five times: he could hear it as if he were in the room, but as if the room were still empty, the lonely stupid ringing. Damn Rico, he thought, letting the phone ring again and again. Damn Rico, damn the twisted little Cuban Jesuit gone wrong, and damn, he said, and damn with the ring of the phone, and damn again and hung up. The receiver clattered into its cradle, and he felt again how painfully slow it was to wake up, how fiercely he must fight to stay above the surface, so to speak, to force every last ache and hurt in body and mind to the service of wakefulness, to a nagging insistence on belief in being awake. Rico was probably out with Alan; Alan, he thought angrily, the little blond jew-boy who's trying to get me out of the way by advising me seriously to go see a psychiatrist. And Rico is helping him too.

He shuddered slightly, envisioning conspiracy and betrayal: the swift, sure honest-eyed kiss of treachery, the bright, the clear, the trustworthy Judas; and the appalling thing was that it took place on such a pitifully small scale, the love life of a colony of worms. The disgust, and the hate, were waking him, slowly, as one fever will fight another and overcome it.

He took up the phone again and called Rhys. One could always talk to Rhys, no matter how far they had gone apart. Long ago, before the drinking, as he thought, they had been close friends, working furiously together, reading two and three books in an evening and listening to Bach from two to four in the morning. And then—there had been no break, not even a coolness; but they went their ways and saw rather less of each other. When he was drunk and wanted to talk out of turn, he often still climbed to Rhys' room, and he would talk wildly for fifteen minutes, often incoherently, and then Rhys would deliberate heavily, and say at last, "Well, John, it's difficult . . ." which in itself would be somewhat reassuring; and then they would exhaust a small stock of polite and cynically erudite remarks about obscure poets, or faculty members, and it would be over.

"Hello, Rhys? This is John–Bradshaw. . . . I hope I didn't disturb you?"

"Not at all," said Rhys, in the coldly amiable tones that meant he was disturbed.

"Look, Rhys, . . . you mustn't mind me; I'm not drunk, but I took twelve grains of amytal last night when I was. I've just managed to get out of bed and I'm a little–woozy." He was, in fact, woozier than he had thought; there was that dull weight on his forehead that was worse than pain, more unknown and more fearful therefore.

"What I wanted to know was could you meet me for a drink, about fifteen minutes from now?"

"No, I can't," said Rhys. "You sound troubled. I don't know medicine, but isn't twelve grains rather much?"

"The prescribed adult dose is a grain and a half. I wish you'd come out for a drink. I want to talk to you. Really, you know, it gets to be too much, sometimes . . . everywhere you go people are such bitches. . . ."

"What the hell is wrong, John?"

"Oh,–look, I'm liable to ramble a bit–I'm not very awake and the drug is still pretty strong–Oh goddam it Rhys, I've been betrayed, I–"

"Again?" A politely skeptical coolness.

Steady, he thought to himself; he was weak and falling again, and before answering he bit his lower lip hard, till the blood ran, to save himself from sleep.

"I mean it," he said stubbornly.

"Yes," said Rhys; and John recognized the tone Rhys used to nice drunks. "Yes, people are . . . difficult sometimes."

"Rhys, I'm not drunk. I want to talk to you. Why won't you have a drink with me?"

"Because I don't feel like it, John."

"Rhys, you think I'm drunk. I'm not, Rhys. It's the amytal. I couldn't be drunk, Rhys, I just got up, I've slept since two this morning."

"I know you're not drunk, John," said Rhys coldly. "I'm busy, and I think you ought to go back to bed. You don't sound very well."

"I only want to talk to you about Rico. You think I'm drunk."

"What's Rico done now?"

"I want to talk to you, Rhys."

"Well . . . ?"

"Not on the phone."

"All right then, good night."

"Rhys—"

"Good night."

He waited for the dead click at the other end, and then placed the receiver carefully down. That had been a shameful performance; he was not drunk, but he could not have been more maudlin in any case. Rhys would be nodding his head sagely at this very moment: poor John Bradshaw. Oh, damn Rhys. It was unfair of him. He might have had the common courtesy to listen to me, Rhys the careful, Rhys the undrunk, the dullard so proud of his dullness; one could summon up at will that favorite image of Rhys the damned, sitting deep in his armchair after a peculiarly bitter confessional period, sitting like a tolerant father-confessor, saying slowly between puffs at a cigarette, "Gawd, all you people live such exciting lives—it must be so difficult for you—you come and tell me about drinking and drugs and your homosexual experiences—

and I sit here on my can, taking it all in, living my dull life. . . ." And he would sit there on his can, looking as old as he could, and staring into the fire, saying "they also serve," or some such. Poor Rhys! And so anxious, too, for you to know that he was only pretending dullness (which God knows he was not) and that he was a man of deep spiritual crises; as he would say, and so smugly, "My blowups all take place inside." All right. Let Rhys take that attitude. He wasn't required.

He got to his feet and walked slowly about the room, still thinking about Rhys, beating one little fist determinedly into the other hand and thinking with melancholy savagery, 'cut away the non-essentials, cut them out.' Rhys was a non-essential, Rhys always worrying about his writing, his piddling poetry, his painful anxiety that you read his newest work, that you pat him on the head, that you say nice things. . . . As for himself, he thought, there would be a book one day . . . a book after this long silence, after the non-essentials had been cut away and meditation had burned some great stone to form inside him, a book that would say all these things that had to be said, against the lying time, against the lying treacherous people, against Rhys, against Rico, against Alan, against (he sneered) all these smilers with their dull knives. One voice in this wilderness would not waste time crying out for help, for cries would only bring the wolves along faster. And through this, beneath the pain and the hate and the disgust and still half-prevailing sleep, he knew that he was crying out.

He went into the bathroom and looked at the bottle of amytal. There were at least twenty-five grains left; he smiled a little to remember the time when one grain could give him a solid night's sleep, the rapid necessity to step up the dose, the doctor at the hygiene building telling him pedagogically that he was by definition a drug-addict, his crazily epigrammatic crypticism to the doctor ("Jonathan Swift was by definition not a well man, and a neurotic to boot"), his cheerful announcement to Rhys (Rhys again): "You may call me De Quincey, I'm depraved." It was the precipitous, the plunging rapidity with which it had happened, this drug business, that astounded him and started slight inadmissible fears from their careful rest. How one thing led to another! in such seemingly inconsequential succession of one pettiness on the next, until, looking back from the most extravagantly fantastic heights of improbability, from the most unwarranted excesses and distortions, one was surprised and shocked to note how accurately and how unerringly every smallest act, word and gesture quietly conspired to build such a wildly rococo and out-of-the-way edifice,–such a goblin's architecture that at one moment one shuddered to think how it drove one on to the end, and at the next dismissed the whole structure with a smile for its implausibility. He stared fixedly at the bottle, imagined himself reaching out for it, tried to imagine himself refusing, and could only get a more or less chromo reproduction of a man in a magazine advertisement with his head turned disaffectedly away from a cup of coffee, saying: "Nope, I keep away from it. Keeps me up nights." This did not seem to him a satisfactory image of moral grandeur; with a smile he took up the bottle and locked it away in the filing cabinet on his desk. Then, puzzled, he looked at the key to the cabinet; what to do with that? He took it with him into the living room. He stood in the very center of the carpet, shut his eyes and turned around thrice, as though he were absurdly playing some children's game of blind man's buff; with his eyes still tightly closed, he threw the key straight before him, heard it tinkle in landing, then turned around twice more before opening his eyes. A glance about the room satisfied him that the key was not in evidence, not obviously anyhow. It might be days before he came across it. Unless the chamber-maid picked it up in the morning. He could imagine that she might hand it to him, asking whether he had lost it, and imagine himself saying no, I wonder how it could have got here . . . but one couldn't do that; all one's correspondence was in the filing cabinet, and notes for a couple of essays as well. Anyhow, it would be easy to find the key again, when it was really required. Meanwhile, one could . . . imagine it lost.

He decided to give Rico one more chance, and dialled his number again. The equivocal ringing—does it ring if you're not there to hear it?—angered him; he thought it possible that Rico and Alan were in the room, refusing to answer, he could hear them guessing who it might be, smiling complacently, drifting from smiles into their moonings and caressings, their adolescent, ill-informed lecheries—but no, neither one of them would have the strength to let the phone ring and keep on ringing; across each ugly infirm purpose would flash thoughts of importance, of some great person, some missed opportunity, the thought especially: it might be something better. And they would answer the phone. Rico particularly would answer the phone, compliant opportunist, affection's whore . . . had he ever done differently, or been anything else? Rico? who told (with pride) how he had been seduced by the house-maid when he was fifteen, and how three weeks later he had gone to his mother and got the girl discharged on some pretext.

No, they would answer the phone, he knew, and since they had not . . . Perhaps they weren't even together; he cut the call short and dialled Alan's room. Alan's roommate answered:

"Hello."

"Hello, is Alan there?"

"No, he went out half an hour ago."

"Was Rico with him?"

"I think he was going to meet Rico. Is there any message I can give him?"

"No thanks."

"Your name . . . ?"

"No thanks," he said coldly and replaced the receiver. He

thought desperately for a moment that he might call Rhys again, then rejected the idea. There was no sense in begging. He felt tired again; the weight in his forehead had turned into a headache, and his eyes tended to water. The slight exertion of walking about the room made him want to go to bed, but he refused, and to clinch his refusal, began to get dressed. A drink was probably what was needed, he thought. A drink, and an hour out of this room. There was the mood he had been in all too often lately: his room depressed him, almost as much as did a library, for example; and the best things in the room,—the Matisse over the victrola, for example—they were so recognized, so much the very breath of his tepid climate that they became unbearable, and music was unbearable, and work as well, and it all seemed to him the ugly and ready-to-hand diversion afforded a man sentenced to life imprisonment. Not the ugly, but the commonplace disgusts, he thought. If they put Matisses in the street-cars, one would counter by hanging advertisements on one's walls. Yet he felt unsatisfied outside his room, again like a prisoner so acclimated as to shun freedom; a walk, however short, tired him inordinately, and climbing two flights to the room made his head throb as if the blood would burst out. He felt now that he required a drink; he would go to St. Clair's, nor did he disguise from himself the fact that half his motive was to find Rico, and that if Rico were not at St. Clair's he might be at Bella Vista, or McBrides, or the Stag Club; or he might be in town at the Napoleon or the Ritz or the Lincolnshire.

By the time he had finished dressing he found himself nearly exhausted. He had to sit down on the couch and turn out the light, and it was then that he began to think about the key to the filing-cabinet. He felt that he had perhaps been foolish, with his infantile stratagem. He might need the key in a hurry, for his notes, or to answer a letter, or—no need to disguise the fact from himself—to get the amytal when he came in drunk; it had to be conveniently to hand, or he would get no sleep. He must recognize the fact by now, he argued: he required the amytal, he was a mature individual, still sane, heaven knows, more sane than most of his dull acquaintances, he would not over-dose. And anyhow, the test was in the will to stay off the stuff, not in locking it away, there was no help in that. To be able to keep it before his eyes, that bottle, to look at it steadily, and steadfastly not to take it—at least not more than was absolutely necessary—there was the thing. Besides, suppose he needed it in a hurry, sometime, and the key had got lost—there were any number of ways that could have happened: it might have fallen into a crack in the floor, might have slid under the carpet, might even have landed down the radiator gratings, irretrievable short of large-scale operations that would require the janitor.

Hastily he turned on the light, began to look around. It was not that he wanted any now, or would take any tonight; but this was the saner thing to do, he must know.

The key was discovered with ridiculous ease, under the bookcase. He picked it up and laid it carefully in the middle drawer of his desk. And unformed to speech or even to clear thought, but present in his mind, was that justification, that ritual against reason, of a postulated higher power, of unspecified nature, watching over the episode, the feeling, carefully swathed in obscurity: Providence didn't want me to hide the key, or I wouldn't have found it so easily.

Put vaguely at ease, he began to get on his overcoat, and then decided to call Rhys again, buoyed up by this same vague assurance that he would, by however narrow a margin, do the thing which was to be done, that the thing would be right because he did it. But there was no answer, and for some reason, he was more infuriated at this than at Rico's absence—a little relieved, too, for Rhys would have been annoyed; but angry, angry that Rhys should not be there, should have gone out after making some excuse to him. Betrayal, he thought, furiously and without power. Rhys too. Although loneliness was his habitual way, it was by preference, because it suited him to be alone, but this, the loneliness by compulsion, was a new thing. He felt a terrible isolation, the phone seemed to him now only an instrument of the Inquisition, to teach him his loneliness as it were by rote, and he had the sudden sense that whatever number he called, it would be closed to him by that instrument. In fact, he thought in satiric anger—in fact this whole room is given only to people who want to be left alone. It is made to teach them the measure—that is, the unmeasurable quality—of isolation, of being absolutely alone. Harvard College built it that way—they get a lot of lonely ones around here.

The brief walk in the cold, up Dunster street and across the Square to St. Clair's, fatigued him excessively; he recognized that last night's dose had not nearly worn off, and that the cold had the unusual effect of making him want to lie down and go to sleep just wherever he was, in the street even. It was almost like being drunk, that disgusting soddenness with drink that made it Nirvana just to stop moving, anyhow, anywhere. He kept up his heart to a degree by repeating his little catechism of betrayal, his interdict on Rico and on Rhys, all the fictions of his misery forming into churches for his martyred self: here was a first station, where one knelt to beg forgiveness for being rude to Bradshaw; and here a second, where one knelt to do penance for being out when Bradshaw called, here another for thinking Bradshaw drunk when he wasn't, here another for the general sin of offending Bradshaw; and a last, where one prayed for the grace of Bradshaw: Oh Bradshaw, we do beseech thee . . . and a return for the petty humiliations, and a hundredfold paid back each error, and he knew it for pitiful, but nevertheless went on, in a rage of cynical benevolence, to forgive Rico, to forgive Rhys, to forgive them and cut them away from his side, and to go on in the thorough lonely discretion of his anger.

When he entered St. Clair's the first person he saw was Rhys, big, rather stout, and darkly dressed as usual, sitting by himself at a corner table. Rhys waved and beckoned to the chair opposite, and John sat down there.

"You're avoiding me," he said without thinking; his anger came to a head and he wanted a fight.

"If I were avoiding you, would I come and sit in a bar?" asked Rhys politely, and it was like being hit across the face.

"Then why did you tell me you couldn't go out?"

"I didn't say I couldn't go out. I said I didn't feel like going out." Rhys was nettled, and showed it by getting more and more polite.

"If you don't want to see me, I won't sit here."

"Don't be silly. Sit around and have a drink."

Rhys, he thought, was playing for a dull peace and it was not to be allowed; he must be disturbed, made to give himself away. He ordered, and got, a large martini, and sipped it in an uneasy silence.

"You should have gone to bed. You look as if you were trying to kill yourself." Rhys gave in and said something.

"What the hell would you care?" he asked rhetorically, hoping at the same time that Rhys would say something friendly and reassuring.

"How is it possible for anyone to care? You're not very responsive to care, you know."

"Oh, some have managed." He lit a cigarette. It tasted very bad, but it was against the sleep that even the drink seemed to drive him at. The place where he had bit his lip was still tender, it hurt when he spoke.

"You alienate even those," said Rhys. It was for him as though he had said 'where are you, John?' and reached out a hand in the darkness; it was such an unwelcome thing to be forced to find people when ordinarily they came and disclosed themselves.

They finished their drinks in silence and ordered more.

"Now what's this about Rico?" said Rhys at last.

John emptied his glass again, slowly, before answering. "It's only that from now on," he said, "I'm going to play dirty too. If you don't what chance have you got?"

"I always thought of Rico as more or less irresponsible," said Rhys, "but–"

"It's not only Rico, God knows. He can be excused: if you were bounced out of a parochial school in Cuba and landed at Harvard with the prospect of eight million bucks when you came out–alors. Not alone Rico, no. It's everyone. And you too, sir. Don't you understand: I'm playing your way now, the safe way you all play, don't give anything with one hand that you can't get back with both, any time. And if I can't beat these Jesuits at their own game–well, what the hell . . ." he shrugged his thin shoulders, deliberately blew smoke across the table between them.

Rhys determined to show no annoyance, to maintain objectivity. So he sat with hands out equally on the table, looking like the balance-pans of the blind goddess.

"Essentially stupid attitude to take," he said. "I mean–granting that people do present . . . difficulties at times–still, just how much have you got hurt?"

"Got hurt, hell. That's not–"

"You don't need to answer me," continued Rhys with a show of calm. "I'm just suggesting the question as something for you to worry about."

"Don't go on; you had it right the first time, when you said something about responsibility. You just make an ass of yourself when you put it on the piddling level of 'getting hurt.' It's only a question of how the essential non-pirate is to live in a world of pirates."

Rhys had no immediate reply to this, so they ordered more drinks and John continued:

"Romans and Orthodox Jews make the best pirates because even if they do put pretty far out to sea after plunder, they've both got a sailor's snug harbor to get to again. The Catholic can drop anchor in a church, the Jew carries his absolution along on shipboard. But they aren't the only ones, not by a long shot. It applies to everyone you know . . . piracy isn't so safe a game for them, but if you think for a minute–"

"I wish you wouldn't pretend to sit in judgment when you're looking so pitifully ill. You remind me not so much of the Christian Way as of Nietzsche."

And suddenly John felt the fatigue again, the wish to give it up; what was the use in arguing with Rhys. The drink was having an inordinate effect because of the amytal. He knew it would be difficult to get up, next to impossible to walk home.

"Hell," he said. "It's only an argument for you. Forget the whole thing." And then: "Will you take me home?"

"What's wrong? Not feeling well?"

"I'm sick to death of sitting here with you, listening to your well-fed brain. I want to leave and I can't do it by myself. I'm asking you: as one last favor, would you see me home? Let me assure you, sir, it will be the last. I shan't disturb you and your values again."

"Please don't be melodramatic with me, John," said Rhys in a quiet rage.

"Can't you see that's not the question?"

"Don't you think you'd feel better if you sat here without drinking for a few minutes?"

"Oh for heaven's sake, sir, don't be reasonable with me. I've asked you a question, will you–"

He felt a draught on his back from the open door. Shivering extravagantly, with the hope that Rhys would think him ill, he turned and saw Rico and Alan standing beside his chair.

"Wha's wrong, little one," asked Rico, slightly drunk, smiling with his beautiful teeth.

"Rico!" He held out his hand, forgetting Rhys, forgetting Alan. "Rico"—and more softly, as though drawing the other into conspiracy—"will you take me home? I can't go myself."

"Sure, little one. I can take you home. Come, give me your hand." Rico laughed, his laugh and his glance taking in the whole room, stranger and intimate alike, as though to disclaim all embarrassment and responsibility, as though to enlist their sympathy not for John but for self-sacrificing Rico who had to take him home.

"Come," he said. "Up on your feet."

He got to his feet slowly enough, his eyes half fading from their focus. The floor seemed to rock beneath him, his ears filled with noise, and it was as if he stood on a separate planet that rocked backwards and over in space, out of sight of Rhys who sat there with an embarrassed expression on his face. Then suddenly he knew he was heavily in Rico's arms, and in one instant synapse of sobriety he heard himself saying to Rhys "I hate you more . . ." and Rico saying roughly "Come on," pulling at his arm. Then the two little voices were again swept away in a wave of sound against his brain, formless sound at first, that resolved itself into a rhythm and at length into words spoken from far away: "Drink and drugs that done him in," or some such; and then—drink and drugs—he could no longer hear for noise, but the enormous voice of Rico was in his head saying "Come on, come on," and all at once they were in the street and the cold stung his eyes and the sweat on his cheeks.

Rico and Alan had taken him by the arms, close to the shoulder, and were dragging him along. Whenever he stumbled they set him right with a jerk that lifted his feet off the ground.

"Wait," he said. "Sick."

And while they stood silently by holding him, Rico holding his head forward, he was sick, with a horrible violence, in a little alley off Dunster street. His stomach, almost empty to start with, twisted painfully at the finish, and he lost consciousness.

When he came to he was alone in his room with Rico. He could not see Alan anywhere. He rested on his bed and Rico was taking his clothes off. There was no longer any rest, or desire to sleep; there was only pain in his stomach and an actively hurtful weariness.

Rico finished stripping him, folded him in between the sheets. "You'll be OK in the morning," he said. "You were sick as a bitch. How d'you feel now?"

"Rico," he whispered. "Don't go away, Rico." He felt distantly that he was a child, in his child's bed at home; he had done a wrong thing, and Rico would be angry, with the efficient necessary anger of a mother.

"Kiss me, Rico," he said. "Kiss me good night." And then, as Rico made no move to comply, he said: "You're mad at me . . . ?" with a pathetic dubious note of shame in his voice, and Rico stooped and quickly kissed him on the cheek.

"Now good night, little one."

"Don't go, Rico. Stay here tonight."

"I can't. You'll be all right now."

"But I won't, Rico. I won't. I'll be sick again." He grew panicky with new fear. "I swear I'll be sick again," he said. "The minute you leave. Don't leave, Rico."

Then, in a tone of malicious invalid craft, he said accusingly: "You gave Alan the key to your room, didn't you?" Breathless, he went on: "You told him to wait in your room, didn't you."

Rico's face gave him away; it was true, it could only be true. "That's why you want to leave," he went on. "I know why." Quietly he began to whimper, and the tears rolled down his face. Then in a desperate martyrdom he said in a choked voice: "I'll kill myself if you go. I'll kill myself the minute you go out that door."

"Nonsense, what would you do it with, little one." Rico was not very good at situations like this; he felt vaguely that he should comfort, should sacrifice himself a little and help; but he had no intelligent means of doing it, being frightened not by a lie, but by a lie that would involve him later.

"I'd take all the amytal. I would. It would be enough. You'd see it would be enough. Rico, don't be a bastard. Don't go away."

"You mustn't do that, John. You mustn't think of it."

"And you can't find the amytal either. I hid it." There was a terrible cunning in his voice, he was determined to have the drug. It did not at that time matter to him whether it was a lethal dose or not; it was to spite Rico, to hurt him, to say to him: 'See what might have happened. The guilt would have been yours, you would have murdered me.'

Rico went to the bathroom to look for the amytal.

"You can't find it, you can't," he mocked in a thin voice cracked with approaching hysteria. "Go away, damn you. Go away."

Rico came back into the room.

"You won't do it, John."

"Get out."

"Promise me you won't do it."

"Get out."

"If you don't promise I can't do anything."

"I said get out."

Rico was faced with something beyond his comprehension, and he took the only way he understood.

"All right," he said sullenly. "I guess it's your life." And having thus washed himself clean in his own eyes, he walked out.

There was no question of decision, now he was alone. It was again that unfaced trust in a higher power, in some back world watching. With unnecessary stealth he got out of bed and, entirely naked, went to the desk, got the key and opened the filing cabinet. He took the bottle into the bathroom and poured all the pills into a highball glass, which he filled with warm water. This decoction he took back into the living room, where he sat down on the couch by the phone and began to drink. When the glass was empty there remained a considerable residue of damp powder at the bottom, so he refilled the glass and started again, more slowly, from time to time stirring the mixture with a pencil. At last he had finished. From experience, he knew there would be about fifteen minutes to wait.

He turned on all the lights, not feeling like getting into bed again. As he stood naked in the corner by the light-switch he was taken suddenly with a frenzy. The thing was done, it was done. Was it right? was it so at all? The indecision after the event frightened him, he imagined the maid finding him in the morning and with a certain sense of abject shame rushed to put his bathrobe about him. How to know? He questioned if he should be saved, and then, as he became somewhat more calm, there occurred to him another of those tests of providence, another cryptic question to which the oracle might smilingly equivocate over his special case.

He took up the phone and dialled Rhys' number. If Rhys answered he would explain and have him get a doctor. If there were no answer . . . and as he listened to the ring he felt certain there must be. It was not so much the test of fate, but the thought that he must speak again to Rhys, apologize, absolve, ask forgiveness.

There was no answer. Unwilling to believe, he put the phone down on the table and let it ring. The answer was given, but unsatisfactorily only more or less given, with the smiling ambiguity of power. He went to the window and opened it, then sat back on the couch. It is doubtful that he thought any more of death, of the probability or the certainty. He listened to the dried icy branches of the trees scratch together in the wind, down in the courtyard; and it is doubtful that he thought of leaving anything behind, of regret, of the irrevocability of death.

For his room, warm with the lights full on, seemed to him some tall citadel of the sun, with a certain congenial ease of sunlight upon it, and when the sleep came down, it drifted in like the cool sudden shadow of a cloud, that only made him shudder slightly.

JUNE, 1941

Howard Moss, *Summer School, 1942*

1922–

Howard Moss, who is on the staff of The New Yorker, *has published a book of verse,* The Wound and the Weather. *Moss published "The Zoo" in the* ADVOCATE *just before attending the long wartime Harvard Summer session in 1942.*

THE ZOO

Ballooning from New York, my cosmos hints
A daring summer clapped among the woods;
But browsing interests, profligate of sense,
Annihilate these dangerous attitudes.

Appeasing lions lope perhaps to ground
Inhabited by any dullard creature;
But trapeze-touched, no animal is bound
To claim one country acre for his future.

Let orange monkeys, tropically astute,
Climb any false particular baboon;
If love claims only this as loot,
I would have lions for my afternoon:

A zoo's excitement, cultivated roars,
A peacock consummated by design,
The muscled rhyming of a leopard's paws
To mock the strict perversity of time.

MAY, 1942

Norman Mailer, '43

1923–

Norman Mailer, author of The Naked and The Dead, *won* Story Magazine*'s annual college short story contest in 1941. After the war, Mailer studied at the Sorbonne.*

MAYBE NEXT YEAR

THE TRAINS USED TO GO BY, USED TO GO BY VERY fast in the field past the road on the other side of my house. I used to go down there and walk and walk through the fields whenever mom and pop were fighting, fighting about money like they always were, and after I'd listen awhile, I'd blow air into my ears so I couldn't hear them, then I'd go out in the field, across the road from my house and slide down the steep part of the grass where it was slippery like dogs had been dirty there, and then I used to climb up the other side, up the big hill on the other side, and walk and walk through the fat high grass until I would come to the railroad tracks where I'd just keep going and going and going.

Why don't we have any money, we never have any money, what kind of man did I marry, what good is he, what good is he, look at him, look at his boy there, look at your boy there, look at him, he takes after you, look at him walk away like he never hears us, look at him, no good like you, why don't you ever get any money?

The grass sticks would be rough and sharp sort of, like sharp pages in a book, and I had to talk with my hands in my pockets so I wouldn't cut my fingers. They were tall, the grasses, and sometimes they would hit me in the face, but I would hit them back, only that used to cut my fingers, and I'd start crying, but I stopped soon, because there was nobody around, and I knew that when there was nobody to hear me, I always stopped soon, although I never could figure it out, because I always could cry for a long time, and say I was going to run away and die if people were around.

I can't help it if I'm not making money, my God there's limits to what a man can do, nag, nag, nag, all the time. My God I can't help it, there's limits, there's depression, everybody's losing money, just worry about keeping the house, and don't compare the child to me, the God-damn child is splitting us up the middle, I can't help it if he's a stupid kid, he's only nine, maybe he'll get smarter yet, I can't help it if he's dumb, there's a depression going on I tell you, everybody's losing money, there just isn't any money around.

The railroad tracks made a funny kind of a mirror. I could see myself in them, one of me on each side, I was so tall in them, but I was awfully short, as short as my arm, but I was awful tall, I looked as tall as pop, except as tall as if I was to see pop all the way in the distance coming up the hill to our house, when he looked as tall as my arm, but I knew anyway that he was oh ten times bigger than me.

Why is the boy always disappearing, why don't you find him, you haven't a job, you just sit around, you might keep him near you, you might teach him to be like you, and sit around all day, and make it easier for me so at least I wouldn't have to look for him, but you can't even teach him that, I never saw such a man like you, they didn't make my father out of men like you.

If I walked and walked along the tracks, there was a spot where I could get to a place where all the big slow trains came into town. If I was careful I could sneak up in the grass near to where the men who jumped off the big trains camped in the fields.

They were dirty old men, they just sat around, and smoked pipes and washed their dirty old shirts in the yellow water spot where I used to go swimming before mom started yell yell yell about the dirty old men and wouldn't let me swim there.

They're filthy old things, you'll get sick and die, they're diseased, they're diseased, why did the town let them camp and flop in a meadow like that, right on the town limits, what's the good of living out of town when our only neighbors are bums, what's the good, what's the town mean, why aren't they put in the coop where they belong, why should they be flopping so near our house in a meadow?

I didn't like the men, they used to talk and laugh to themselves all the time, sometimes they would sing songs. I knew they were dirty men cause mom said they would give me diseases, but one time I came up and talked to them, when I went out mom and pop were shouting, and the men looked at me, one of the old ones who was sitting on his old stork bundle bag sort of, got up and looked at me, he made fun of me, he said sonny got a dime for a poor old man to have some coffee, and then all the men started laughing, haw haw haw kind of laughing. The other men came around me, one of them said he was going to take my shirt and use it for a snot-rag, and they all laughed again, the big man in the middle of them making believe he was going to throw dirt at me only I didn't know he was going to fool me until I started crying, and he laughed too, and dropped the dirt.

That boy is going to get in trouble, why don't you take care of him, keep him around you, he goes off into the meadow, and God knows what those bums are going to do to him, they're all vile, they don't live like men, they're not men I heard, they're no more men than you are, both of you are, why don't you take care of him, he'll turn out weak in everything like you, those bums will get him in trouble.

Pop came over, grab-me picked me up, and carried me upstairs, and licked me, and locked the door on me, and then he went downstairs, and he and mom yelled and yelled right through my crying. I waited and waited for them to hear me, but I must have fallen asleep because the next thing it was morning, and I didn't remember stopping and rubbing my hands on my nose to wipe off the crying. They unlocked the door before, I sneaked downstairs, the front door was open and mom and pop were sitting around front, not saying anything, I hated them, I ran out the door between them, and hid around the side of the house. Pop and mom came running out, they ran the wrong way calling to me, they were looking for me, and they weren't smiling, but they were talking nice the way they did when they didn't mean it, just like when they wanted to catch our dog, and that made me feel sad, and oh I felt just terrible, and then when they started coming back I didn't want to get another licking so I ran away without their seeing me, and sneaked across the road further down, into the field, and up the slippery hill, run run running way off until I got to the railroad tracks. I sneaked along them to where the dirty men with the disease were, and I hid down in the grass, and hid behind some to look at them, but they were all gone, there weren't any of them, but the old man who had made fun of me the day before, and he was lying on the ground crying and yowling like he was hurt or dead.

I walked over to him, he looked at me, he started crawling to me, I could see it was his foot that was hurt cause it was all bloody like, and bleeding near the knee. Help me kid, help me kid, he kept yelling.

Go ahead, hit the child, hit it, hit it, it deserves it, playing with dirty old men, hit it, it's a terrible child, it never listens to us, there's something wrong with it.

The old man looked like a snake, and I stepped back to run away from him, but he kept crawling after me, yelling don't go away kid, I won't hurt you, please don't go way kid, but he looked like a snake, only bleeding. I yelled at him, I said go away, you're a dirty old man, but he wouldn't stop, and I picked up a rock, and threw it at him, it missed him, but I threw another rock, and it hit him in the head, he stopped moving to me, he was crying something terrible, there was a lot of blood all over his face.

Why kid, why kid, why kid, why hit me.

You're a dirty old man, leave me alone, I don't like you, you're a dirty old man.

Kid for God's sakes help me, I'm going crazy kid, don't leave me here, it's hot here kid, it's hot here kid.

Then I picked up a stone, and threw it at him again, only I didn't see if it hit him because I was running away. I heard him crying, screaming, and I was scared, but I kept running, and then I said I hate them, I hate them, the grass kept cutting at me, I couldn't run with my hands in my pockets, kept cutting at me and cutting at me, I fell down, and then I got up and kept running home.

I walked down the last part of the hill, and across the road, and when I got back mom and pop were sitting around again, and I started crying. I cried and cried, they asked me what's the matter, what's the matter with you, why are you crying, but I just kept saying the dirty old man, the dirty old man.

And mom said I thought they all were kicked out of town, I don't know how any of them were left, you're not lying?

I'm not lying, I'm not lying.

And pop got up, and said to mom I told you not to do it, you get an idea in your head, and you can't stop, those men were beaten, I don't know how any were left in the dark, we had flashlights, but there might have been, it's the boy's own fault, he had no business going around there today, and anyway he wasn't hurt, he didn't start crying until he saw us, I saw him before he saw me.

And mom said, if you were a man you'd go over there now, and finish them off, you wouldn't even go last night without any help, if I were a man I'd thrash the man that touched my boy, but you just sit there and talk talk talk that it's the boy's fault.

Pop got up, and walked around and around, and he said it isn't the boy's fault, but it isn't the man's either, and then he stood up, and said I'm not going to do anything about it, what with the boy between us, and the job ruined, and everything Goddamn else, I might be one of them myself, maybe next year, and then pop stood up and walked off down the road only farther out of town, not the way the old man was. I could see that pop's shoulders were screwed up around his neck, and then I was happy, because all I could think of was that I'd seen two big men cry that day, and maybe that meant I was getting bigger too, and that was an awful good feeling.

JUNE, 1942

APPENDIX

T. S. Eliot, '10, an Advocate Friendship

by W. G. Tinckom-Fernandez '10

Conrad Aiken, in a letter to the editor, wrote that W. G. Tinckom-Fernandez, "was father, uncle, guardian, and guiding star, to all of us, Tom included, and brought the moribund ADVOCATE *to new vitality for a college generation...." Mr. Tinckom-Fernandez' essay was written for the* ADVOCATE's *T. S. Eliot issue, printed in 1938.*

ON THIS OCCASION WHEN MOTHER ADVOCATE GIVES accolade to T. S. Eliot she celebrates the first occasion when one of her sons has acquired international renown before reaching middle-age, not only as a poet, dramatist and critic but as the spokesman of intellectual youth on both sides of the Atlantic.

My assignment is to present Eliot as an ADVOCATE editor. Because the privilege of contacts with a choice personality befell me. I find myself reviving memories of an ADVOCATE friendship instead of the casual relations of editorial activities. In doing so, however, I realize that I raise hopes of a vivid personal portrait such as that undergraduate friendship justifies; whereas I find myself facing a problem which Eliot, the literary critic, has often encountered.

To look back over more than a quarter of a century and try to recapture a personality from a remote and limited period, especially of one who was then as shy and reticent as he is probably still, is a difficult task. This is not to say that the necessarily brief friendship was not intimate and rewarding, nor that Eliot was wholly different as an undergraduate from the personality which he has since revealed in his poems, plays and critical opinions. Let me say, however, that while he was then no less concerned with literature than he is today, to regard the undergraduate writer as one who was even then conscious of literary destiny among his fellow editors of the ADVOCATE is to do him an injustice.

Small wonder that in retrospect those episodes, conversations and ideas of our undergraduate days become hopelessly kaleidoscopic. What we were like then and what we wanted to do and become are things which elude us who are now armed with experience and chastened by realities. Having to readjust our lives after two major crises like a world war and a world depression, the poets of our troubled generation seem to be "world-losers and world-forsakers."

Thus the ambitions and desires of our youth have long since made their quaint compacts with Necessity. In our twenty-fifth anniversary class report Eliot told us of his lean years in England as a school teacher on a pittance with a dinner thrown in, and as a bank clerk with a free tea at four o'clock. Was it irony that led the poet to add that he liked banking? Recalling his sensitive nature, and the inspissated gloom of a London bank interior, that rather sounds like the sort of humor that was permitted in the last carriage of a funeral procession in the Cambridge of our day!

I am also aware that such glimpses and memories as survive precariously today remind us that our personalities at that period of our lives did not have so much finality in them as they pretended to. Withal, there is the temptation to rationalize in our endeavor to overcome what James Huneker somewhere called "the pathos of distance."

II

It was in the old ADVOCATE sanctum under the eaves of the Harvard Union that I first met Eliot. As I was the first to be elected from our class, I was able to watch the other 1910 candidates. Eliot was the most promising of these, and as he was the next to be elected we began a friendship based upon such literary tastes and enthusiasms as we shared or induced each other to share.

But Eliot's ADVOCATE days were numbered. In his sophomore year he decided to complete his course in three years and take a master's degree. Thereafter the sanctum saw less of him; his comments in a minuscular hand on the contributions of candidates soon ceased along with his own. Only now and then did he come to initiations and punch nights to expand, in the midst of our hilarity, into his quiet, subtle humor; and we saw as little of him at the Stylus Club and the Signet Society. As president, during the first half of our final year, I made a desperate effort to get editorials from him, but by then he was working harder than ever in the Graduate School. To his classmates and the ADVOCATE board he became a recluse, and I used to run him to earth in his room.

But he was not lost to undergraduate life. He was always ready to lay his book aside and fill his pipe. With his analytical mind his curiosity was insatiable as to the meanings and motives in the literary and social currents of our day. He was always the commentator, never the gusty talker, and seemed to cultivate even then a scholarly detachment. And there was a lot to talk about, for the university was then peculiarly, and perhaps for the last time, a kind of national clearing-house, a laboratory, such as would delight the pedagogues of today.

As the Ph.D. degree had just become a pedagogical fetish, the university attracted a host of aspirants for doctors' and masters' degrees from all over the country, and that microcosm, Harvard College, with its elective system of study, exposed us undergraduates to a variety of stimulating contacts and experiences. I like to account for Eliot's flair for eclectic scholarship, which is revealed in his poems and which is perhaps their outstanding characteristic, by recalling the intellectual excitements in this competitive atmosphere which the swarm of graduate students from small and large colleges created in our class-rooms, for we rubbed shoulders with them in undergraduate as well as graduate courses. In that experience Harvard to us seemed truly a university.

I have no doubt that in Eliot's case all this was a vivid, formative influence, as indeed it was in the lives of all our generation at Harvard during those last years of the elective system. If the College seemed to us to lose its identity in this almost alien, as it were cosmopolitan, atmosphere, at least it had more of the atmosphere and fellowship of the medieval university than Harvard's cloistered undergraduates today enjoy in those replicas of Oxford and Cambridge on the banks of the Charles.

What if certain graduate courses received us undergraduates with sublime toleration, even reluctance? Our barbarian airs and graces saved those courses from the heavy-witted Teutonism with which the Ph.D. aspirants tried to flavor them. Our professors were more amused than flattered by the atmosphere of *lèse-majesté* with which these earnest souls surrounded them, and in turn doubtless appreciated our undergraduate anticlimaxes. How often during a lecture was the absurdly rapt attention of those grinds disturbed, if not shocked, when someone of our group, after a riotous evening in Boston or Cambridge, would begin to nod and finally pass into unabashed slumber? It was Professor William James who, during a lecture, upset a post-graduate questioner with, "What is mind? No matter! What is matter? Never mind!"

The unfailing punctuality of these strangers within our gates irked instead of reproached us; we sometimes wondered if that exemplary phalanx had left the class room since the last lecture. And yet, we had all the breaks. None of the graduate grinds was ever late because, running to a lecture, he had almost bumped into Henry James at the corner of Linden and Massachusetts, and knocked off his hard, high-low-crowned English hat which resembled a Regency coachman's, and picked it up with breathless apologies, and then politely waited upon a sentence which had a beginning and a middle, but which tailed off unfinished in a despairing smile. If any of them had had this experience, it should have furnished him with a doctor's thesis on that distinguished novelist's style, since appropriate subjects for theses were always uppermost in their minds.

And if during lectures these greasy grinds had their laugh when they selectively poised their pens over their notebooks while we industriously plied ours like "pickers-up of unconsidered trifles," it is a surprising amount of information that we managed to pick up. We learned to swim by going beyond our depth. But we had our innings when those post-graduates from the sticks appeared in the ADVOCATE sanctum to submit contributions which, when published, were proudly sent back to their home town and *alma mater*.

III

So much for the intra-mural influences of Eliot's day. The result was, for one of his precocious mind, a healthy sophistication, which is quite another thing from the sophistry which, a lecturer told us, Bacon ascribed to the medieval university. And since Eliot wrote some of his early poems during his last two years of college, it is worth our while to ask why they were not published until 1925 by that professional world of letters to which we aspired. The answer is that the New York world of editors and publishers reminded the young writer that the cautionary Victorian advice of being seen and not heard was still in force.

I recall the sensation caused in the ADVOCATE sanctum when the editor of the *Literary Digest* wrote asking for samples of ADVOCATE poets which he wanted for a survey of American undergraduate verse. Of the samples submitted, needless to say, none of Eliot's was used by the *Digest* editor.

Today young writers, even those in college, are cultivated and encouraged by editors and publishers to submit their work. Not so in our day. As yet the young writer, especially the poet, was not supposed to have anything worth saying. Of course there were certain publishers who would gladly publish your poems at your own expense, and the custom was more common than is known. The late Edwin Arlington Robinson, whom I came to know in New York, told me that his first book, "Captain Craig," was subsidized. And when I met Eliot's English contemporary Rupert Brooke in New York, still unknown in 1913, he told me that he had paid for the publication of his first book of poems in London.

In the light of these conditions and influences, within and without Harvard in our day, it is not surprising that the writers of 1910 have been, like Eliot, rebels, though not all have remained so. For that world we faced three years before the World War was a smug, somnolent world: as yet the word Armageddon was only used by divinity students to scarify their first congregations. It will sound like rationalization to say that, although we entered college soon after the century opened, by the time we left we found, or rather sensed, an atmosphere of *fin-de-siècle*, even of disillusion, in the literary and political world. The note is evident in our classmate

Walter Lippmann's first three books. Reading once more Eliot's essay "For Lancelot Andrewes" I have wondered in what mood he first discovered this stanza of Dryden's which he quotes in that study:

> All, all of a piece throughout!
> Thy Chase had a Beast in View;
> Thy Wars brought nothing about;
> Thy lovers were all untrue.
> 'Tis well an Old Age is out,
> And time to begin a New.

As regards belles lettres, the field was dominated and monopolized by a coterie of pundits, a sort of superannuated, mutual admiration circle. Their prestige might have been said to rest upon an axiom like "that which is new is not true, and that which is true is not new." Some occupied academic chairs of literature and others were editors. The magazines always found room for their long colorless odes which we characterized as "spindaric." There were, however, notable exceptions, two of whom were sons of Mother Advocate. One was that inspired poet and teacher, Professor George Woodberry '77, of Columbia, whose poems appeared too seldom, and the other was one of the founders and during its best years the editor of the original *Life*, Edward S. Martin '77, who welcomed us to his pages. He was a modern survival of Chaucer's "verray parfit gentil knight." His son was our classmate.

These were formative influences for Eliot and his generation of writers. Almost too late in college we heard of the literary revolt abroad, which in time found American supporters like the poets Amy Lowell, John Gould Fletcher of the *Harvard Monthly* and the ADVOCATE's Conrad Aiken. And let me proudly add that it was in our ADVOCATE that Ezra Pound's first book of verse was reviewed, with Eliot and myself among his admirers. It was Eliot who first told me of the Vers Libre movement, of the work of Paul Fort and Francis Jammes; and he was to go over to the Sorbonne for study and to assess these literary influences which, stifled by the War, were to end in the literary and artistic nonsense that was appropriately termed Dada.

Meanwhile Eliot had found what he wanted in Paris and returned to Harvard for his Ph.D. study. I can testify to the fact that he had now already begun to shape his own technique of verse form and style, for, after leaving Cambridge to become a cub reporter on the *New York World*, I kept up a correspondence with him, and he sent me copies of these early poems, among which I recall the "Preludes," "Cousin Nancy," "The Boston Evening Transcript" and "Aunt Helen." There may have been others which have not since been published, and I regret that another Harvard man to whom I showed them never returned them. The point is that these poems waited until 1925 for publication, and it is surprising to find that even those of the post-war period do not as yet begin to date; each character seems to have its note of universality.

Those who bring against Eliot the charge of a wilful or perverse obscurantism should remember that these poems crystallize the suppressed ideas, emotions, aspirations of a period of catastrophe, when the experiences of our stratified world, the world of Aunt Helen Slingsby and the Lady of the Portrait, were destined for Limbo. It is not only that some medium was necessary for a distillation of these crowded, complex and inarticulate moods and experiences, but that Armageddon liquidated that world. By what miracle could a conventional or traditional frame-work contain and adequately convey their significance?

Thus it seems as if Eliot set himself the task of assessing, with his fastidious sincerity and scholarship, the myriad contacts and experiences of a transitional epoch. There was so much to record of this Human Comedy whose characters with their moods, attitudes and whispers were destined to create international crises, that Eliot's elliptical mode of expression alone could celebrate. Even the Boston of our day was less "a state of mind" than a world of characters, some of whom we met in the portraits of Sargent's exhibition of 1908 in Copley Hall. In depicting this scene Eliot seems to have borrowed from the canon of classical Chinese painting, where linear perspective is modified by the tone values and shading of atmospheric perspective. It is futile to classify him as a symbolist, an imagist, an impressionist or a surrealist, since all these things are the concern of the modern creative artist. The poet, moreover, often found himself assuming the rôles of biographer and historian. Incidentally, it is not surprising that Eliot has shared in the silly stricture which Oscar Wilde passed on Browning—of using poetry as a medium for writing prose.

While Eliot's meticulous classification of fugitive types, situations and motives may seem like rummaging in an intellectual attic among outworn emotions and ideas, certainly these things also have their tears and laughter. And so his types, his characters, are never ludicrous; they become prototypes instead of caricatures. J. Alfred Prufrock, Sweeney and his landlady Mrs. Turner, Aunt Helen Slingsby and the Lady of the Portrait, all have their dignity and their lawful occasions. If they seem like memories of our dead lives, that quality makes them the stuff of literature. And if Eliot's poetry sometimes suggests an atmosphere of *fin-de-siècle*, that is because of the curious time-lag which seems to haunt our tardy American reactions to the social, spiritual, intellectual, and economic currents of the Europe towards which we so reluctantly and ruefully turn for orientation, and which by sacrifice of our lives and treasure we were to help to save in 1917.

IV

When the young and untried writer faces the compromise which he must make with the professional world, by a self-preservative instinct he chooses a milieu in which that compromise is not likely to be threatened with spiritual and literary extinction. Thus it was natural that, when his academic apprenticeship was over, Eliot should prefer to take his chances at making a living in London. As writers the idea had come to us in college when we discussed Ezra Pound's case. Pound, like Eliot, was a gifted poet and scholar. After teaching for a brief period in Pennsylvania, he had gone to London for literary recognition, and his first poems, which reached us here in 1908, were published there. In the fall of 1913 I decided to exchange the journalism of New York for that of London, and Eliot came to see me off when I sailed on this forlorn hope from Boston. Thus the idea of London must have been in his mind during those last years in Cambridge when he was beginning to write with professional ambitions.

Before he left, however, I used to descend on him at his summer home in East Gloucester on my way to Maine. There I saw him in a quiet, charming family circle of parents and sisters, whose affectionate understanding of his arduous scholarship and his untried gifts must have been an inspiration for him in those lean years he later faced in a foreign land. He used to take me sailing in his catboat, and he could handle the sail with the best in Gloucester harbor.

Although I lost touch with him when he finally went abroad, it is sad to relate that this friendship died when it should have been revived. A guilty conscience compels me to admit that I did not see him while I was in London in the months before and after the Armistice. And if those months were not propitious, I failed again to see him while I was working in London as a newspaper correspondent during

1924–26, and once more when I passed through to Constantinople in 1927 as special correspondent of the *New York Times.* Our only excuse for such seemingly perverse omissions is that the world is too much with us in earning our living. But, like so many poets, Eliot remained in that cold British world until it gave him his first recognition, and repaid it by becoming its citizen.